NEW WORKS IN ACCOUNTING HISTORY

edited by

RICHARD P. BRIEF
LEONARD N. STERN SCHOOL OF BUSINESS
NEW YORK UNIVERSITY

PASTORAL ACCOUNTING IN COLONIAL AUSTRALIA

A CASE STUDY OF UNREGULATED ACCOUNTING

GARRY CARNEGIE

Routledge
Taylor & Francis Group

LONDON AND NEW YORK

First published 1997 by Garland Publishing, Inc.

2 Park Square, Milton Park, Abingdon, Oxon OX14 4RN
711 Third Avenue, New York, NY 10017, USA

First issued in paperback 2016

Routledge is an imprint of the Taylor & Francis Group, an informa business

Library of Congress Cataloging-in-Publication Data

Carnegie, Garry D..
    Pastoral accounting in colonial Australia : a case study of unregulated accounting / Garry D. Carnegie.
        p.   cm. — (New works in accounting history)
    Includes bibliographical references and index.
    ISBN-13: 978-0-8153-3037-0 (hbk)
    ISBN-13: 978-1-1389-9478-2 (pbk)
    1. Animal industry—Australia—Accounting—History. 2. Accounting—Australia—History. 3. Accounting—Australia—History—Sources.
I. Title. II. Series.
HF5686.A56C37 1997
657'.863—dc21
                                            97-33178

TO COLLEEN, LAUREN AND JOEL

FOR THEIR INTEREST, PATIENCE

AND UNDERSTANDING.

CONTENTS

PART II   EXAMINATION OF SURVIVING PASTORAL BUSINESS RECORDS

Chapter 4   Research Methodology

Chapter 5   Backgrounds of Pastoralists Whose Business Records are Examined

Chapter 6   Pastoral Accounting Records in Review

ABSTRACT

Set in colonial Australia, this explanatory, investigative study examines the dimensions of accounting information prepared for pastoral industry engagement in the Western District of Victoria during 1836-1900 and the local, time-specific environmental factors which shaped these dimensions. Based on examinations of surviving business records, the study provides evidence of the structure and usage of pastoral accounting information in an unregulated financial reporting environment. As an interpretive historical study, it attempts to provide explanations of the accounting practices observed.

Prior to this investigation, very little was known of the nature of pastoral accounting information prepared in the pre-Federation era of rapid transformation in the Colony of Victoria. This study features a research sample of 23 sets of surviving business records, representing a range of records available for examination. It acknowledges that there are many key environmental factors which affect accounting. The identification of these factors relies upon the examination of the relevant accounting literature, an elucidation of the pastoral industry and station environments and a review of the backgrounds of the pastoralists whose surviving records are examined.

This study found a broad range of financial and volume records prepared for engagement in the pastoral industry by the entities comprising the research sample. In the absence of accountability relationships, there was an emphasis on the maintenance of personalized ledgers combined with various records of non-financial operating statistics for internal control. There was also a general focus on the use of operating statistics for performance measurement. The nature of information prepared for accountability purposes and for the government had a stronger financial focus. Professional accountants facilitated this increased emphasis on the measurement of financial outputs. Thus, the impact of externalities was central to the development of accounting. There is evidence to suggest that Western District pastoralists did not find reporting systems which focused on the measurement of financial outputs to be effective for the running of day to day station affairs. The emphasis by professional accountants on financial recording and the preparation of periodic financial statements for their view of pastoral entities appears to have isolated them from the real value-creating processes in pastoralism.

Cultural, educational, legal and political, professional, economic and other factors are tendered as probable environmental influences on the accounting practices observed. The use of culture in this field-based historical research represents an extension of a burgeoning literature on the impact of culture in shaping the accounting environment of a country.

There are five major implications of this study. Firstly, it illustrates the importance for archival researchers in accounting to focus on understanding the structure and usage of accounting information in the organisational and social context in which it was prepared. Secondly, it shows how culture can emerge as a key contextual factor in accounting history studies. Thirdly, it provides some evidence which suggests that a key determinant of the professionalization of accounting in pre-Federation Australia was the expansion and enhancement of the domain of double entry accounting. It also provides insights into the present dominance of the financial accounting function and the emphasis on financial reporting issues by the organized accounting profession in Australia. Finally, it provides evidence of a regard for efficiency of production by pre-Federation Western District pastoralists which predates similar concerns in contemporary manufacturing and the public sector for the evaluation of input/output relationships in both physical and financial terms. Opportunities for further field-based case study research are also proposed.

ACKNOWLEDGMENTS

This volume stems from my doctoral research undertaken at Flinders University of South Australia. Many people and institutions have contributed in various ways to the preparation of this work and some of these must be thanked here. I am indebted to my supervisors, Professor Lee D. Parker, now at the University of Adelaide, and Dr Peter O'Brien, for their guidance, encouragement and support. Professor Shahid Ansari of California State University, Northridge, provided helpful advice in the initial stages of the research, and Mr Ken Morris of the University of Ballarat rendered helpful comments on early drafts of many of the thesis chapters. Useful discussions on the implications of the research findings also took place with Ms Gweneth Norris of Deakin University. I also thank Professor Peter W. Wolnizer who sharpened my research focus in 1989 during the early months of his appointment as Foundation Chair of Accounting and Finance at Deakin University, and I acknowledge Dr Robert W. Gibson whose long-standing interest in accounting history influenced the shaping of my research agenda.

I am also grateful to those people who kindly made available pre-Federation pastoral business records from private archives. Records of pastoral entities comprising the research sample were supplied by Ms Caroline Shepherd (nee Armytage), Corney family, Cumming family, Dennis family, Hood family, Hope family, Jamieson family (especially the late Mr Robert Jamieson III MBE), Kininmonth family, Lang family, Mackinnon family, Dame Ella and Miss Helen Macknight, Mr Colin McIntyre (now deceased), Officer family, Patterson family and Mr Geordie Russell. I also express my gratitude to Dr John Menzies, and Mr Hugh Strachan (now deceased) for their assistance in the initial stages of this research in providing necessary introductions for tracing surviving business records in private archives.

I also thank the management and staff of the La Trobe Library of the State Library of Victoria, the University of Melbourne Archives, the Noel Butlin Archives Centre of the Australian National University, the Gold Museum, Ballarat, the Geelong Historical Records Centre and the Group Archives of the National Australia Bank Ltd and Australia and New Zealand Banking Group Ltd for their assistance in this research. To those people who in earlier times deposited pre-Federation pastoral business records with these repositories, I express my gratitude. Gratitude is also expressed to the archivists of the Geelong Church of England Grammar School, Geelong College, Melbourne Church of England Grammar School and Scotch College. Dr Philip L. Brown (now deceased) gave helpful advice in connection with the Clyde Company/Russell, G. records. Dr Gordon Forth also gave helpful advice during the early stages of the research. The assistance of the management and staff of the Australian Society of Certified Practising Accountants and Deakin University libraries has been appreciated. Mrs Jan Greenhill of Deakin University efficiently typed the thesis manuscript with utmost dedication while Ms Allison Oemcke prepared this revised manuscript ready for publication with exceptional attention to detail, good grace and enthusiasm. I am also grateful to Mr Brian West of the University of Ballarat for proofreading assistance in preparing this manuscript and to Professor Lee D. Parker again for reviewing the penultimate draft. Finally, my deepest gratitude must be reserved for my own family who have always given their unconditional support and encouragement.

Of course, the usual caveat applies: none of these people nor institutions should be held responsible in any way for the deficiencies, interpretations or conclusions of this work, the full responsibility for which rests with its author.

TABLES

ABBREVIATIONS

AARF   Australian Accounting Research Foundation

AIIA   The Australian Institute of Incorporated Accountants

AML&F   Australian Mortgage (Mercantile) Land & Finance Company

ASA   The Adelaide Society of Accountants

ASCPA   Australian Society of Certified Practising Accountants

CAA   The Corporation of Accountants of Australia

FIA   The Federal Institute of Accountants

ICAA   The Institute of Chartered Accountants in Australia

IIAV   The Incorporated Institute of Accountants, Victoria

UIG   Urgent Issues Group

Pastoral Accounting in
Colonial Australia

CHAPTER 1

INTRODUCTION

In Australia, the Victorian pastoral industry developed rapidly from the mid 1830s when European pastoral settlement commenced on fertile lands which Major Thomas Mitchell had described as "Australia Felix".[1] Those seeking grazing land moved into the Port Phillip District (then part of the Colony of New South Wales)[2] by means of two routes: overland from settled districts in New South Wales and by sea from Van Diemen's Land (known subsequently as Tasmania). Migration from Britain began once news spread of the quality of the land. Known during the squatting era as the Portland Bay District, the Western District of Victoria was the first district settled for pastoral pursuits and is still regarded as a rich pastoral region. According to Kiddle (1961, p.13), the pastoral settlers:

> . . . were soon to regard the Western District as theirs by right of discovery, confirmed by the expenditure of labour and capital they would bring to its development. To them 'Australia Felix' was a British possession in which they could find the riches which would make them happy. They never thought of the land of the cockatoos as belonging to the people who already occupied it, and whose felicity must prove incompatible with their own.

The pastoral pioneers were required to apply a diverse range of skills to survive in a harsh isolated setting. Although there were failures, various pastoralists and their descendants found security and prosperity during the colonial period to 31 December 1900. This pre-Federation period of approximately 65 years was one of rapid pastoral industry development. This development was spurred by the existence of lucrative foreign and domestic markets, the availability of expanses of fertile grazing lands and the employment of workers in an unregulated labour market.[3] According to Forth (1982, p.34) "it was perhaps in the Western District more than any other pastoral region of Eastern Australia that the squatters' golden age was most clearly evident". Throughout the pre-Federation period, the pastoral industry was a vital industry in the flourishing Colony of Victoria (Strachan, 1927, pp.7-8; de Serville, 1991, pp.159-188).[4]

A Scenario for Investigation

A study by Bridges (1975) of the historical development of Australian farm recording from 1788 to 1972 was confined to an evaluation of the available literature on the topic. Apart from a fundamentally descriptive study of a single set of surviving business records by Gibson (1979a), very little was known about the structure and usage of pastoral accounting information prepared in the pre-Federation era of rapid transformation in the Colony of Victoria.[5] To the author's knowledge, there are not any published accounts by other researchers based on examinations of surviving business records of the structure and usage of accounting information prepared for pre-Federation pastoral industry engagement in the Western District of Victoria.[6] Pre-Federation Western District pastoralism presents an opportunity to examine the nature of accounting information prepared in a unique setting involving the advent and development of a significant industry in a region where all infrastructure facilities had to be established upon lands which were described as "beyond the limits of location".[7]

The advent of an organized Australian accounting profession occurred in the mid 1880s.[8] The earliest known professional association of accountants established in Victoria is The Incorporated Institute of Accountants, Victoria (IIAV). Formed in Melbourne on 12 April 1886, the association was registered under the *Companies Statute* 1864 on 1 March 1887 with a foundation membership of 45 (Australian Society of Accountants, 1963, p.25). Incorporated on 13 December 1892 under the *Companies Act* 1890, The Australian Institute of Incorporated Accountants (AIIA) was Victoria's second professional accounting body (Carnegie, 1993b).[9] It was based in the Western District from incorporation to its dissolution on 14 January 1938.[10] The AIIA had a foundation membership of 55 of which 60 per cent resided in the Western District (AIIA, 1892).

According to Bridges (1975, p.14), the "first Australian farm recording system" was devised by Musson and published in 1893 in the *Agricultural Gazette of New South Wales*. Writing specifically for farmers and orchardists, Musson (1893, p.163) sought to prescribe how they could keep accounts to ascertain the "true position" of their affairs and whether the transactions resulted in a profit or loss. Musson (1893, p.162) asserted that "it appears to be nearly the rule amongst farmers to keep no proper set of books from which a balance sheet could be made out, for instance". As Accountant to the Bureau of Agriculture in Western Australia, Buckley (1897) also published a farm recording system. In emphasising farming as a commercial pursuit, Buckley (1897, p.342) also stated "it is quite as necessary that the farmer should keep proper books of accounts as the dry goods merchant, the storekeeper, the banker, or any other commercial man". In that year, the pastoral company Goldsbrough Mort & Co. Ltd produced a booklet which featured a segment on "Station Book-Keeping, &c." and argued "the necessity for an annual analysis of one's progress and financial position" (Goldsbrough Mort & Co. Ltd, 1897, p.44) while Hombsch (1897, p.453) argued "much haphazard can be avoided by the adoption of simple methods of bookkeeping". Another writer advocated the preparation of an inventory and the financial valuation of "everything in connection with farming, livestock, crops, fencing, building, land, &c., &c." (Anon, 1899, p.175).

The first known Australian book on pastoral accounting was written by Francis Ernest Vigars, a Sydney accountant, and published in 1900.[11] Vigars's *Station Book-keeping - A Treatise on Double Entry Book-keeping for Pastoralists and Farmers* was written "for those who make Station Products their chief business" (1900, p.3). However, according to Bridges (1975, p.23), it was written primarily for accountants who predominantly served the rural sector. Musson (1893), Buckley (1897), Goldsbrough Mort & Co. Ltd (1897) and Vigars (1900) all advocated double entry bookkeeping for financial recording.

During the pre-Federation period, financial reporting practices by non-corporate entities were unregulated. Thus, such entities were not exposed to any accounting regulation. This was not so for Victorian public companies which from 1896 were required under the *Companies Act* 1896 to issue an audited balance sheet which disclosed a minimum range of information (Gibson, 1971, pp.39-47; 1979b, pp.24-25). While there were not any financial reporting requirements prescribed for non-corporate pastoral entities to govern the preparation and reporting of financial information in the period to Federation, an income tax was imposed in 1895. Goldsbrough Mort & Co. Ltd (1897, p.44) addressed the implications of income tax for station bookkeeping when it stated "nearly everyone has some annual return of his year's work to make in these times, if only for taxation purposes, so bookkeeping becomes a necessity . . .". Vigars (1900, pp.3-4) did not mention the effect of income tax introduced five years earlier,[12] but stated in the introduction to the book that:

> . . . it must be obvious to all thinking persons, that, in these days of keen competition, a strict record of all business matters undertaken should be kept, and comparisons made from year to year of the *Receipts and Expenditure* and their sources. By this means a Pastoralist can at any time ascertain his actual financial position, and not be led or misled by supposition of such-and-such being his position (emphasis added, not in original).

The earlier study of non-corporate pre-Federation Victorian pastoral accounting undertaken by Gibson (1979a) involved the examination of the McLeod partnership business records relating to Ensay Station which was located in the Tambo River valley on the south side of the Great Dividing Range in Victoria's North-East region. The surviving financial and volume records examined spanned the period April 1868 to August 1872. For this period, Gibson (1979a) identified 293 individual account titles in the ledger of which 255 related to individual station workers including piece-work contractors. Gibson (1979a, p.9) explained there was not much regard for distinguishing capital and revenue items as all costs appeared to be written off as expenses when incurred. Examples were provided of "assets" acquired but which were charged to expense. In the analysis of volume records, Gibson (1979a) focused on the outputs of contract workers such as shearers who were compensated on the basis of performance made plain in shearing tally records. In examining the surviving historical evidence, Gibson (1979a) appeared to view the structure and usage of financial information in the context of contemporary accounting practice at the time of writing rather than portraying the information as a local, time-specific product shaped by a range of environmental conditions of that bygone era. Any explanation of accounting practice is likely to be incomplete and unreliable if the historical evidence is viewed, even in part, from the perspective of the present.[13]

A concern for understanding the past on its own terms underpins this study. This mode of historical enquiry is usually known as "historicism" (Tosh, 1991, pp.12-15). The fundamental premise of historicism is explained by Tosh (1991, pp.12-13) as recognising that:

> . . . each age is a unique manifestation of the human spirit, with its own culture and values. For one age to understand another, there must be a recognition that the passage of time has profoundly altered both the conditions of life and the mentality of men and women - even perhaps human nature itself - and that an effort of the imagination must be made to relinquish present-day values and to see an earlier age from the inside.[14]

Thus, as far as possible, present-day values must be set aside in examining not only historical events but also the mentality of the actors in history. Recreating the past from the inside is a pre-requisite to explaining the past. As accounting is an element of the organisational and social context and as any accounting system is an expression of the society which gave rise to it, the emphasis of this study is on understanding pre-Federation pastoral accounting in the contexts in which it operated. In examining accounting practices within their organisational and social context, one comes to understand the contingent nature of one's own traditions and practices. Thus, accounting history studies of this genre can help to place accounting's present into context and also broaden perspectives of accounting's potential.

Scope and Purpose of the Research

This study is concerned with the structure and usage of pre-Federation pastoral accounting information prepared for non-corporate pastoral entities in the Western District of Victoria whose surviving accounting records were available for examination. These entities included sole proprietorships, partnerships and trusts. This focus on non-corporate pastoral entities provides the opportunity to study the structure and usage of accounting information in an unregulated financial reporting environment. Because of this emphasis on pastoral accounting practice in an unregulated environment, companies are excluded from this study. As explained, company financial reporting practices in Victoria from 1896 to Federation were not entirely unregulated. It was also impossible to incorporate Victorian companies until 1864 when the first Victorian companies' legislation, the *Companies Statute* 1864, became operative. Non-corporate pastoral entities represented the vast majority of participants in pastoral activities in Victoria from the mid 1830s with most of these entities being operated by specific families. In total, 23 sets of surviving business records of non-corporate pastoral entities are examined in this study.

The purpose of this study is expressed in the following statement of objective:

> The express objective of the study is to investigate the nature of accounting information prepared for pastoral industry engagement by non-corporate entities in pre-Federation Western Victoria and to endeavour to explain the accounting practices observed and identify their possible implications for farming and business practices.

Given this research objective, the major general research question posed in this study is:

> What were the dimensions of accounting information prepared for pastoral industry engagement in pre-Federation Western Victoria and the local, time-specific environmental factors which shaped these dimensions?

This study acknowledges that there are many important environmental influences which affect accounting. These environmental influences are commonly organized into groups such as educational, legal and political, professional, economic and cultural (Arpan & AlHashim, 1984, p.4; Arpan & Radebaugh, 1985, p.13; Nobes & Parker, 1995, pp.10-11).

Since the late 1970s the impact of culture in shaping the accounting environment of a country has been recognized in the accounting literature. The cross-national cultural studies in accounting conducted from this time generally explain differences in international accounting practices, standard setting arrangements, the workings of accounting institutions, and differences in the meanings attributed to accounting concepts by reference to cultural differences between the countries involved in the investigations. It is a logical development of this literature for accounting historians to examine culture as one of a range of key environmental factors to assist in explaining historical accounting practices in their local, time-specific contexts. As a function of personal interactions, culture appears in three main layers: national, organisational and occupational. An examination of culture should enable more comprehensive explanations to be drawn of particular accounting practices in bygone eras. The cultural perspective adopted in this study is further examined in Chapter 2.

Even if the pre-Federation pastoral accounting practices were witnessed by the writer in their time-specific contexts, it would have been tenuous to endeavour to rank the key environmental factors identified in order of importance. Hence, no attempt is made in this study to rank the key factors identified in any order of significance. Rather, the study identifies a range of environmental factors specific in location and time to the 65 year period in question to shed light on the contingent nature of accounting practice during and since that time.

Period Selection

The period of approximately 65 years accommodated by this study extends from the date of preparation of the earliest surviving pastoral records available for this study, 1836, to the 31 December 1900. On 1 January 1901, Australia became a Federation. According to Greenwood (1955, p.196):

> Federation in one sense was an act of faith, symbolized for many by the fortuitous but happy combination of events which produced a new nation at the outset of the new century.

Federation meant that a population of almost four million people embarked to control their destiny by means of a national government.

This involved a shift in focus from Colonial governments only to both a Commonwealth government and State governments. This was an era when national development became an objective and where matters national in character were surrendered to the Commonwealth of Australia by the former Colonies. This date of changed political structures and the identifiable end of the colonial era in Australia provides a pertinent point of closure for this study.

Historical Methodology Employed

As previously mentioned, this study of surviving business records places emphasis on understanding accounting in the contexts within which it operated. Historical studies of this genre focus on depicting accounting not as a technique in itself but as one element of the organisational and social context (Hopwood, 1983, 1985; Napier, 1989). Conceptualising accounting in this way involves interpreting the "archive" on its own terms. Interpretive or interpretational history involves explanations as to why episodes took the forms identified from examinations of the available evidence (Previts, Parker & Coffman, 1990a, p.2). An understanding of accounting in its local, time-specific contexts is dependent upon an exploration of the underlying environmental influences in order to provide probable explanations for the structure and usage of the accounting information examined. This interpretive historical study set in the "archive" is concerned with presenting a range of environmental influences which appear to have impacted upon the structure and usage of pre-Federation pastoral accounting information.

This study adopts the field-based case study research method and also makes use of oral sources as explained in Chapter 4. Chapter 4 follows a review of the literature pertaining to this investigation.

Limitations of the Study

A limitation of any study of this nature relates to the inability to examine certain records which previously were part of a larger collection of business records. The nineteenth century records under investigation in this study pre-date the research period by between approximately 90 and 155 years. Inevitably, surviving sets of nineteenth century records available for this study are incomplete. Some records were likely to have been either discarded or lost by those who prepared or made use of the records or by their descendants. Alternatively, some surviving records may have been withheld from examination because they were regarded as "private" or "confidential" while other records may have been temporarily misplaced. As would be expected, there are varying degrees of incompleteness of the different sets of records under examination.

Extensive searches for records in both public and private archives were aimed at reducing the extent to which the available sets of records were incomplete. The biases evident in the research sample selected for this study are discussed in Chapter 4.

Literature Selection

As this study is concerned with accounting in the contexts in which it operated, the literature which elucidates the nineteenth century pastoral industry environment and pastoral station environment is reviewed. This follows the review of the accounting literature concerned with facets of accounting development and the recognition of key environmental factors which influence accounting. As outlined earlier in this chapter, the relevant accounting literature relating to Australian pastoral accounting practices in the pre-Federation period and the advent of an organized Australian accounting profession is addressed. Both primary and secondary sources are examined in elucidating the nineteenth century pastoral industry and station environments. These sources comprise diaries and other papers in manuscript, theses, official government records, newspapers and periodicals, contemporary printed sources and later secondary sources.

Pattern of Analysis

The following text is divided into three major parts. Part One (Chapters 2-3) is concerned with the review of the pertinent literature for this study. The literature relevant to aspects of accounting development and also key environmental factors is examined in Chapter 2, which also explains the cultural perspective adopted in this study. Chapter 3 elucidates the nineteenth century pastoral industry environment and station environment respectively.

Part Two contains four chapters (Chapters 4-7) relating to the examination of the surviving pastoral business records of the entities included in the research sample. Chapter 4 details the methodology of the study and includes a discussion of the research sample, the types of records subject to examination and the process adopted in gleaning oral evidence. Chapter 5 relates the backgrounds of those pastoralists whose surviving nineteenth century records are examined in this study. The account of the research findings provided on a case by case basis is given in Chapter 6. Chapter 7 contains an overview of the structure and usage of nineteenth century pastoral accounting information based on the findings reported in Chapter 6. This chapter identifies generally adopted practices and delineates trends in accounting practices in the period to 1900.

Part Three (Chapters 8-9) presents probable explanations for the accounting practices observed and incorporates the conclusion of this study. Chapter 8 identifies and discusses the key environmental factors which appear to have influenced the accounting practices observed. Chapter 9 includes a summary of the major findings of the study and outlines the study's contemporary relevance. The final chapter also outlines opportunities for future research.

NOTES

1. Major Mitchell first used the name Australia Felix to describe "country ready for the immediate reception of civilised man; and destined perhaps to become eventually a portion of a great empire" which his expedition traversed in the western half of Port Phillip (Mitchell, 1839 cited in Bassett, 1954, p.390). Powell (1970, p.xxv) and Forth (1984, pp.116-118) discussed the subsequent use of the term in defining certain regions.
2. In August 1850, the Port Phillip District achieved separation from the Colony of New South Wales and became the Colony of Victoria (*Geelong Advertiser*, 20 November 1850).
3. Federation of the six colonies within Australia into the Commonwealth of Australia took place on 1 January 1901. On Federation, the Colonies became known as States (Turner, 1973, pp.327-356, which was first published in 1904).
4. Hugh M. Strachan was a pastoralist, woolbroker and sugar grower whose father, John F. Strachan, commenced wool trading activities at the newly established Port Phillip settlement in 1836 (Were, J.B. & Son, 1934; de Serville, 1991, p.340). Strachan (1927) was issued for private circulation only (Billis & Kenyon, 1930, p.27).
5. This volume presents a revision of Carnegie (1994) from which Carnegie (1995) was distilled. Carnegie (1993a) reported on pre-Federation pastoral accounting of the Western District's Jamieson family.
6. An instance of New South Wales station accounting in 1913 is featured in Gibson (1974) who reported on John A. Rogerson's recollections of station bookkeeping and accountants. John A. Rogerson was born in 1897 and had extensive pastoral management experience in both New South Wales and Queensland.
7. Early pastoral licence certificates were titled "License to Depasture Crown Lands beyond the Limits of Location".
8. Founded in Adelaide in November 1885 and incorporated on 30 March 1886 under the *Associations Incorporation Act*, 1858, The Adelaide Society of Accountants (ASA) is the first known professional accounting body established in Australia (Parker, 1961; Walton 1970a, pp.1-6; Gavens, 1990, p.386). The ASA had 19 foundation members,

not all of whom were fully occupied as accountants (Parker, 1961, p.339).

9. The Federal Institute of Accountants (FIA) was incorporated under the *Companies Act* 1890 on 17 July 1894 (Maskell, 1944, p.208) and was hence the third accounting body to be incorporated in Victoria. Both Howden (1900) and Henning (1980, p.209) stated incorrectly that the FIA was the second accounting body to be incorporated in Victoria.

10. The Australian Securities Commission "Production System Organisation Details Enquiry" made on 9 December 1991 showed that the AIIA (Organisation Number 004 044 544) was dissolved on this date.

11. Vigars's book appeared in five editions (second edition, 1901; third edition, 1909; fourth edition, 1914; fifth edition, 1937).

12. Bridges (1975, p.23) stated that Vigars (1900), in giving his reasons for writing the book, referred to the "impact of recent income tax legislation". However, on examination, the statement of Vigars cited in Bridges (1975, p.23) was found to have appeared in the fourth edition only.

13. Hopwood and Johnson (1986, p.46) argued that earlier generations of accounting historians "expended enormous time and energy searching early double-entry records for 'antecedents' to modern financial reporting".

14. In writing about the perspective, Elton (1969, p.31) referred to the need "to understand a given problem from the inside".

PART I

LITERATURE REVIEW

CHAPTER 2

ACCOUNTING DEVELOPMENT AND ENVIRONMENTAL FACTORS

Accounting originated in countries other than Australia and had reached various stages of development in different parts of the world by the early nineteenth century. As Australia comprised six British colonies, it is important to recognize that accounting practice had reached a certain stage of development in Britain by 1788 when New South Wales, subsequently known as Australia, became a British settlement, and that colonialism played a role in the spread of legal and accounting practices from Britain to Australia. As explained in Chapter 1, this study of the structure and usage of pre-Federation pastoral accounting information endeavours to provide probable explanations for the accounting practices adopted during the period 1836 to 1900. To provide such explanations, it is firstly important to address relevant aspects of accounting development prior to European settlement of the Western District and to address the major environmental factors identified in the literature as impacting upon accounting practice in any country.

This chapter has two main sections. The first section addresses aspects of accounting development but particularly accountability considerations and the role of colonialism. The second section provides an analysis of environmental factors and, in particular, focuses on explaining the cultural perspective adopted as a theoretical position in this study.

Accounting Development

Accounting development may be defined as the state of the art or discipline of accounting in a society to a particular point in time. It is recognized that accounting occurred in early times in cases of the entrepreneur as the sole owner and operator of an enterprise and also where there was segregation of "management" and ownership. Pattillo (1965, p.24) contended that accounting for one's own use was the "first stage of accounting development". Accountability considerations have also had an important bearing on accounting development as the advent of an obligation to account where circumstances previously did not involve the possession of resources in some agential capacity has implications for the recording and reporting of the consequences of business activity. Colonialism facilitated the spread of legal and accounting practices and contributed to accounting development in colonial societies (Seidler, 1983, pp.60-61). Both accountability considerations and colonialism are now discussed in more detail.

Accountability Considerations

By necessity, the notion of accountability involves two parties, an accountor (or agent) and an accountee (or principal). According to Ijiri (1975, p.ix) "the 'accountability relationship' normally requires an accountor to account for his activities and their consequences for the benefit of an accountee". An accountability relationship can arise under "a constitution, a law, a contract, an organisational rule, a custom, or even by an informal moral obligation" (Ijiri, 1975, p.ix). A feature of the accountability relationship is that the accountor will safeguard the resources of the accountee. This commonly involves the maintenance of records relating to the use of resources to facilitate the rendering of an account to a provider of those resources. Accounting records have traditionally provided evidence of an accountor's "stewardship" of the accountee's resources.[1] In this context, Belkaoui (1985a, p.6) noted that accounting records "provide a history of a manager's *stewardship* of the owner's resources" (emphasis in original).

Accountability relationships are not new and have been observed throughout history (Wallace, 1985, p.18; Walsh & Stewart, 1986; Mills, 1988, 1990, p.55). Such relationships have been provided for under the English legal system, the foundations of which were laid in the latter half of the twelfth century.[2] The earliest accountability relationship under common law was that between lord and bailiff and, according to Milsom (1969, p.239), it was around the institution of the bailiff's account that "the legal ideas of account first grew". Around this time, the system of writs was instrumental in extending and differentiating the common law (Lovell, 1962, p.104; Mills, 1990, p.58). In effect, a writ constituted the Royal response to a private individual's petition for redress and was drawn up by Chancery on payment of a fee. Among the writs available was the writ of account. As explained by Mills (1990, p.59):

> The purpose of the writ was to compel an accounting, an examination of an agent's stewardship transactions. It was designed as a remedy where an agent had refused or otherwise failed to render an account privately before his principal, which common law required. . . . In effect, the writ ordered the sheriff to secure the defendant's presence in court for the purpose of rendering an

account of the plaintiff's money or other property, the defendant having held it in some agential capacity.

These writs permitted suit against three types of agents: "the bailiff or estate manager; the guardian in socage; or the receiver" (Mills, 1990, p.59). In the case of partnerships, a receiver could be sued on account when one or more partners sought an accounting from an associate. As described by Fifoot (1970, p.270), the standard declaration made in such actions was to require the defendant to "render his reasonable account of the time during which he was the receiver of the monies of the plaintiff, accruing by any cause or from any contract whatsoever to the common profit".

During this period in England, the need for agents to account to their principals was evidently an accepted tenet of commerce. As described, this need led to a non-statutory requirement becoming institutionalized by means of the process of providing for legal remedies in the case of a lack of accountability by an agent. Legal intervention in such instances is not surprising. As Goldberg (1965, p.9) observed, the phenomenon that accounting practices "are subject to constraints of law is simply a recognition that they are of sufficient significance in the lives of a sufficient number or proportion of people in the community to warrant the attention of the lawmakers".

According to Previts and Merino (1979, p.15), "colonial" accounting developed in accordance with the increased propensity for joint ownership of business enterprises. Previts and Merino (1979, p.15) contended that:

> . . . colonial businessmen were able to create joint ventures to provide sufficient capital to undertake new, relatively specialized, and often risky ventures. When joint ownership increased, the adoption of early double entry and the requisite proprietary accounts expanded.

It appears that Previts and Merino (1979) were acknowledging the impact of changing business structures on the structure and usage of accounting information. Implicit in their contention is recognition of emerging accountability relationships involving the need to structure accounting records to facilitate the periodic review or reporting of financial information to those with an ownership interest in a firm.

The advent of the company form of business organisation also had implications for accountability relationships and was a major influence on accounting in general during the second half of the nineteenth century (Pattillo, 1965, p.24; Yamey, 1962). Yamey (1962, p.25) argued that the widespread adoption of double entry accounting probably occurred from the latter part of the nineteenth century.

Agency relationships have been linked to the origins of accounting. For instance, Yamey (1962, p.15) claimed that:

> The origins of accounting and indeed of written records are probably to be found in the need of an "accounting" officer to render a statement of money and other assets received in his charge on behalf of his employer, or disbursed on his behalf. There was need for a check on the honesty and reliability of subordinates.

Similarly, in focusing on evidence of Greek and Roman accounting, de Ste. Croix (1956, p.38) argued:

> We must always remember . . . that the whole purpose of ancient accounting was not to measure the rate of profit or loss but to keep accurate records of acquisitions and outgoings, in money and kind, and to expose any losses due to dishonesty or negligence.

Despite the presence of these arguments in the literature, there is also recognition that accounting occurred in early times where the entrepreneur was both the sole owner and operator of an enterprise (Pattillo, 1965, p.24).

Surviving business records are an important source of historical evidence to test or support views on accounting practice. This study involves examinations of surviving business records of non-corporate pastoral entities in situations where accountability relationships both did and did not exist. As a consequence, any differences in accounting practice between the two states of affairs can be identified along with any variations in practice following a change in particular cases from one form to the other. This will allow conclusions to be drawn about the nature of accounting information prepared solely for one's own purposes as opposed to that prepared for a wider audience.

Colonialism

The colonisation of countries often resulted in the adoption of the notion of accountability accepted in the home country and the advent of institutions whose mode of operation bore a close resemblance to those based in the home country. Even in cases where a country was not colonized, the accounting influence of whatever country became the major cultural or business participant was likely to have been experienced. Despite the role of colonialism in importing accounting practices, colonial accounting reflected a range of environmental factors specific in location and time. For instance, Baxter (1956) indicated that although barter was still practised to some extent in Britain in the eighteenth century, it was very common in America. Baxter (1956, p.272) offered two prime reasons related to the functioning of the American economy for this difference in propensity to barter:

> First, each community was small in numbers; and, if a market consists of few dealers, the chances are high that A will both sell to and buy from B - particularly as both men may be somewhat unspecialized and so have a wide range of wares on offer. Second, money was scarce and bad.

According to Baxter (1956, p.275) and R.H. Parker (1986, p.85), the role of accounting in an economy which lacks banks and ready money is to lubricate barter. "Bookkeeping barter" entails the entering of personal accounts in ledgers to record an exchange which involves the use of money as a unit of account in cases where it is not used as a means of payment. Bookkeeping barter is common in isolated communities. It occurred, for example, in early New South Wales (Parker, 1982).

As a British settlement, the educational, legal and political, and economic systems adopted in the six British colonies in Australia were broadly based on those prevailing in Britain. Moreover, the British model of an organized accounting profession was subsequently adopted in Australia from the mid 1880s (Brentnall, 1938, p.64; Parker, 1989, pp.12-19; Carnegie, 1993, pp.61-62; Parker & Carnegie, 1997).

Environmental Factors

Schoenfeld (1983, p.153) explained the basic approach adopted by accounting historians of earlier times in stating:

> Accounting history has been pursued as a descriptive analysis of accounting developments; authors usually concentrated on specific periods or sets of available records. Normally these are interpreted in terms of modern accounting; this results in findings which stress either similarities or differences. To explain such differences mostly specific economic events or developments are identified as influencing factors. In all cases in which accounting history is analyzed over extended periods of time, such individual studies are drawn together to provide the necessary evidence. Finally time periods are identified, which appear to show sufficient similarity in accounting developments to permit generalizations.

This emphasis on the identification of specific economic events or developments to explain differences between current and past practices was indicated by Schoenfeld (1983, p.171) to have been taken in Baxter (1950), Littleton and Yamey (1956), ten Have (1976) and Chatfield

(1977). Baxter (1946, 1983) provided a further illustration of a focus on economic factors on contending that the development of colonial accounting was a function of market specialisation which brought less reliance on "two-way" trade in a period where the currency became disciplined. Such a sweeping explanation for the development of colonial accounting appears to ignore the complexities of a colonial society under rapid transformation. However, Baxter (1956, p.287) was not completely satisfied that economic factors could "tell us everything that is needed to explain the change". This doubt was encapsulated in the question posed: "May not the character of colonial life - for instance, a relaxed tempo in business, and a relish for negotiation - have had something to do with financial methods?" (Baxter, 1956, p.287). Schoenfeld (1983, p.154) also explained that this traditional approach to accounting history involved "provincialism" or the identification of changes in accounting practice within a particular region or country. Such narrow horizons often produced conflicting evidence of the growth and development of accounting when the examinations of practice extended to other countries or regions.[3]

While the identification of specific economic events or developments assumes importance, it is now recognized that a broad range of influences impact upon accounting (Schoenfeld, 1983; Belkaoui, 1985b, pp.28-29; Loft, 1986; Fleischman, Kalbers & Parker, 1996; Fleischman & Tyson, 1997). According to Fleischman, Kalbers and Parker (1996, p.315) the horizons for the investigation of accounting history have been widened "to incorporate social, psychological, cultural, and political parameters to complement more traditional economic explanations of change". Further, the contemporary accounting literature recognizes that accounting practices vary from country to country and that it is normally inappropriate to make generalisations about accounting developments generally based on studies in any single country or region of a country.

Classification of Environmental Factors
Various authors including Schoenfeld (1983), Arpan and AlHashim (1984, pp.15-25), Arpan and Radebaugh (1985, pp.13-23) Belkaoui (1985b, pp.28-54), Radebaugh and Gray (1993, pp.42-54) and Nobes and Parker (1995, pp.10-20) have classified variables identified as influencing accounting practice into major categories. In developing a conceptual framework for analysing differences in international business practices, Farmer and Richman (1966, pp.75-80) organized environmental characteristics into four major groups: educational, legal and political, economic and sociological. Such factors are seen to affect accounting practices as accounting provides information about business

activity (Arpan & AlHashim, 1984, p.4; Arpan & Radebaugh, 1985, p.13; Radebaugh & Gray, 1993, p.43).[4]

The strength, size and competence of the accounting profession is also regarded as an important factor in shaping accounting thought and practice in a certain country (Nobes & Parker, 1995, pp.17-18). This fifth factor is referred to as "professional" in this study although the advent of an organized accounting profession first took place in Scotland in 1853 (Parker, 1978, pp.54-55; 1989, p.13). The concept of how members of a social stratum establish and preserve their status, and how collective mobility is attained has been termed "social closure" (Larson, 1977; Macdonald, 1985, p.54; West, 1996). West (1996) examined the factors identified in the literature as determinants of the professionalization of accounting. These factors include traditionally espoused professional ideals such as altruism and specialized knowledge and more recently identified notions such as political acuity, relations with the State, gender and social class.

This study adopts the term "cultural" rather than "sociological", "sociocultural" or "social" as explained in the discussion below on the cultural perspective adopted. Based on the above discussion, the categories of major environmental influences accommodated in this study are: educational, legal and political, economic, cultural and professional. These influences assume potential importance in endeavours to understand accounting in the contexts within which it operated. Whilst there exists generalized understandings of the educational, legal and political, economic and professional influences upon accounting, the cultural perspective adopted in this study as a theoretical position requires specific explanation which follows.

Culture

Culture has only recently been recognized as an important environmental factor impacting the accounting environment of a country (Frank, 1979; Nair & Frank, 1980; Belkaoui, 1985b, pp.29-39; 1989; Hofstede, 1987; Schreuder, 1987; Gray, 1988; Bloom & Naciri, 1989; Riahi-Belkaoui & Picur, 1991; Radebaugh & Gray, 1993, pp.53-54). It is a logical development of this literature for accounting historians to examine the impact of culture in studies of accounting's past. Culture has been broadly defined as "the totality of equivalent and complementary learned meanings maintained by a human population, or by identifiable segments of a population, and transmitted from one generation to the next" (Rohner, 1984, pp.119-120). More briefly, Rohner (1984, p.113) referred to culture as "a system of meanings in the heads of multiple individuals within a population". Hofstede (1980, p.25) defined culture similarly as "the collective programming of the mind which distinguishes the members of one human group from another". Culture as a function of personal interactions appears in three main layers: national, organisational and occupational. National culture is the programming of most members within a nation; organizational culture is the particular programming shared by most persons within an organisation and occupational culture is the programming shared by those in an identifiable field of endeavour, such as banking, hospitality, and real estate (Hofstede, 1987, pp.1-2). In order to operationalize this very broad concept of culture, Hofstede (1987, p.2), distinguished four levels at which culture manifests itself: symbols, heroes, rituals and values. An essential feature of social systems is the existence of a system of societal norms, or cultural values shared by groups of individuals within a nation (Gray, 1988, p.4). Values are defined by Hofstede (1987, p.4) as "broad tendencies to prefer certain states of affairs over other states of affairs" and are regarded as the "deepest-seated level" in the hierarchy of manifestations.

The cross-national cultural studies in accounting have focused on the impact of culture on the accounting environment of a country. These cultural studies involving comparisons across different countries have focused on accounting practices (Frank, 1979; Gray, 1980; Nair & Frank, 1980), accounting standard setting arrangements (Bloom & Naciri, 1989), the working of accounting institutions (Belkaoui, 1989) and the meanings of accounting concepts (Riahi-Belkaoui & Picur, 1991). In contrast, Ansari and Bell (1991) adopted a cultural perspective in examining, by observation, the accounting practices of a *single* organisation, a Pakistani ice cream company during the period 1967 to 1989.

The cultural perspective adopted by Ansari and Bell (1991) is embedded in the works of cultural anthropologists, but particularly those of Geertz (1973, 1983, 1988). The pith of what Geertz terms "interpretive anthropology" is to understand events and institutions in their socio-historical context (Geertz, 1983, p.7). Geertz (1973, p.89) defined culture as:

> . . . an historically transmitted pattern of meanings embodied in symbols, a system of inherited conceptions expressed in symbolic forms by means of which men communicate, perpetuate, and develop their knowledge about and attitudes toward life.

Ansari and Bell (1991, pp.8-9) explained the cultural perspective adopted as follows:

> Along with music, art and literature, social institutions, such as accounting and control systems, are seen as symbolic forms

through which a society expresses its collective world view. To understand these institutions, we must first understand how the acquired world views used by individuals shaped such systems and what they come to symbolise for them.

Under this cultural perspective, culture provides organisational participants with interpretive schemes for processing experiences. Over time, an individual's pattern for interpreting events becomes that person's world view.[5] Therefore, culture plays a key role in the process of forming world views. It follows that accounting systems come to define and be defined by culture as the context within which world views are determined.

Unlike Hofstede (1987), who adopted a more functionalist perspective in distinguishing four levels of culture, Ansari and Bell (1991) believed that culture is manifested in all the ways in which people organize their lives. That is, not just in the identification of, for example, heroes or rituals but art, architecture, accounting, law and so on are all manifestations of culture. The cultural perspective adopted by Ansari and Bell (1991, p.8) "treats organisational or national culture as the *context* within which *local* practices can be explained" (emphases in original). Ansari and Bell (1991) used the cultural perspective to explain how and why certain types of accounting systems existed in the organisation at various stages during the period involved. Their study showed how culture supplies the interpretations that individuals use to make sense of their experiences and demonstrated the power of culture as an explanatory variable in a local, time-specific context. Dissimilar to the present study, Ansari and Bell (1991) focused on the accounting practices of a single organisation. Further, unlike the Ansari and Bell (1991) study, the accounting practices reported upon in this study were not witnessed by the author in their time-specific contexts. Notwithstanding, the cultural perspective adopted by Ansari and Bell (1991) is applied in this study as a theoretical position in addressing culture as a major environmental factor.

Culture is not the only concept needed to understand behaviour in sociocultural contexts. Others include "social system" and "society". Although the constructs of culture, social system and society are interrelated, they should be analytically distinguished from each other (Parsons, 1973, p.34; Rohner, 1984, pp.127-130). According to Rohner (1984, p.128):

Many culture theorists take as their model of culture and social system the linguist's model of language and speech. According to this metaphor, culture is to social system as language is to speech. Here both culture and language are construed as systems of meanings, and both involve mental rules that "guide" behavior (that is, guide the social system and speech, respectively).

Knowledge of culture (that is, a symbolic meaning system) alone is an uncertain basis for predicting social behaviour (that is, the social system) (Rohner, 1984, p.127). This historical study of surviving business records is clearly not concerned with predicting the behaviour of participants. Hence, it is appropriate to use the term cultural in this study rather than sociological, sociocultural or social, all of which are perceived to have wider connotations.

Summary

In contemporary accounting research there is recognition that a broad range of environmental factors affect accounting practices. In this study, it is recognized that accounting in an earlier age was also affected by a broad range of environmental factors. The major environmental factors accommodated in this study are: educational, legal and political, economic, cultural and professional. Such factors assume potential importance in endeavours to understand accounting in the organizational and social context in which it operated. The use of culture in accounting history studies is intended to provide a further dimension for understanding accounting in its local, time-specific contexts. This focus is not found in studies which attempt to explain accounting's past by reference to economic rationales alone.

To assist in recognising the major environmental factors which shaped Western District pastoral accounting practices, it is vital to elucidate the nineteenth century pastoral industry environment and the pastoral station environment. This portrayal appears in the following chapter.

NOTES

1. Birnberg (1980, p.73) addressed the evolution of the stewardship concept over time and identified four periods: pure custodial; traditional custodial; asset-utilization and open-ended.
2. Refer to Pollock and Maitland (1968) for a comprehensive account of the historical development of the English legal system.
3. Provincialism occurs, for example, because historians from places like the UK and USA largely confine themselves to English language sources while European historians very often draw on a totally different set of sources.
4. While Arpan and AlHashim (1984, p.5) referred to "sociocultural" factors, Arpan and Radebaugh (1985, p.17) preferred to title these as "cultural" factors. Radebaugh and Gray (1993, pp.53-54) described such

factors as "culture, or societal values". Arpan and Radebaugh (1985, p.13) and Radebaugh and Gray (1993, p.42) also stated inaccurately that Farmer and Richman (1966, pp.75-80) used the term "sociocultural" for factors which had been described as "sociological".

5. In simple terms, what this means is that when two individuals are confronted with the same event, for example, the decision to retrench staff, the way they interpret this event and make sense of it is based on their acquired world views. Hence, one person may view the retrenchments as efficient and worthwhile while the other may view them as cruel and avoidable. (For a discussion of world views and their ability to explain empirical observations in labour conflict, see Sabel, 1982).

CHAPTER 3

NINETEENTH CENTURY PASTORAL ENVIRONMENT

This chapter attempts to elucidate the nineteenth century pastoral environment in order to assist the identification of key variables which appear to have impacted upon the structure and usage of the accounting information of the pastoral entities whose surviving business records are available for this study. It comprises two main sections: the pastoral industry environment and the station environment. These may be regarded as the macro and micro representations of the nineteenth century pastoral environment.

The pastoral industry environment section examines the development of the industry in the Port Phillip District/Colony of Victoria from the mid 1830s to 1900. It explains the main economic and legal and political developments affecting the pastoral industry and details changes in prevailing world views depicting national culture as society moved from a "settler capitalism" to a "colonial liberalism" mode. The pastoral station environment section examines the station conditions experienced by the pastoralists and the station workers during the period to Federation. It explains the isolated Western District stations as small communities of varying interdependent populations and points to the lifestyles of those working and living in these communities at different stages during the pre-Federation period. Educational developments are also addressed along with assessments of varying employment practices and conditions on Western District stations compared with those at pastoral stations in New South Wales and Queensland. Possible connections between the respective environments examined and pastoral accounting practice are considered at the close of each of the two main sections in this chapter.

Pastoral Industry Environment
This examination of the pre-Federation pastoral industry environment comprises five sub-sections: settlement to 1850, 1851 to 1870, 1871 to 1890, 1891 to Federation, and overview. A discussion then follows of

the possible impacts of this environment on pre-Federation pastoral accounting practice.

Settlement to 1850

European settlement on the fertile lands of the Western District is claimed to have commenced on 19 November 1834 when Edward Henty landed at Portland Bay in the then known Port Phillip District.[1] According to Billis and Kenyon (1930, p.27), it was not until May 1835 that the "real" pastoral settlement of Port Phillip took place when John Batman, as representative for a group of pastoralists from Van Diemen's Land, made his historic visit to the site of the City of Melbourne. By the end of 1836, there were around 100 sheep farmers in Port Phillip including the Hentys at Portland Bay, although most of these had squatted on land around Melbourne, Geelong and Werribee (Sutherland, 1977a, pp.139-141).[2] However, it was not until after Major Mitchell's visit to the Henty's establishment in 1836 that the influx of settlers to the then known Portland Bay District occurred (Kiddle, 1961, p.35). Until 1838, the depasturing of stock in the Colony was without fee, licence or authorisation. Then, a run licence fee of 10 pounds was set without limitation of area or carrying capacity although few paid the fee in the first year as only 58 licences were taken out.[3] The number of licences issued in 1839 increased to 69 (Billis & Kenyon, 1930, p.5). The pastoral settlers in the later years of the 1830s had to push farther into the interior to seek runs and by late 1839 it had become difficult to find new runs.[4]

According to Billis and Kenyon (1930, p.42) "the excursions of many of the early pastoral settlers of Port Phillip in search of runs were exploration feats of no mean merit". The significance of this era of pioneering pastoralism is summed up in the words of Strachan (1927, pp.7-8) who stated:

> No chapter in the history of the colony is more interesting than the records of the early stocking and the first settlement, from small beginnings, of the stations, which afterwards became recognised as some of the most valuable properties in Australia. These records reveal the splendid and determined characters of many of the pioneers, all of whom encountered such difficulties that only the most resolute survived. By their determination and fortitude, they built, on the most substantial foundations, the colony's great pastoral industry, which is the one factor, more than any other, that can be regarded as the backbone of finance, commerce, and the general prosperity of the entire community.

The pioneering pastoralists lived in primitive conditions but most of them were able to increase their flocks and herds despite the isolation, vagaries of the weather, absence of proper transportation and other infrastructure facilities. They also met with the indigenous population, the Aborigines, who were ultimately displaced and diminished in number as pastoral settlers pushed further into the interior (Kiddle, 1961, pp.127-130 & 301-302; Critchett, 1990).

In 1839 an annual assessment based on stock numbers was introduced under the Act 2 *Victoria, No.27* in order to cover the cost of mounted police known as the Border Police. The annual assessment, payable half-yearly, was at the rate of one half-penny for every sheep including weaned lambs; one penny for each head of cattle above the age of six months; and threepence for each horse aged six months or over. This legislation also required the six monthly reporting of the numbers of persons resident or employed on a station. The stock assessment was removed in 1853 and reintroduced in the following year at enhanced rates (Billis & Kenyon, 1930, p.5). By around the mid 1840s there were 282 pastoral runs of between approximately 5,000 and 75,000 acres and some larger runs covering the entire Western District (Kiddle, 1961, p.44). Until 1841, the Western District pastoralists enjoyed a boom period but were then hit by an economic depression which spanned the period to 1844 (Roberts, 1935, pp.224-258; Kiddle, 1961, pp.133-137; Fletcher, 1976, pp.118-125).

There are varying explanations of the main factors which contributed to the 1841-44 depression or "the great crisis" as termed by Roberts (1935, pp.224-258). Roberts (1935, p.234) attributed the main cause of the depression to excessive speculation which was driven by an excess of capital. Although wool prices halved from two shillings to one, Roberts (1935, p.241) argued that "squatting could still pay with wool at a shilling a pound". Alternatively, Fitzpatrick (1941, p.110) believed that the main cause of the crash was the 1839 crises in the English money market which led to a reduction in foreign investment. Butlin (1953, pp.318-328) discounted each of these explanations and contended that the pastoralists had over-expanded and had relied too heavily on a continuation of the high returns of the previous years. During the depression banks both closed and foreclosed.[5] Credit was virtually impossible to obtain and many pastoralists who had heavily extended themselves in the boom period felt the brunt of misfortune (Kiddle, 1961, p.135; Cannon, 1973, p.20; Fletcher, 1976, p.121).

Following the depression, pastoralists experienced a period of solid recovery and expansion. By 1850, the value of the wool clip was £1,614,241 compared with £566,122 ten years earlier (Fletcher, 1976, pp.122-123). Further evidence of expansion and growth in the Colony

of New South Wales (including the Port Phillip District) is found in
Table 3.1 as reproduced from Fletcher, 1976, p.120.

**TABLE 3.1: Expansion of Population, Agriculture, Sheep
and Cattle Raising in New South Wales
(including Port Phillip) 1830-50**

	Population	Acreage cultivated	Cattle	Sheep	Wool exported (lbs)
1830	46 402	70 695	248 440	504 775	899 750
1835	71 592	79 256	n.a.	n.a.	3 893 927
1840	129 463	122 906	n.a.	n.a.	8 610 775
1845	173 377	138 237	1 159 432	5 604 644	10 522 921
1850	265 503	144 647	1 374 968	7 092 209	14 270 622

Note:
The figures for 1830 come from the 1828 census - no census was taken in 1829 or 1830.

Sources: *New South Wales Colonial Secretary, Returns of the Colony, 1830 to 1850.*

By 1848-49, the Port Phillip District of the Colony provided around 60
per cent of the Colony's wool clip based on sheep depastured as
evidenced in Table 3.2 as reproduced from Roberts (1935, p.448).

**TABLE 3.2: Position at the End of this [Roberts] Survey,
1848-9**

	New South Wales (proper)	Port Phillip
Number of squatters	1 041	824
Area of runs, sq. miles	54 821	30 304
Average area of a run	34 000 acres	24 000 acres
Sheep depastured	2 358 000	3 146 000
Cattle depastured	644 000	244 000
Licences paid	£18 812	£13 009
Average per sq. mile	8/10	8/7
Average annual cost of depasturing each sheep	1½ d.	1d.

This table also shows that the average run area in the Port Phillip
District at this time was 24,000 acres. However, the average station size
in the Western District in 1848-49 was probably less than this figure as
the Western District was more closely settled than any other district in
the Port Phillip District (Kiddle, 1961, p.44).

The early pastoral settlers in the Port Phillip District experienced currency problems in the years before the establishment of a system of banking and before the standardisation of the currency. Currency problems eased as bank agencies were established and local banks were founded. The creation by banks of branch networks also eased the problems (Kiddle, 1961, p.41). According to Kiddle (1961, p.41):

> Before the establishment of bank branches in Melbourne, Geelong and Portland, indeed for long afterwards, the squatters paid for goods and gave wages in orders on their agents made payable to the bearer.

The local currency consisted of a diverse mixture of sterling, dollars, "holey" dollars, dumps and rupees. It was not until 1849 that standardisation was achieved when only British coins were in circulation (Butlin, 1953, pp.175-189). In August 1850, the Port Phillip District achieved separation from the Colony of New South Wales and became the Colony of Victoria.

1851 to 1870

Less than twelve months after separation on 7 July 1851, the *Geelong Advertiser* published the first announcement of the discovery of gold in Victoria. This lead to a substantial increase in the population of the new Colony which rose from 77,345 in 1851 to 540,322 ten years later (Kiddle, 1961, p.203). Although station labour became scarce and difficult to retain as workers moved into the goldfield regions, the pastoralists recovered from the mining era as good mutton and beef were in constant demand, and wool consigned to Europe was carried cheaply due to the substantial increase in ships bringing people to Australia (Strachan, 1927, pp.35-36; Billis & Kenyon, 1930, pp.128-130; Shann, 1930, p.185). The pastoralists also benefitted from an English wool market which had been rising steadily since 1849 (McNaughtan, 1955, p.116).

The influx of new settlers inevitably lead to calls to throw open crown lands then occupied by pastoralists (to "unlock the land") (Kiddle, 1961, pp.213-232; Cannon, 1973, pp.126-145). "Settler capitalism" is a term used by Macintyre (1991, p.88) to describe the development of the Colony of Victoria in the first two decades of squatting occupation.[6] According to Macintyre (1991, p.89), "the productivity of settler capitalism concentrated wealth in the hands of a minority and restricted opportunities for the bulk of the population". From around the mid 1850s there developed a culture referred to as "colonial liberalism" which embodied the rejection of world views implicit in settler capitalism (McNaughtan, 1955, pp.98-144; Dunstan, 1984, pp.15-16 &

55-56; Macintyre, 1991, pp.88-89). Opposition to squatting occupation of prime grazing land developed among the rapidly expanding numbers of mining, working, business and professional people in Melbourne and other urban areas. As stated by Macintyre (1991, p.5), the urban liberals "sought to establish a sphere of freedom in which all citizens could meet each other, safe from interference and liberated from the hierarchical bonds of traditional society". The liberals were against the pastoralists who, as the liberals characterized them, placed their interests before the public interests. The ideal of a closer settled Victorian countryside worked by the independent yeoman farmer rather than the pastoralist was advanced by the liberals (McNaughtan, 1955, p.115; Dingle, 1985, p.102).

The liberals soon gained political influence and, according to Dunstan (1984, p.15), liberalism provided "much of the framework and language of politics". Policies were adopted to unlock the land as part of the reforms seen as essential to equalize people in a liberal society. The pastoralists faced land reform from a position of strength having been assisted by favourable trends in the industry. Of course, having opened up and developed the land, the pastoralists thought of the land occupied as their own. They were anxious to ensure their stations remained substantially intact and that legal ownership of pastoral land was secured. As explained by McNaughtan (1955, p.116):

> . . . the tense political atmosphere made compromise more difficult each year as the clamour to "unlock the land" grew and the squatters became intransigent. As a result the land Acts of the early sixties were declarations of war for the possession of the Crown lands - the reformers never doubting that the victory would go to "the people".

However, following the enactment throughout the 1860s of land reform Acts known as the Nicholson Act, the Duffy Act and the Grant Acts, ownership of the overwhelming bulk of the grazing land in Victoria went to the pastoralists (McNaughtan, 1955, p.118; Powell, 1970, pp.82-87, 104-110 & 128-132; Macintyre, 1991, p.101; de Serville, 1991, p.161).

The pastoralists adopted various techniques in their battle for control of the land including the use of pre-emptive rights, improvement and auction clauses and dummying. Dummying involved the selection of land under rights of selection by those sympathetic to the pastoralist such as family and friends, station hands and travellers for subsequent transfer to the pastoralist. An effective technique used to block unwelcome selectors was to secure the water resources on a station by acquiring the land fronting rivers and that surrounding fresh water lakes. In other instances, selectors were bought out. Many of these selectors were not interested in the land for their own pastoral pursuits but were regarded as land "sharks" or blackmailers who were satisfied in being bought out at a high price (McNaughton, 1955, pp.111-122; Kiddle, 1961, p.273; Powell, 1970, pp.59-144). The Western District pastoralists who were the strongest and wealthiest in the Colony secured the pick of the district's pastoral land (Powell, 1970, p.79; de Serville, 1991, p.161). As would be expected, the pastoralists' shrewdness and acquisitiveness was not widely appreciated as they "thumb[ed] their noses at the political hopes and ideals of the age" (de Serville, 1991, p.161). However, according to Macintyre (1991, p.102), "once the genie of land ownership was released, the liberals had to live with the consequences".

During the 1860s the Victorian pastoral industry was required to be "capitalized" as land previously held under licence was purchased. Pastoral companies such as the Australian Mortgage (Mercantile) Land & Finance Company (AML&F) responded to demands for finance as the lands became unlocked (Bailey, 1966, pp.14-23) as did the banks and insurance companies (McNaughton, 1955, p.118). However, the seeds for the capitalisation of the industry were planted earlier (Bailey, 1966, p.50). New licence holders were required to put up much more capital than the squatters who, on sale of their operations, capitalized improvements together with their flocks which multiplied quickly on expanses of productive land. During 1868-69, the Victorian pastoral industry experienced a crisis caused by drought and sharply declining wool prices following a prolonged boom in wool prices to 1867. The pastoralists faced this crisis carrying a much higher level of indebtedness due to their land acquisitions earlier in the decade than had prevailed in earlier times. The acquisition by Victorian pastoralists of Riverina land with access to river frontages was a reaction to this crisis.[7] Hence, the Victorian pastoral crisis was a contributing factor to the boom in Riverina properties in the early 1870s (Bailey, 1966, pp.36-48).

1871 to 1890

The 1870s-80s period is commonly regarded as the "boomtime" in nineteenth century Victoria (Kiddle, 1961, pp.329-361; Colligan, 1990, pp.4-9). The pastoralists were enjoying a period of prosperity which had become an "established order" with favourable world markets, a swelling local population and the implementation of sheep handling improvements which raised the weight of individual fleeces (Kiddle, 1961, p.468). However, many pastoralists were carrying debt finance during this period for a range of reasons including the funding of land acquisitions, the erection or extension of sheds and huts, and the construction of substantial homesteads or extensive improvements to existing homesteads which were dotting the Victorian countryside (Butlin, 1957; Kiddle, 1961, pp.273 & 307-328; de Serville, 1991, pp.169-172). Many Western District pastoralists had also expanded their interests by acquiring stations in the Riverina and further afield, often through the use of borrowed funds (Bailey, 1966, pp.78-84; Shaw, 1981, p.58).

The 1870s period witnessed the introduction of death duties (1870) and land tax (1877) in Victoria.[8] The government had come to the conclusion that although it could not prevent the growth of large estates it had the ability to introduce measures to dismantle them. The celebrated land tax was assessed only on those estates in excess of 640 acres and was determined on the basis of the carrying capacity of the land. In its first year, the payment of land tax involved only 855 landowners (Macintyre, 1991, p.102; de Serville, 1991, p.161).[9] Death duties and land tax represented an attack on wealth which was deemed appropriate to advance the liberal ideals. The introduction of land tax rather than income tax suited the prevailing views. Parnaby (1951, p.104) explained that the land tax:

> . . . had a wide appeal. It attracted merchants anxious to avoid the income tax suggested by the late premier, McCulloch; it appealed for the same reason to city manufacturers. Small farmers were satisfied that the ministry should restrict it to estates over 640 acres. The Treasurer saw here financial relief for the government; doctrinaires [liberals] believed that it would break up the big estates; . . .

To the disappointment of the established pastoralists, the Australian union movement began in the next decade when shearers' unions were formed in 1886. An office to enrol shearers in a union opened at Ballarat in the Western District on 3 June, 1886 (Kiddle, 1961, p.481). As explained by Kiddle (1961, p.481), "shearers were the elite of the bushworkers. 'Ringers' or champion shearers were heroes not only to those who worked with them, but to the general country population". The shearers were grumblingly accepting of their conditions until around the mid 1880s when pastoralists tried to reduce the shearers piece-work rates in line with a decline in wool prices. In response, the first shearers' unions were formed at Wagga Wagga and Bourke and by the end of 1886 about 9,000 shearers in Victoria were union members. Many Victorian pastoralists decided to fight the advent of unionism and the demands for increased rates for union members. In 1888, the Western District Sheepowners' Association was formed and non-union labour drawn largely from the ranks of selectors in pastoral areas was employed on many stations (Kiddle, 1961, pp.481-483). The appointment of non-union labour frustrated the unionists and a period of confrontation ensued.

1891 to Federation

The final decade of the Colony of Victoria began amid widespread economic gloom especially in Eastern Australia as the boomtime had come to an end (Blainey, 1958, ch.10; Butlin, 1961, ch.12; Butlin, 1964, ch.6.3; Cannon, 1967, pp.21-28; Boehm, 1971; Turner, 1973, pp.291-326).[10] The boomtime years brought over-expansion to the pastoral industry (Butlin, 1957, p.10). For the pastoralists who had lost the ascendancy over the urban liberals (Serle, 1971, ch.3; Sherington, 1990, p.69; Connell & Irving, 1992, ch.3), the 1890s brought a period of bad seasons, plummeting wool and livestock prices and also land values, bank closures and shearers' strikes. The pastoralist, especially one who was carrying much debt from the excesses of the earlier decades, was under siege (Butlin, 1957, pp.9-10; Kiddle, 1961, pp.468-507; Bailey, 1966, pp.157-172). The AML&F which dealt in Colonies other than Victoria experienced two separate waves of foreclosures in 1890-1 and again in 1898-9 (Bailey, 1966, p.157). As explained by Kiddle (1961, p.482) "the [Western] District and the country were plunged into an economic cataclysm from which the spirit of boundless optimism never fully recovered".

The economic depression years of the early 1890s ran the Colonial government in Victoria into serious deficit and led to the advent of income tax on incomes in excess of £200 under the *Income Tax Act 1895* (Mills, 1925, pp.89-92; Fayle, 1984, pp.674-675; vanden Driesen & Fayle, 1987, p.29).[11] Unlike death duties and land tax, income tax was not targeted only at pastoralists and other wealth holders. However, pastoralists with estates of over 640 acres were opposed to the income tax because they perceived the imposition of both land tax and income tax as a double taxation regime (*Victoria, Parliamentary Debates, Session 1894-5*, pp.1708-1722). Under the income tax legislation, 1894 was the first year for which returns of income were required to be prepared.

The situation in the middle of the decade was summarized by John Cooke, an Australian Manager of AML&F, in stating:

In five years - from Dec/Jan 1889/90 until Dec/Jan 1894/95 I find the average depreciation in values of our shipments of wool to London has been not far short of 40 per cent. Side by side with this, the fall in stock values has been still more pronounced. The fall in sheep values over the period may fairly be stated at 50 per cent (cited in Bailey, 1966, p.165).

During 1892, Cooke revalued the station properties on which AML&F's lending was secured. This resulted in writing off 25 per cent from book values. These write-offs proved to be insufficient and, in 1896, a further £120,000 was written off to take account of bad seasons. While these properties were largely located in New South Wales, the 1890s brought heavy falls in Australian pastoral investment and reductions generally in the value of pastoral property (Butlin, 1964, pp.61-62). Due largely to the impact of non-interest-bearing loans, AML&F's net profit after tax declined with £106,463 in 1890 to £39,657 in 1897. Profits stabilized at around this level until 1902 when they vanished following the company's second wave of foreclosures (Bailey, 1966, pp.157-166).

Further indication of the effects of the economic depression in the 1890s upon the pastoral industry in Eastern Australia is found in Butlin (1958). For New South Wales, Queensland and Victoria, Butlin (1958, p.2) showed the sheep population and percentage distribution for selected years. The information reported for the period 1862 to 1902 is reproduced in Table 3.3. (The table is also found in Butlin, 1964, p.67.)

TABLE 3.3: Flock Distribution by Colonies (Selected Years only)

	Sheep Population (millions)			Percentage Distribution (%)		
	NSW	Qld	Vic	NSW	Qld	Vic
1862	6.2	4.3	6.2	37.2	25.6	37.2
1866	11.6	7.3	8.8	41.8	26.4	31.8
1876	24.5	6.7	11.7	57.1	15.6	27.3
1880	32.3	6.4	8.7	68.1	13.5	18.4
1887	42.8	12.3	10.7	65.0	18.6	16.4
1892	55.5	20.9	12.9	62.1	23.4	14.5
1902	26.6	7.2	10.5	60.0	16.3	23.7

This table shows that during 1892-1902 sheep numbers declined in New South Wales, Queensland and Victoria although the decline in Victoria was not as pronounced as in the other two jurisdictions. The table also indicates that the portion of sheep in Victoria declined during the period of 30 years to 1892 as new pastoral areas were settled in New South Wales and Queensland.

Butlin (1958, p.5) also provided information about the percentage distribution of the sheep population in Victoria. Table 3.4 shows the relevant information for the period 1862 to 1905. (The table is also found in Butlin, 1964, p.69.)

TABLE 3.4: Percentage Distribution of Victorian Sheep Population

	N. East	Gippsland	Central N.	Central S.	Western	Wimmera
1862	7.5	1.0	11.3	17.6	28.8	33.8
1874	8.5	0.8	11.0	14.1	34.6	31.0
1881	8.1	1.2	11.0	19.4	31.2	29.1
1891	10.9	2.3	13.2	16.6	28.8	28.2
1905	9.9	4.1	12.5	18.5	27.5	27.5

This table indicates that the average portion of Western District sheep relative to the total population of Victorian sheep was around 30 per cent for the period of 43 years from 1862. As the table shows, the Western District was the leading sheep district in Victoria for most of this period.[12] Western District pastoralists were also renowned for their focus on quality. Keenly contested sheep and wool shows held at Skipton, Ballarat, Geelong and Melbourne assisted in the improvement and development of flocks (Billis & Kenyon, 1930, pp.186-187; Kiddle, 1961, pp.372-376; Notman, 1989, pp.37-46).[13]

Overview

Historians, especially economic historians, have emphasized the significance of the pastoral industry but particularly the wool industry to the development of Australia (Strachan, 1927, p.8; Shann, 1930, pp.386-408; Barnard, 1957; Wadham, Wilson & Wood, 1964, pp.97-99). In the period to 1900, pastoral stations had become heavily capitalized and well fitted to cater for the local and overseas demands for wool, beef and mutton. In Victoria, the pastoralists had experienced both the highs and lows of the industry during a period of rapid transformation in the Colony from the mid 1830s to 1900. Even though most of the pioneering pastoralists in the Western District did not live long enough to witness the Federation of Australia, they left behind substantial and productive establishments, many of which are significant properties in today's pastoral industry although virtually all of these are smaller in terms of acreage.

Possible Implications of Pastoral Industry Environment for Accounting Practice

The above discussion points to various factors which potentially influenced pre-Federation pastoral accounting practice in the Western District. The imposition of requirements, as occurred in the pre-Federation period, to submit information to government for levy collection purposes may have created an obligation to collect and record certain types of information. Nevertheless, prevailing world views, such as those implicit in colonial liberalism, impact upon the nature and applicability of laws introduced to facilitate the collection of government revenue. Along with national culture, the ability to enforce laws, as existed in pre-Federation society, may also have been a determinant of accounting practice. Currency problems, particularly at isolated Western District stations, would have been expected to give rise to barter transactions with possible implications for accounting practice. Other economic factors such as economic depressions may have influenced the timing of the introduction of government levies, as shown to be the case for income tax in colonial Victoria.

Station Environment

The examination of the station environment in the pre-Federation period is divided into three sub-sections: station establishment and development, pastoral prosperity and station working conditions. There follows a discussion of the possible impacts of this environment on pre-Federation pastoral accounting practice.

Station Establishment and Community

Obligated to become an explorer, the pioneering Western District pastoralist was required to establish a future home on land which was described as "beyond the limits of location". According to Strachan (1927, p.8):

> Even then, in most cases, his troubles were but begun, for he was many miles from his nearest neighbour; he had no transport facilities; no means of rapid communication in emergency; stores and provisions had to be carted, sometimes over almost impossible obstacles, and there was the constant danger of complete loss of stock by fires, blacks and wild dogs.

Initially, the squatters lived in small sod or timber huts or tents and undoubtedly found the living conditions to be uncomfortable given the vagaries of the weather and their isolation.[14] However, despite the various difficulties, many of these pioneers were able to expand their stock numbers on the fertile Western District lands.[15]

The pioneering pastoralists required increasing numbers of station hands including shepherds and boundary riders as the number and size of herds and flocks grew. There was a corresponding need for more shearers to handle the increasing wool production. At first the station hands and shearers were obtained from the ranks of former convicts who came from either Sydney District or Van Diemen's Land. They had to be closely watched given their habits (Billis & Kenyon, 1930, p.80; Cannon, 1973, p.40; Lang, n.d., p.7). These "old hands" or "lags" as they were described were often older than the pioneering pastoralists who employed them. They contributed much to the knowledge of inexperienced pastoralists and taught immigrant shepherds bush survival techniques. Very few of these old hands married and most died on stations not having reached positions of influence in the Port Phillip District/Colony of Victoria. They were provided with the basic essentials of life and experienced a solitary life, favoured over one of want, hunger and oppression as often previously experienced (Billis & Kenyon, 1930, pp.80-81).

It was common for early Western District station hands to go to Melbourne or Geelong with months' or a year's earnings and to spend much of the money with innkeepers in a few days' dissipation (Billis & Kenyon, 1930, p.80). Such a journey was often a major exercise. For instance, a trip on horseback from the Darlington region to Geelong took three travelling days (McGregor & Oaten, 1985, p.6). Curr (1968, p.439) pointed out some changes in the behaviour of station hands in writing:[16]

> . . . a desire for property sprung up amongst them; so that although the old convict custom of going to town once a year "to have a spree", or spend in three or four days' drinking the earnings of the twelve months, did not go out of fashion altogether, it at least became modified, by the men investing a portion of their wages in the purchase of horses, guns, prime sheep, dogs, or something of the sort.

In spite of their habits, the old hands were, according to Billis and Kenyon (1930, p.80), "well fitted for the work of assisting in the settlement of new country". Curr would appear to have agreed in his summation of the working relationship experienced with ex-convicts. Curr (1968, p.440) stated:

> As they improved in their conduct I naturally came to have a kindly feeling towards them, which soon became mutual; and though I was a little stern with my rogues, and kept them at arms-length, I experienced several instances of goodwill on their parts which proved their disinterestedness.

It was recognized that an old hand was normally a better proposition for station work than a new immigrant (Kiddle, 1961, p.51; Cannon, 1973, p.40).

Not all pioneering pastoralists in the Western District enjoyed a lifestyle any better than that of the early station workers. The economic depression of the early 1840s took its toll on many young pastoralists as explained in John G. Robertson's letter of 26 September 1853 to La Trobe reported in Bride (1969, pp.154-169).[17] John G. Robertson stated:

> Numbers of the young gentlemen who came out to this colony about that time, with a few hundred pounds, took up runs with 300, 400, and 500 sheep, clubbed together, and expected to make fortunes in a few years, from the way they spoke, and the way in which they managed their sheep farms. Few of them knew anything of mechanics, and they were totally unable to make comfort for themselves or their servants. In consequence of which they fell back lower in morality and energy than many of their men, for dirt and filfth (sic) were noticeable in *places* and *persons*, and their pride was, who would rough it best. They even went so far with their indolence as to drop shaving themselves, and it was no bad criterion to know how a man managed his station if the owner was seen looking out through a large wisp of hair on his face. The three eventful years, which will long be remembered in this colony, of 1841-2-3, swept off most of these young gentlemen with their herds and all. About twenty of the squatters in the Portland Bay District (that were fast men) were sold off (emphases in original) (Bride, 1969, pp.157-158).

As the depression passed and the old hands died, the immigrants of the labouring class arrived to work on the stations. These workers became known as the "new hands" or "new chums" (Billis & Kenyon, 1930, p.82; Curr, 1968, p.444). They were of different backgrounds to the remaining old hands who were predominantly survivors of convictism. According to Curr (1968, p.444):

> In my experience the new chums . . . were the least satisfactory servants, often sober men; as, besides being poor hands in the bush, they were generally dissatisfied, and had a very faint idea of obeying orders. Old soldiers were better in this respect, but less intelligent than others, and generally drunkards.

The new hands, unlike the old hands whose rugged existence as convicts toughened them for the exigencies of pioneer life, needed to be broken-in to station life (Cannon, 1973, p.39-40).

As the stations were isolated in remote regions, station communities were formed as accommodation and stores were provided by the pastoralists in the absence of town facilities. These unique small communities centred around station homesteads with their clusters of outbuildings had interdependent populations ranging to over one hundred people including those in outlying huts or out-stations (Forth, 1979, p.28). Bands of itinerant shearers would walk from shed to shed as a moving population. Although the shearers were remunerated on the piece-work basis the more permanent station hands who attended to stock and constructed station facilities such as buildings, stockyards and dams were normally appointed on an annual basis at an agreed amount. Food rations supplemented the agreed rates. Payment for labour, particularly for station hands was often satisfied by the issue of supplies such as tobacco, boots and clothing items, blankets, pipes, postage stamps and alcoholic beverages. Hawkers travelled the Western District in their drays "with every conceivable article likely to be required by the station proprietors or their hands" (Kiddle, 1961, p.84). The stations also rendered hospitality to strangers travelling through the region or those seeking work. As many as six or eight strangers were accommodated overnight at stations bordering on the main interior tracks from the coastal townships. If a traveller's social status did not seem to be proper, accommodation would be found in the men's hut rather than the station homestead (Kiddle, 1961, p.84). In the absence of towns, the stations provided a base for local district activities such as horse racing. According to Notman (1989, p.15), a race meeting was held at Bamgamie (or Langi Willi) station on Mt. Emu Creek in 1844.

The out-stations served as the base for shepherds and hut-keepers and would normally be visited once or twice a week by the pastoralist for the purposes of delivering rations and for checking the numbers and condition of the sheep. These huts were small and primitive but provided a rough shelter to the men who watched over and tendered between 500 to 1000 sheep on the unfenced runs from sunrise to sunset. In the evenings, the sheep would be moved to hurdle yards close to the huts for protection from the Aborigines and marauding dingoes. Travellers would find shelter in the huts if they were not within easy reach of the station homestead. The usual needs of the men located at out-stations were food, alcohol and a rough shelter, although the pastoralist tried to restrict the availability of alcohol. Although life in an out-station was monotonous and a lonely existence, it provided a grounding for those who moved into positions as stockmen and overseers (Kiddle, 1961, pp.59-61; Cannon, 1973, pp.41-42).

The gold rushes of the early 1850s upset the balance of operations on most Western District stations as station hands and shearers left for the gold fields to find their fortune (Strachan, 1927, p.35; Kiddle, 1961, p.198; Palmer, 1973, pp.74-75).[18] The difficulties experienced by pastoralists during the period are typified in the oral reminiscences of John Lang Currie of Larra station as recorded by Lang. According to Lang, Currie reminisced in 1897 as follows:

I remember one time, after purchase of "Larra", Dodds, the Manager, and I were left to carry on the place alone, all the men having left for the Diggings. It was very hard work - at it night and day - and would have killed us soon. The dingoes were very bad at night; we could not keep them out of the hurdle yards where we herded the sheep. We had, at first, two flocks but when the men left, we boxed them together into one. Dodds and I would go off in the morning, one to one side of the run and the other to the other side, and try to keep the sheep together. At night the dogs would come in packs sometimes. Shearing was coming on, and the wool had to come off. I heard that an immigrant ship, the "Marco Polo", was expected, so set off at once for Melbourne. I went straight on board and engaged half a dozen men. They were good honest Scotchmen, hard-working men and they did not desert me for the diggings.

We set off at once for "Larra" - none of them had ever shorn sheep before, but, by the end of shearing, were good workers - Dodds I had just left to carry on alone as best he could. We muddled through that time somehow.

Robert Marshall was one of these men; it must be nearly fifty years ago now. He left me for the diggings for twelve months only. (Later on Robert Marshall held the position of shepherd and later on of boundary rider at "Larra" and was finally pensioned off and lived at "Larra" until his death about 1907). They got the wool off however. It was a most satisfactory feeling to know there was enough wool to carry the place on till next shearing. The men got 30/- per 100; wool about same price as previous years (n.d., pp.6-7).[19]

Eventually, many disappointed former station hands returned to station work while new arrivals sought work on stations on the realisation that the gold rush days had come to an end. However, the influx of gold immigrants, some of whom were prone to have little regard for the notion of private property, combined with the shortage of station hands in the early 1850s had served to expedite the introduction of fences. Fences reduced the propensity for pastoralists to employ shepherds as previously occurred under free-range grazing.

In many homesteads from around the 1850s, most activities, with the exception of prayer meetings and meals, were forbidden on Sundays. Prayer meetings were often compulsory for family members, station hands and house servants (Kiddle, 1961, pp.93 & 112-113; Cannon 1973, p.188). Kiddle (1961, p.112) pointed out that "for most practical purposes squatters' country was untouched by organized religion until towards the very end of the forties". Notwithstanding, church services began in the Henty woolshed at Portland in 1837 (Bassett, 1954, p.410). Mary Robertson of Warrock station, spouse of George Robertson, insisted on daily prayer meetings and was prone to announce the name of any participant who was not concentrating on worship (Hetherington, 1964, p.25). On some stations, churches were built either as separate buildings or as an extension to the homestead to provide a place for worship and often where itinerant preachers conducted services (Cannon, 1973, p.189). In the Western District, for instance, a church in the form of a specially equipped room was incorporated into the Ozencadnuck station homestead (Hamilton, 1981, p.107; Hamilton, 1991, p.37).[20]

In the 1850s and 1860s a number of inland Western District towns developed, many of which sprang up to service the station communities. Typically such a township would include a store with post office, hotel, blacksmith's forge, saddlery, church and government school. As an illustration, Woorndoo, which was officially declared a township in 1868, serviced stations such as Salt Creek, Eilyer, Bolac Plains, Mt. Fyans and Hexham Park. The town's sporting history provides an indication of station comradeship as the first cricket match played on 24 November 1869 was between teams from Salt Creek and Hexham Park stations (Green, 1968). The participants probably played with a sense of community spirit similar to that which would have existed had they been representing a township. The children attending the town school included those of station hands from nearby stations.

Pastoral Prosperity

A large scale Australian pastoralist specialising in sheep, as most did in the Western District, was advantaged in a period marked by rising world wool consumption during 1860-90 (Cannon, 1973, p.177; Forth, 1982, p.34). The most outstanding expression of a pastoralist's prosperity was the building of a solid and substantial homestead. Cannon (1973, p.183) perceived these homesteads to be "lavish mansions" necessary to replace "the unpretentious single-storey timber homestead[s] with which they had replaced the old bark huts". Many of these impressive homesteads came to be regarded as social centres where leading families in the Colony and some of the Colony's distinguished guests came to be entertained (Cannon, 1973, pp.183-186; Forth, 1982, p.36). Virtually all of the substantial Western District homesteads featured extensive gardens including expanses of lawn, rose plantations, bountiful flower beds, hedges, European trees, fruit tree plantations and rotundas. Around the homesteads on many Western District stations were improvements judged as necessary for socialising such as croquet lawns, artificial lakes and designated areas for the conduct of sporting events such as polo, tennis or cricket. Peacocks and fantail pigeons were, in some instances, part of the landscape around a station homestead.

Indoor servants came to be an essential part of the homestead population and their number grew in line with increased pastoral prosperity (Kiddle, 1961, p.289). Although Western District pastoralists continued to take an active interest in the running of their stations, the practice of employing an overseer to supervise daily station activities became commonplace (Kiddle, 1961, p.284; Forth, 1982, pp.35-36). In line with their increasing prosperity, Western District pastoralists, as evidenced in Chapter 5, came to educate their children at private boarding schools such as Scotch College, Geelong Church of England Grammar School, Melbourne Church of England Grammar School and Geelong College[21] and, in many cases, the children completed their education at colleges and universities in England. These educational developments contributed to the increasing sophistication of Western District society and the creation of social networks. As an illustration, William Moodie stated:

> I have often, when travelling outback, been asked if I ever went to Scotch College. When I replied "No, but I had brothers who did", that was near enough for a bond of friendship and made a theme for conversation at once (Palmer, 1973, p.96).

Forth (1982) referred to the pastoralists' "Golden Age" in the Western District as the quarter of a century following their victory in the battle for the lands. During this Golden Age, large scale pastoral operations became more profitable due to "the adoption of less labour-intensive and more economic forms of stock management, the impact of new technology (particularly in the area of transportation) and the introduction of selective breeding programs" (Forth, 1982, p.34). The security found by the pastoralists following the resolution of the land tenure issue and the prosperity they attained was accompanied by endeavours by certain wealthy pastoral families to be seen as a type of "colonial landed gentry" (Forth, 1982, p.34). Indeed, according to Kiddle (1961, pp.512-513), in many cases the second generation of Western District pastoralists spent the fortunes made by the pioneering pastoralists in "riotous living".

Cannon (1973, pp.177-95) wrote about the rise to power of the Australian pastoralists and the class created as a consequence of their success. Cannon (1973, p.177-178) was not an apologist for the pastoralists when he argued:

> The external signs of the creation of this new class were the stout fencing of their freehold acres, the building of large mansions and town houses, employment of household servants, intermarriage

between leading families, hierarchical social behaviour based on degree of wealth, education of offspring at exclusive schools, absentee landlordism, substitution of the polite description 'grazier' or 'pastoralist' for the cruder 'squatter', and many other phenomena characterising privileged classes which try to place themselves above the general experience of mankind.

Following his visits to Australia in the early 1870s, the English novelist Anthony Trollope wrote "that the life of the Victorian landowner is very much as was that of the English country gentleman a century or a century and a half ago" (Edwards & Joyce, 1967, p.445).[22] Trollope also stated:

> As were country houses and country life then in England, plentiful, proud, prejudiced, given to hospitality, impatient of contradiction, not highly lettered, healthy, industrious, careful of the main chance, thoughtful of the future, and, above all, conscious, - perhaps a little too conscious, - of their own importance, so now is the house and so is the life of the country gentleman in Australia (Edwards & Joyce, 1967, p.445).

According to a Colin Campbell, who spoke at the Skipton Show dinner in 1871, Western District pastoralists were entitled to be proud of their achievements since improvements in the breed of merino sheep since the Western District Pastoral and Agricultural Society began in 1859 were "miraculous" (reported in Billis & Kenyon, 1930, pp.186-187).

Forth (1982, p.36) addressed the obstacles which the pastoral pioneers had mounted and stated:

> . . . the successful emigrant squatters took pride in the fact that they were the survivors of a protracted struggle during which they had overcome environmental and economic obstacles as well as various attempts on the part of their fellow colonists to dispossess them.

Irrespective of the justification for their elevated position in society, the increasing wealth of the pastoralists and its related influence remained under the constant notice of station personnel but more particularly the shearers who moved from station to station noting the on-going improvements and trappings. As discussed in the previous section, the shearers became discontented with their lot.[23] Sections of the press of the day sided with the shearers, as pastoralists were portrayed as "living off the fat of the land at the shearer's expense" (Ronald, 1978, p.149). Tension in the shed led to a series of shearers' strikes from 1890-4.

Kiddle (1961, p.480) commented on the levelling ideal in Australian society and argued:

No matter what a man's quality, if he achieved success he was suspect. Considering the moral standards of colonial society this suspicion was often justified. The most suspect, of course, was the squatter whose Scots upbringing led him to value worldly success as a reward for rectitude.

As a minority, the pastoralists had difficulty combating the levelling ideal especially when publications such as the *Bulletin* were actively promoting the ideal as part of the national consciousness (Kiddle, 1961, p.480; Forth, 1982, p.37). However, according to Kiddle (1961, p.480), the Western District society "was closer knit and nearer to the Old World model".

Station Working Conditions

Conflict between pastoralists and labour was not as widespread or as intense in the Western District as was the case in Western New South Wales and Queensland. On pre-Federation Western District pastoral conditions, Kiddle (1961, pp.480-1) argued:

> Squatter masters were often paternal in their attitude, and those who worked for them, because their working conditions were usually good, were more settled and contented than they were elsewhere. Nevertheless the ideal [levelling ideal] was present amongst the selectors and travelling workers of the District as it was amongst those of New South Wales and Queensland.

Similarly, Forth (1982, p.38) stated that the better industrial relations climate in the Western District was because of:

> . . . the relatively large number of permanent resident employees found on most Western District stations, the small farming background of many of the casual workers employed, and the fact that the district squatters appear (sic) to treat their workers in a more liberal fashion than was usually the case elsewhere.

In contrast, the outback stations in New South Wales and Queensland employed a greater proportion of casual itinerant workers (Kiddle, 1961, p.481; Forth, 1982, p.38). Understandably, the casual workers of small Western District farming backgrounds would have been disinclined to reject an income stream from shearing which supplemented their income from farming. As a consequence, they had a propensity to overlook the union demands to place industrial pressure on Western District pastoralists.

In discussing "pastoral morals", Collier (1911, p.269) referred to the prevalence of honesty in commercial dealings (such as the sale of a station) and stated in connection with the pastoralists' Golden Age in the Western District that "the uncommercial relations were also at their sweetest and best". Forth (1982, p.38) pointed out that there were various accounts of how the Western District pastoralists were "just and reasonable men who treated their employees in a humane fashion". One of these accounts is provided by James Charles Hamilton, a Western District station owner in the nineteenth century, who wrote in 1914 at the age of 76 years that "nearly all my men were friends, and would do anything for me, and I treated all travellers well" (Hamilton, 1981, p.70). Another is provided by John G. Robertson, as recorded in Bride (1969, p.160), who stated in his letter of 26 September 1853 "there is not a station in the Portland District better managed for its size, both as regards economy and care of man and beast in it". When properly treated, the permanent station hands showed loyalty towards the pastoralist who employed them and an attachment to the property on which they toiled and lived (Forth, 1982, p.38). William Moodie rendered an example of long term relationships with two itinerant workers in the Western District. As stated by William Moodie in Palmer (1973, pp.109-110) "one shore for us for twenty-eight years and the other pressed wool for twenty-seven years. This only ended when the Unions destroyed the good feeling between us". Another Western District pastoralist, Peter Learmonth, was also a miller who "gained the respect of his subordinates" (*Hamilton Spectator*, 20 July 1893). According to Dunstan (1991, p.1), Thomas and Andrew Chirnside at Werribee Park reigned like "benevolent barons" over their pre-Federation station operations.

There are many instances in the Western District of long-serving station hands in the nineteenth century. For instance, at Murndal station which employed about 23 permanent station hands around the 1880s, approximately one-third of these had been born on the station. Almost all of the permanent hands lived on the station including some who had lived there since birth (Forth, 1982, p.38). Some specific examples of long term station engagements follow. According to Wood (1991, p.34), James Bloomfield commenced work at Woodlands station in 1857 and both he and his four sons contributed to the operations on Woodlands for the next 70 years. In 1883, Angus Campbell became the overseer at Merrang station and continued in that role until 1897. At least six of his 13 children worked at Merrang in various capacities during that period. Further, Tom Claridge started work at Merrang in 1884 and members of that family continued to be employed on the station until 1948 (Hood, 1991, pp.65-67). Alexander (Sandie) McCallum became an employee of James Leonard Kininmonth at Mt. Hesse station in 1882 and in 1886 became the station manager, a position he held for the next 40 years (Kininmonth & Kininmonth,

1987, pp.64-65). Mention was made earlier of Robert Marshall who worked at Larra station for over 50 years from the early 1850s.

The view of the typical pre-Federation Western District pastoralist as a paternalistic provider would explain resentment towards the advent and growth of the union movement. Samuel Pratt Winter at Murndal station was evidently offended by the act of station hands joining unions. Winter saw this trend as leading to the breakdown of the "mutually advantageous" master and servant relationship (Forth, 1982, p.38). According to Forth (1982, p.38):

> The paternalistic Winter who considered himself responsible for the welfare of all who lived and worked on his station, believed that acceptance of union conditions in effect released both master and servant from their rightful obligations to each other.

William Moodie expressed similar disappointment in stating, "I have always felt that the absurd tactics adopted by the Workers' Unions destroyed the good feeling that existed between employers and employees . . ." (Palmer, 1973, p.110). Nevertheless, the spread of the levelling ideal in the 1890s had an impact in the Western District.

It seems that general resentment towards the nineteenth century pastoralists may have been augmented by the apparent loafing of the pioneering pastoralists who had retired from active station duties and the perceived excesses of the second generation of pastoralists. In earlier times when their stations constituted few facilities, the pioneering pastoralists often worked long hours alongside their station hands. In the Western District, for instance, Charles M. Gray told of how his bullock-driver, Paddy Crawly and himself worked together in 1851 to bring the timber needed to build a cottage at Nareeb Nareeb station a distance of about twenty miles (Gray, 1932, p.17). Evidence of another example is found in an obituary notice for Charles Hamilton Macknight, formerly of Dunmore station, published in the *Australasian* on 10 May 1873 which stated, "Mr Macknight was said to have been more than a match for the best of the hired navvies in the daily use of spade, pick and barrow". Trollope wrote that the Victorian pastoralist ". . . becomes an idle man. He comes down to breakfast at nine, and is impatient for his dinner before six, thinking that the clock must be losing time. . . . Loitering is common . . ." (Edwards & Joyce, 1967, p.448). Sons of pioneering pastoralists who had completed their education in England often appeared to lose touch with the work ethic which had provided the platform for their parents to build pastoral empires under more trying pioneering conditions. In the estimation of Cannon (1973, p.190):

> . . . such sons often deteriorated into shadow images of their stern
> old parents, with no function in life but to pretend to manage their
> properties upon inheritance, to interfere ignorantly with
> important political developments, and to grow old, gross and
> ineffectual. No wonder the golden age of squattocracy had hardly
> begun before it was over, flickering fitfully in the great halls of its
> semi-deserted mansions.

Consistent with the notion that the halcyon days were over, Kiddle (1961, p.513) contended that those of the third generation of Western District pastoralists were obliged to work hard for their income.

Possible Implications of Station Environment for Accounting Practice

The foregoing discussion of station environment points to certain factors which potentially influenced pre-Federation pastoral accounting practice. It has provided evidence that a typical Western District station was a remote, interdependent community under the paternalistic control of the pastoralist. Underpinning the operation of a station community was a broad spectrum of interpersonal communal exchanges between those involved with the community. Such unique conditions possibly influenced pre-Federation pastoral accounting, particularly in periods before the advent of government and other calls for accounting information. Government levy collection arrangements typically reflect certain ideals and often have both economic and reporting consequences. The application of the imposts outlined may have contributed to change in the structure and usage of pre-Federation pastoral accounting information. The backgrounds and habits of early station workers may have affected the types of recording systems introduced while the practice of paying shearers on a piece-work basis also possibly had accounting implications. As explained, the education of the progeny of pioneering Western District pastoralists at private boarding schools and in some cases at other educational establishments would have contributed to the increasing sophistication of Western District society and also had possible implications for pastoral accounting practice.

Summary

This chapter on the pastoral environment in the nineteenth century has elucidated the development of a vital industry in a society which underwent a rapid transformation and the emergence of pastoralists on stations as a distinctive social set in the Australian fabric of life. Importantly, this chapter provides prerequisite background to assist in the later identification of the major influences upon pre-Federation pastoral accounting practice in the Western District. The section on the pastoral industry environment, as the macro representation of the pastoral environment, addressed the major economic and legal and political developments and cultural factors evident in the period to 1900. The nineteenth century pastoralists experienced the peaks and troughs of pastoral life throughout the pre-Federation period and many did not survive the economic depressions of the period. Alternatively, the peaks provided the pastoralists with the ability to accumulate wealth rapidly and, together with their families, to enjoy the privileges and opportunities this wealth afforded them. It was found that the prevailing world views of an increasingly diverse society affected political and legislative developments which involved the adoption of reforms to dispossess the pastoralists of the land they occupied and, once this battle was essentially won by the pastoralists, to impose financial burdens upon pastoralists in order to break up the large-scale station holdings.

At the micro level of the station environment, the isolated Western District stations were shown to be small interactive communities of interdependent populations. The evidence suggests that Western District pastoralists were often of a paternalistic nature and generally provided good working and living conditions. It seems that a typical Western District pastoralist provided a satisfying lifestyle for permanent station workers which was possibly not fully appreciated or understood by many of those in Melbourne and the larger towns. The pastoralists' isolation and wealth generation ability contributed to educational developments which involved their children's attendance at private boarding schools in Melbourne and Geelong and, in many cases, at schools in England and at universities in Melbourne and England. The material success of the nineteenth century pastoralists came under increasing notice. They eventually experienced a backlash from the itinerant station workers who saw fit to form unions to fight their employers for better conditions in a period when the pastoralists were depicted as being too greedy. However, the Western District pastoralists generally appeared, in the short term, to face somewhat less disruption than their New South Wales and Queensland counterparts in the battle which emerged.

Given all the developments which took place from the mid 1830s, station life in the Western District at the turn of the century was unquestionably more sophisticated and complex than it was when the pioneering pastoral settlers were constructing their first sod or timber huts on lands "beyond the limits of location".

NOTES

1. Squatting was the colonial way of describing the process of settling or "sitting down" on the land. According to Billis and Kenyon (1930, p.20), the word "squatter" in Australia "was first applied by the Government officials to the stockholder depasturing his herds and flocks on lands of the Crown".
2. Sutherland (1977a) was first published in 1888.
3. A run consisted of the home station where the pastoralist or station manager resided and several outlying huts which were known as outstations. According to Billis and Kenyon (1930, p.22), "the 'run' comprised the lot; but the word 'station' was the collective name and not 'run'".
4. Pioneering Western District pastoralists such as Niel Black [1840] and James Ritchie [1841] had to purchase stations from those who had arrived before them (Kiddle, 1961, p.45).
5. In 1843, the Banks of Australia, Sydney and Port Phillip closed leaving only four banks in the Colony (Kiddle, 1961, p.135; Fletcher, 1976, p.121).
6. Denoon (1983) interpreted the term "settler capitalism" to describe the mode of production adopted in settler societies in the southern hemisphere during the nineteenth century and to 1914. Denoon's (1983) comparative study of six settler societies involved Argentina, Australia, Chile, New Zealand, South Africa and Uruguay.
7. Located in New South Wales, the Riverina "lies essentially between the Murray and Murrumbidgee Rivers, but in common usage the area extends northwards to include the flat land surrounding the Lachlan River" (Bailey, 1966, p.78).
8. Respectively known as the *Duties on the Estates of Deceased Persons Statute* 1870 and *The Land Tax Act* 1877.
9. In readiness for the introduction of a land tax, the government prepared a register of pastoral landowners in Victoria with estates in excess of 640 acres. Heading the list was William John Clarke with 164,444 acres while the last listed of the 855 landowners was John McNicol with a holding of 643 acres (de Serville, 1991, p.161).
10. Turner (1973) was first published in 1904.
11. This Act provided for different rates of income tax to be charged depending upon whether the income was derived from personal exertion or property, (sec.5). For the year ended 31 December 1894, the rates of income tax on taxable amounts of personal exertion income were as follows: fourpence for every pound sterling up to twelve hundred pounds; sixpence for every pound sterling over twelve hundred pounds and up to two thousand and two hundred pounds, and eightpence for every pound sterling over two thousand and two hundred pounds. The rates of income tax applicable to taxable amounts of property income were based on the same income bands but were double those charged on taxable amounts of personal exertion income.

12. On analysing the information in Tables 3.3 and 3.4, the Western District accounted for, an average, approximately 7.5 per cent of the total sheep population in New South Wales, Queensland and Victoria during 1862 to 1902.

13. During the 1860s, the Skipton Show became world renowned (Palmer, 1980, p.92; Shaw, 1981, p.58).

14. Descriptions of early station huts are found in Nunan (1971, p.6) and Cannon (1973, pp.22-31).

15. For instance, in a letter dated 26 September 1853 to Charles Joseph La Trobe from John G. Robertson of Wando Vale station, it was stated "I commenced with 1,000 sheep; at the end of five years there were 7,300 sheep on the run" (Bride, 1969, p.159). At the time, La Trobe was Lieutenant-Governor of the Colony of Victoria.

16. Curr (1968) was first published in 1883. Edward Micklethwaite Curr was a pastoral pioneer in the Western Port District who first arrived in the Port Phillip District in 1839. He held Wolfscrag and Tongala stations among others. According to Roberts (1935, p.442), Curr's recollections of pioneering days "may be taken as a type of the life of a successful squatter".

17. Bride (1969) was first published in 1898.

18. Palmer (1973) is an edited version of the memoirs of William Moodie a Western District pastoralist whose father, John Moodie, settled with his family at Wando Dale station, in the early 1850s.

19. According to surviving Larra station records the rate cited of 30/- per 100 was around 100 per cent higher than the rate paid in the year before the gold rush.

20. Hamilton (1981) was first published in 1914.

21. These four private boarding schools were founded in 1851, 1854, 1858 and 1861 respectively (Bean, 1950, pp.43-44 and 59).

22. Anthony Trollope's *Australia and New Zealand* was published in 1873. Edwards and Joyce (1967) edited the reprinted version of Trollope's chapters on Australia which was published by the University of Queensland Press.

23. Charles M. Gray, a pioneering Western District pastoralist who arrived at Port Phillip from Scotland in 1839, provided an insight of the difficulties experienced during this period. He sold his Nareeb Nareeb station in 1886 "parting with it with deep annoyance now being caused by sheep shearers and others" (Gray, 1932, p.20).

PART II

EXAMINATION OF SURVIVING
PASTORAL BUSINESS RECORDS

CHAPTER 4

RESEARCH METHODOLOGY

Historians' work is often defined as being either narrative or interpretive. Interpretive history involves explanations as to why episodes took the forms identified from examinations of the available evidence (Previts, Parker & Coffman, 1990a, p.2). Importantly, those historians adopting historicism as a mode of enquiry, as discussed in Chapter 1, recognize that the phenomenon under investigation was shaped by environmental conditions specific in location and time (Kitson Clark, 1967, pp.25 and 204-207; Tosh, 1991, pp.10-22). On the other hand, narrative history relates episodes in a non-analytical manner and presents history as more of a story rather than focusing on explanations of its components (Previts, Parker & Coffman, 1990a, p.2). Studies which attempt to augment our understanding of accounting's past are potentially more helpful than descriptive studies in placing accounting's present into context and in considering accounting's future.

This interpretive historical study adopts the field-based case study research as the prime research method and makes use of oral sources. The field-based case study research method is based on qualitative, holistic analysis and allows a multiplicity of variables to be taken into account (Previts, Parker & Coffman, 1990b, p.149).[1] It attempts to represent and analyse situations as they took place in their organisational and social context (Buckley, Buckley & Chiang, 1976; Kaplan, 1986). The case method is applied on a longitudinal basis in this study of the actual records of past entities.[2] Oral evidence was obtained in interviews held with a small number of elderly descendants of pioneering Western District pastoralists to elucidate family backgrounds and pre-Federation pastoral conditions, and also to gain insights into the use of accounting information in Western District pastoralism to 1900.[3] Although interviewees such as Robert Jamieson III (now deceased) were already at least one generation removed, these remembrances of narratives and descriptions of events and people in the past are symptomatic of endeavours to embrace all sources.

The first section of this chapter comprises a discussion of key aspects of the research sample. There follows an explanation of the nature of the surviving business records accommodated in this study and also a description of the process adopted in gleaning oral evidence.

Research Sample

Discussion of the approaches adopted in determining the research sample and in tracing surviving business records precedes a review of the composition of the research sample.

Determining the Research Sample

The sample of non-corporate pastoral entities for this study is drawn from those entities which operated Western District pastoral stations that are identified in *Pastoral Pioneers of Port Phillip* by Billis and Kenyon (1974) as either original runs or subdivisions of those runs except those which arose under closer settlement schemes. The investigations undertaken resulted in the location and examination of 23 sets of surviving business records pertaining to such stations which comprises the study's research sample of pre-Federation pastoral accounting records.[4] For pastoral families, a set of business records relating to a Western District station comprises either the records of the original pastoralist or those of the descendants of that pastoralist where the pastoralist died before 1901 or both. To remove any bias toward the nature of accounting information prepared in the final stages of nineteenth century pastoralism, pastoral entities were not included in the sample where the only surviving Western District business records available were prepared in the 1890s.[5] As this study is concerned with pastoral accounting in the Western District of Victoria, business records relating to stations operated by a Western District pastoral entity in other parts of the country do not form part of the collection of available nineteenth century records for examination in this study.

The sample size of 23 sets of surviving business records represented the range of sets of records available for examination which met the above criteria for selection. Although other sets of records meeting the selection criteria may have survived, they were either not traced or were unavailable for examination at the time of the investigations. A sample size of less than 23 sets of records could have been selected, however, it became apparent on a review of a preliminary sample of five sets of records that certain sets of records were incomplete in terms of their time span in that they did not cover the entire period of pastoral occupation identified from other sources. Hence, the selection of the largest possible sample assists in overcoming this limitation. Further, the sample size of 23 sets of records provides a spread of records prepared in different parts of the Western District so as to avoid, as far as possible, the impact of any isolated influences in the region such as the presence of a public accountant in a particular township.

Given the approach to sample selection as outlined, a bias exists toward the examination of records relating to large-scale stations which, in effect, were isolated communities comprising up to 100 people. Pastoral operations on such stations were different in scale to those conducted by selectors who, under rights of selection, could lay claim to lands of up to 640 acres dating from the late 1850s. Although the selectors who farmed land were important to the development of Western District pastoralism and the social fabric of the region, this study's focus is intended to incorporate the examination of the earliest surviving business records available and patterns of development to 1900. Hence, the surviving business records of pre-Federation Western District selectors whose lands previously formed part of large-scale station holdings are not subject to investigation in this study.[6]

A further bias exists in this study which relates to the level of success of the pastoral entities included in the research sample. The survival of nineteenth century pastoral business records is contingent upon, at least in part, on the values of family members responsible for the collection, storage and preservation of such records. It is also indicative of the apparent success of the pastoral operations involved, as business records in particular are prone to be in short supply when an entity fails or when a family disconnects itself from land with which records were associated. The existence of records pertinent to this research implies, in general terms only, that the pastoral entities involved were survivors for varying periods in the pastoral industry. It may be argued that survival in the pastoral industry is more likely where there is oversight of resources employed through the maintenance of business records appropriate to the pastoralist's needs. However, an examination of any link between the maintenance of business records and pastoral survival is outside the scope of this study.

Having identified particular biases in this study, it is not asserted that the findings reported are representative of the structure and usage of accounting information prepared generally for colonial pastoral entities in the Western District or in other regions of the Colony or in other British colonies in Australia or even beyond. Rather, the study presents evidence of the nature of accounting information prepared by those entities whose business records have survived and were accommodated in this study. In so doing and in submitting probable explanations of the accounting practices observed, our understanding of pastoral accounting practice in the pre-Federation period is anticipated to be augmented.

Tracing Surviving Business Records

In a study of the papers of the Winter Cooke family, a pioneering Western District pastoral family, Forth (1984, p.39) asserted that "day to day financial and stock details and annual stud books, station diaries, wage books records were rarely considered worthy of retention". Consequently, an intensive search was mounted in order to trace surviving pastoral business records for this study. In order to overcome the asserted shortage of nineteenth century business records, the investigations encompassed searches for relevant information in both public and private archives. Table 4.1 provides the archive location details at the time of examination of available sets of surviving business records.[7]

TABLE 4.1: Archive Locations at Time of Examination

Entity (23)	Location of Records
Armytage	La Trobe Library
	Private archive, Melbourne
Beggs	Gold Museum, Ballarat
Black Bros. (& Smith)	La Trobe Library
Clyde Company/Russell, G.	La Trobe Library
Corney	Private archive, Tulse Hill
Cumming	La Trobe Library
	Private archive, Myrngrong
	University of Melbourne Archives
Currie	La Trobe Library
	Private archive, Titanga
Dennis	Private archive, Tarndwarncoort
French	La Trobe Library
Hood	Private archive, Merrang
Hope	Private archive, Darriwill North
Jamieson	Noel Butlin Archives Centre
	Private archive, Stony Point
Kininmonth	Private archive, Mt. Hesse
Mackinnon	La Trobe Library
Macknight and Irvine	Private archive, Melbourne
McIntyre	Private archive, Geelong
Millear, Maidment and	La Trobe Library
Austin/Millear	
Miller and Tulloh	University of Melbourne Archives
Officer	Private archive, Mt. Talbot
Ritchie	University of Melbourne Archives
Robertson/Patterson	Private archive, Warrock
Russell, P.	Geelong Historical Records Centre
	Gold Museum, Ballarat
	La Trobe Library
	Private archive, Langi Willi
Russell, T. *et al.*	Noel Butlin Archives Centre
	Private archive, Ocean Grove

The searches of public archives were extensive and included examinations of catalogues at the La Trobe Library section of the State Library of Victoria, the University of Melbourne Archives, and the Noel Butlin Archives Centre (formerly the Archives of Business and Labour) at the Australian National University, Canberra. The *Guide to Collections of Manuscripts Relating to Australia* was also examined in order to facilitate the identification of suitable collections. Enquiries aimed at determining whether suitable records existed were also made at regional historical centres comprising the Geelong Historical Records Centre, the Ballarat Gold Museum, and various historical societies which operate in townships in the Western District of Victoria. The historical societies contacted were the Camperdown, Colac, Hamilton, Harrow, Heywood, Koroit, Mortlake, Port Fairy, Portland, and Warrnambool societies. Whilst only the Ballarat Gold Museum and the Geelong Historical Records Centre held relevant records in their collections, the approaches to the Hamilton and Port Fairy historical societies led to introductions to persons who either held, or knew the existence of, surviving nineteenth century pastoral business records pertaining to Western District station properties.

It was anticipated that many important nineteenth century business records would be held by descendants of the pastoral pioneers, particularly those who held Western District lands which had been operated by the same family for at least 100 years. The determination of the locations of private archives involved an important Western District custom of being introduced to those who could advise on the matter of the availability of records relevant to the research. At the commencement of the study, both John Menzies of Camperdown, a medical practitioner, and Hugh Strachan (now deceased) formerly a semi-retired pastoral company executive, kindly provided introductions to people with long-standing pastoral connections all of whom were contacted about this study. Many of these enquiries led to meetings, normally at pastoral properties, and consent in virtually all cases to examine any surviving nineteenth century business records in possession. Having provided an understanding of the nature of the research and established the confidence of these supporters, further introductions, on occasions, would be provided and hence a chain of enquiries resulted throughout the Western District. Reporting of the research study occurred through local media outlets to supplement these searches of public archives and personal enquiries based on introductions.[8] Although these indirect approaches to trace suitable records generated some enquiry, they did not directly lead to the unearthing of any sets of records relevant to the research. Nevertheless, this formed part of a strategy of adopting both direct and indirect approaches to seeking out applicable primary materials.

In some instances, relevant nineteenth century pastoral business records examined in this study were found in both public and private archives. In such instances an examination of the records in the public collection alone would have been deficient based on the existence of other relevant records which, on suitable enquiry, were available for this study. Hence, the enquiries aimed at tracing relevant surviving business records in private and public archives resulted in the availability of the most complete collections for examination at the time of the investigations. Of the 23 sets of surviving business records, nine sets were held in private archives, eight sets were held in public archives and six sets involved collections held partly in public and partly in private archives on the occasions these records were studied.

Other avenues of enquiry were pursued in both the private and public sectors in order to trace relevant nineteenth century business records relating to the pastoral entities included in the research sample. In the private sector, extensive enquiries were made to trace surviving business records of banks, pastoral companies and also accounting and legal firms which had business dealings with these pastoral entities. On occasions, these enquiries led to the discovery of records relevant to the research including those that had been vested with public archive centres. Table 4.2 provides details of the locations of surviving nineteenth century business records of entities which were identified as having had dealings with different pastoral entities included in the research sample.

For public records, the Victorian Public Records Office was a major point of contact. The Victorian Public Records Office holds various records lodged in connection with the advent of deceased estates including statements of assets and liabilities prepared for deceased nineteenth century pastoralists. These statements were drawn upon extensively in this study. For instance, comparisons were made where possible of the valuations of assets and liabilities reported in surviving ledger records with those shown in such statements. Similar statements available through the Probate Division of the Supreme Court of New South Wales were also examined in cases where relevant. Unfortunately, the original copies of Colony of Victoria income tax returns dating from the year ended 31 December 1894 were unavailable as they had been destroyed. As elaborated upon in Chapter 8, some primary records of the AIIA are located at the Victorian Public Records Office.

TABLE 4.2: Locations of Records of Other Entities

Other Entities	Location of Records
*Banks**	
Bank of Australasia	Australia and New Zealand Banking Group Ltd, Melbourne
Bank of Victoria Ltd	National Australia Bank Ltd, Melbourne
National Bank of Australasia Ltd	National Australia Bank Ltd, Melbourne
Union Bank of Australia Ltd	Australia and New Zealand Banking Group Ltd, Melbourne
Pastoral Companies	
Australian Mortgage Land & Finance Co. Ltd	Noel Butlin Archives Centre
Dalgety and Co.	Noel Butlin Archives Centre
Dennys Lascelles Ltd	University of Melbourne Archives
Goldsbrough Mort & Co. Ltd	Noel Butlin Archives Centre
Strachan & Co. Ltd	University of Melbourne Archives
Union Mortgage & Agency Co. of Australia Ltd	Noel Butlin Archives Centre
Accounting Firms	
Yeo, Brentnall & Merrin	University of Melbourne Archives
Legal Firms	
Ardlie, William	University of Melbourne Archives
Blake & Riggall	University of Melbourne Archives
Clarke & Barwood	Noel Butlin Archives Centre
Lyne & Sylvester	University of Melbourne Archives

*   The banking archives are not open to the public and may be accessed with permission, as occurred in this study, on a case by case enquiry basis.

Composition of Research Sample

The research sample of 23 sets of surviving nineteenth century business records of Western District pastoral activity comprises 22 sets of records of pastoral families or partnerships involving such families and one set of records of a co-partnership (Clyde Company) which involved investors abroad. The earliest surviving record available for this research is a ledger of the Clyde Company which dates from 1836. Table 4.3 shows for each of these 23 pastoral entities their commencing dates of pastoral occupation and the respective station names along with the relevant Billis and Kenyon (1974) references to those stations. A roughly determined measure of the extent of pastoral activity conducted by pastoral entities comprising the research sample as a proportion of Western District pastoralism can be ascertained. As depicted in Table 4.3, the 23 sets of surviving business records relate to 38 identifiable stations.[9] Of these holdings, 35 were recorded in Billis and Kenyon

(1974) as original runs or subdivisions of those runs for purposes evidently other than closer settlement schemes.[10] These 35 runs represented approximately 12.5 per cent of the 282 pastoral runs in the Western District by around 1845 (Kiddle, 1961, p.44).[11] It is acknowledged that many of the pastoral pioneers may not have prepared any business records.

TABLE 4.3: Pastoral Entities Comprising the Research Sample

Entity (23)	Date of Pastoral Occupation	Station Names	Billis and Kenyon (1974)
Armytage	1857	Mt. Sturgeon Fulham	pp.209 & 253-254
Beggs	1855	Eurambeen	p.206
Black Bros. (& Smith)	1885	Mt. Noorat The Sisters Grassdale Estate	pp.214, 228 & 277
Clyde Company/ Russell, G.	1836	Golf Hill Terinallum Elderslie Leslie Manor	pp.203, 215, 267 & 288
Corney	1840	Wando Vale B Tulse Hill	p.296
Cumming	1856	Mt. Fyans	p.250
Currie	1844	Larra Titanga Gala	pp.210 & 249
Dennis	1840	Tarndwarncoort	pp.226-227
French	1841	Monivae	p.245
Hood	1854	Bolac Plains Merrang	pp.176 & 229
Hope	1840	Darriwill Gnotuk	p.198
Jamieson	1841	Castlemaddie Eumeralla West Bolac Plains Stony Point	pp.176, 189, 206 & 281
Kininmonth	1882	Mt. Hesse	p.220
Mackinnon	1840	Marida Yallock	p.241
Macknight and Irvine	1842	Dunmore	p.202
McIntyre	1843	Ardachy	pp.166-167
Millear, Maidment and Austin/Millear	1858	Edgarley	p.218
Miller and Tulloh	1845	Pieracle	p.264
Officer	1847	Mt. Talbot	p.254
Ritchie	1842	Blackwood	p.176
Robertson/Patterson	1844	Warrock Capaul	p.298
Russell, P.	1843	Carngham Langi Willi	pp.171 & 188
Russell, T. *et al.*	1851	Barunah Plains	p.173

Appendix A contains a map reproduced from Spreadborough and Anderson (1983) which shows the locations of pastoral runs throughout the Western District. It also contains a map (as an insert) which depicts where the Western District of Victoria is located in Australia.

Types of Surviving Business Records Examined

In accounting history studies, business records are commonly categorized as either financial or volume records. This study involves an examination of both types of accounting records that were prepared for use in the operation of non-corporate pastoral entities. Financial records are those which show figures expressed in a unit of currency and include day or cash books, journals, ledgers and financial statements. Financial statements show certain representations based on transactions entered into and include statements of receipts and disbursements, profit and loss accounts and balance sheets. Until 1966, the official monetary unit in Australia was nominated in pounds, shillings and pence. Alternatively, volume records are prepared to show quantitative information of a non-financial operating nature. For pastoral operations, such records pertain to the physical quantities of livestock and stores and to the outputs of production including wool and lambs. Records which showed details of individual stud stock only did not qualify for consideration as volume records in this study as such information, by nature, is merely qualitative.

Other types of surviving business records were also relied upon in this study. These included available letters, diaries, wills, partnership agreements and other written agreements which elucidate the function and concernment of accounting information in nineteenth century pastoralism. Whilst some collections of records available for this study included various papers of this kind, others provided few, if any, documents of this nature. Further, social history items recorded in financial and volume records were also examined as they related to the use of accounting records as a multi-purpose information repository.

Process Applied in Gathering Oral Evidence

A small number of descendants of pioneering pastoralists with a broad knowledge of Western District pastoralism and a strong interest in this study were invited to be interviewees. All interviewees were senior citizens who generously gave their time.[12] The interviews were generally unstructured and interviewees endeavoured to respond to all questions posed.

Oral remembrances were gathered in interviews with Robert Jamieson III (now deceased, formerly of Bolac Plains and Stony Point), Norman & Sheila Dennis (Tarndwarncoort), Eoin Smith (Grassdale

Estate), and Dame Ella and Helen Macknight (Dunmore). With the exception of the interview with Dame Ella and Helen Macknight which was conducted in Melbourne, the interviews were conducted on pastoral properties in the Western District. The experience of conducting these interviews elucidated the strong historical interests of the interviewees and their willingness to relate their substantially unrecorded knowledge of pioneering pastoralism to academic researchers.

NOTES

1. Pollard (1965), Johnson (1972, 1978), Gibson (1979a), Fleischman and Parker (1990, 1991), Chambers and Wolnizer (1991) and McLean (1995) provide examples of the adoption of the case method in accounting history studies of surviving business records.
2. In commenting on pre-nineteenth century accounting, Hopwood and Johnson (1986, p.46) argued that ". . . historians, by not examining the actual records of past companies, completely ignored the development of modern managerial accounting".
3. See Tosh (1991, pp.206-227) for a discussion of the use of oral evidence in historical studies and also Collins and Bloom (1991) for a discussion of the use of oral sources in accounting history research.
4. Fleischman and Parker (1991) provided evidence that a research sample size of around 25 sets of surviving business records is appropriate for accounting history studies of this nature.
5. The Weatherly collections of pastoral business records, located at La Trobe Library (manuscript numbers MS 8921/9617) and on the station, "Woolongoon", were not incorporated in this study as they date from 1895, when the Weatherly family acquired "Woolongoon", and thus did not fit the criteria for selection. The kind assistance of the Weatherly family is noted.
6. The surviving business records of the Christie brothers dating from the 1860s were not incorporated in this study. The Christie brothers were selectors of land at Byaduk near Hamilton. These records are held in a private archive at Wannon and were kindly offered for examination.
7. This table and Table 4.3 are based on the appendix in Carnegie (1995, p.33).
8. A feature on the research titled "Farm accounts under scrutiny" was published in the *Warrnambool Standard* on 23 February 1991 and a radio interview followed on the Western District's 3WV/WL station on 13 March 1991. Another feature titled "Looking Back on Unregulated Accounting" appeared in the November 1991 issue of *Deakin University News*.
9. Bolac Plains was operated by Hood and also by Jamieson but at different times.
10. Tulse Hill, Gnotuk and Capaul stations are not identified in Billis and Kenyon (1974).

11. Of these 35 runs, not all were held in the mid 1840s by the pastoralists whose surviving pre-Federation business records are examined in this study.
12. All interviewees were informed of the purpose of the interview and the expected application of the information gathered.

CHAPTER 5

BACKGROUNDS OF PASTORALISTS WHOSE BUSINESS RECORDS ARE EXAMINED

This chapter relates the backgrounds of the individual pastoralists connected with the 23 pastoral entities whose business records comprise the research sample in order to further facilitate the incorporation of a broad range of contextual variables into the examination of these surviving records. The specific background information presented in this chapter for this group of pastoralists also complements the reporting of the findings of detailed examinations of surviving business records which occurs on a case by case basis in the following chapter. Based on the research sample, general observations of Western District pastoralism for this group are made following this review of the specific backgrounds of the pastoralists involved. These observations, together with the elucidations of the nineteenth century pastoral industry and station environments contained in Chapter 3, provide local, time-specific context within which the structure and usage of pre-Federation pastoral accounting information is explained.

This chapter comprises two sections. The first section contains the specific backgrounds of the pastoralists presented in the same order as found in Table 4.1. The second section provides general observations of Western District pastoralism for this group of pastoralists.

Specific Backgrounds

Armytage[1]
George Armytage was born to George Armytage, snr., and Elizabeth, nee Rose, in 1795 at Ticknall, Derbyshire, England.[2] He was raised in Brussels and in Yorkshire, and settled in Australia after studying engineering in London. George Armytage arrived in Sydney in 1815 and in the following year took up pastoral land at Bagdad in Van Diemen's Land. In 1818, he married Elizabeth, nee Peters, daughter of Thomas Peters, a Lieutenant in the Duke of York's regiment. George Armytage had taken sheep to Port Phillip in 1836 and a decade later had developed

numerous pastoral stations in the Western District including Ingleby, near Winchelsea and Fulham, on the Glenelg River, near Balmoral.

George and Elizabeth Armytage had seven sons and four daughters. Their fourth son, Charles Henry Armytage, was born at Bagdad on 24 August 1824. Charles Henry Armytage was educated in Van Diemen's Land where he gained pastoral experience on his father's properties. He married Caroline Morrell, nee Tuckwell, in 1856 at Winchelsea and had issue ten children. In January 1857, his father gave the Mostyn and Fulham stations to him and in May 1863, after his father's death in July 1862, he acquired Mt. Sturgeon station on the Wannon River in partnership with his brother-in-law, George Fairbairn.[3] This partnership was dissolved in January 1869 and from this time Charles Henry Armytage operated Mt. Sturgeon on his own account. In 1863, he also purchased Como at South Yarra in Melbourne, a property of 54 acres and used this property as his city residence. In addition to his Western District holdings, Charles Henry Armytage also had pastoral interests in South Australia and also mining interests, and was associated with the manufacture of eucalyptus oil after having observed how the Aboriginals used gum leaves to cure scratches. He died at Como on 26 April 1876 leaving his wife, nine children and net assets valued for probate purposes at £130,040. The Estate of Charles Henry Armytage operated Fulham and Mt. Sturgeon throughout the remaining pre-Federation period and beyond.

The second of Charles Henry's five sons, George Herbert Armytage, became the station manager of Fulham around January 1887 after gaining pastoral industry experience with Dalgety and Co. He was born at Fulham on 16 March 1860 and was educated at Toorak College and Brighton College, England. He married Amelia Fanny, daughter of John Chatfield Tyler of Toorak, and had issue three children. The third son of Charles Henry, Harold Augustus Armytage, appears to have taken over the running of Mt. Sturgeon around September 1886. He was born at Fulham on 28 March 1862 and was educated at the Geelong Church of England Grammar School and Brighton College, England. George Herbert and Harold Augustus were only 16 and 14 years of age respectively on the death of their father. George Herbert Armytage died at Toorak on 18 December 1925 and Harold Augustus Armytage died unmarried at Melbourne on 19 September 1926.

Beggs[4]

Francis and George Beggs were sons of Francis Beggs, snr., a merchant. They were born at The Grange, Malahide, Dublin, Ireland. Born on 29 September 1812, Francis Beggs was engaged in farming his father's Malahide estate and other estates after he attended Trinity College,

Dublin where he matriculated in 1828. He married Maria Lucinda, daughter of Thomas Warren White, barrister-at-law, who was called to the Irish Bar in 1821. George Beggs was articled to John Faris, solicitor but decided to settle in Australia with Francis and Maria Lucinda and Sophia Montgomery Beggs, a sister of Francis and George. They arrived at Port Phillip on 17 March 1850. George Beggs later married Charlotte Elizabeth, nee White, sister of Maria Lucinda.

After running the Mt. Yallock station near Avoca, George Beggs purchased Eurambeen station near Beaufort in September 1855 in partnership with Humphrey Gratton.[5] Francis Beggs acquired the Gnarkeet station near Lismore and remained there until 1859 when he sold that station and purchased the interest of Humphrey Gratton in Eurambeen. The partnership of G. & F. Beggs continued until 17 January 1879 when George Beggs died leaving his wife, three of four children and net assets valued for probate purposes at £28,100. Eurambeen was divided into two parts, Eurambeen East became part of the Estate of George Beggs while Francis Beggs operated Eurambeen West and also Eurambeen East under a lease from the estate. Francis Beggs died on 29 December 1880 leaving his wife, nine of ten children and net assets valued for probate at £28,416. At that time Theodore Beggs, the seventh child of Francis, took charge of the family properties on behalf of the respective executors. Theodore Beggs was also an executor of his father's estate. Both George and Francis Beggs served their local community by means of their positions on district councils. George Beggs was a member of the Beaufort and Carngham District Roads Board from May 1863 to August 1867 and was a chairman of that Board. He was also a councillor of the Ripon Shire Council during 1873-1879 and served as President in 1875. Francis Beggs joined the Ripon Shire Council in 1879 on the death of his brother and served as a councillor until August 1880.

On 30 December 1886, a partnership comprising Theodore Beggs and his two brothers, Robert Gottlieb and Hugh Norman, leased Eurambeen and other family properties.[6] This "Beggs Brothers" partnership was dissolved in 1913. Theodore Beggs was born on 17 August 1859 and was educated by a private tutor. Robert Gottlieb and Hugh Norman Beggs were born on 21 September 1861 and 6 June 1863 respectively and were also educated by a private tutor although Hugh Norman attended Wesley College, Melbourne. After completing his education, Hugh Norman Beggs gained banking experience at the Bank of Victoria, Beaufort Branch, before embarking on his pastoral career. Both Theodore and Robert Gottlieb Beggs served as councillors of district councils. Theodore Beggs was a councillor of the Ripon Shire Council during 1887-1891 and 1892-1913 and served as President in

1890. During 1910-28, he was the member for Nelson Province in the Victorian Legislative Council. In 1918, Theodore Beggs married Agnes Jane, daughter of Herbert Reginald Robert Walpole, a descendant of Sir Robert Walpole, English Prime Minister. Robert Gottlieb Beggs married twice, firstly, Maria, nee Balcombe in 1882. She died in 1883 and in 1905 he married Amy, daughter of Colonel P.R. Ricardo. In 1897, Hugh Norman Beggs married Mary Catherine Reeves, daughter of Henry Sandford Palmer, former high sheriff for County Tipperary, Ireland.

Black Bros. (& Smith)[7]

Niel Black was born at Kilbridemore in the Cowal district, Argyllshire, Scotland on 26 August 1804. He was the second son of Archibald Black, a tenant farmer, who died in 1808, and Janet, nee Buchanan. Niel Black was the managing partner of Niel Black & Co., a co-partnership involving British-based investors which operated various Western District stations. There were various changes in the personnel of Niel Black & Co. in the 30 years to 1869 when the partnership was dissolved and the pastoral lands were distributed by lot amongst the partners. The southern portion of the Glenormiston station went to Niel Black, which he named Mt. Noorat. About three years later, Niel Black purchased The Sisters station which had gone to another partner in the former firm. Niel Black died at Mt. Noorat on 15 May 1880 leaving his wife Grace Greenshields, nee Leadbetter, three sons all of whom were born in Victoria, and net assets valued for probate purposes at £179,208.

After a period, the three Black brothers, Archibald John, Steuart Gladstone and Niel Walter, operated the stations formerly held by their father and traded as the "Black Bros". Archibald John Black was born on 27 September 1859 and was educated at the Geelong Church of England Grammar School, Trinity College, University of Melbourne and Trinity College, Cambridge. Born on 14 April 1862, Steuart Gladstone Black was educated at Kew High School, Geelong Church of England Grammar School and Trinity College, Cambridge. Both brothers earned a B.A. from Cambridge and Steuart Gladstone was also awarded an M.A. from Cambridge. The brothers were largely responsible for the establishment of the Glenormiston Butter and Cheese Factory Co. and Trufood of Australia Ltd. Archibald John Black was a councillor of the Hampden Shire Council for many years and served as President for four terms. He married Agnes, daughter of Dr. Daniel Curdie of Tandarook station, and had issue four children. Steuart Gladstone Black held the seat for the Nelson Province in the Victorian Legislative Council during 1901-1904. He served on the Mortlake Shire Council during

1889-1898 with two terms as President and also on the Hampden Shire Council during 1912-1923 and was President for one term. Steuart Gladstone Black married twice, firstly, Mary Anne, daughter of Daniel Mackinnon of Marida Yallock, who died in 1900 and, secondly, Isabella McCance, nee Moat and altogether had issue four children. Born on 13 June 1864, Niel Walker Black was educated at Kew High School, Geelong Church of England Grammar School, Ormond College, University of Melbourne and Emmanuel College, Cambridge. Always in delicate health, he died in 1908 when the ill-fated "Waratah" sank without trace on a voyage to England.

John Smith was born at Lochgoilhead, Argyllshire, Scotland on 26 February 1840 to Donald Smith and Mary, nee Swan. His father was a sheep farmer on a small land holding in Argyllshire and his mother's family were also sheep farmers at Loch Awe, Scotland. Donald Smith brought his family to Australia in 1852, arriving at Portland. Donald Smith soon acquired Balochile station near Coleraine. After gaining pastoral experience at Balochile, John Smith became the station manager for Niel Black at Mt. Noorat station around 1871. He held this position until December 1885. For a short period from around 1880, John Smith held an interest with R. Buchanan in the Tallangatta station in Victoria's North-east. On 14 December 1885, John Smith, in partnership with Archibald John and Steuart Gladstone Black, purchased Grassdale Estate near Branxholme. John Smith was the managing partner of Grassdale Estate until 2 November 1905 when he became the sole owner of a smaller acreaged Grassdale Estate. John Smith married Euphemia Adamson, nee Walker, on 27 April 1881 and had issue three sons. He took an interest in community and pastoral affairs and was a councillor of the Portland Shire Council from 1892-1921. He died at Grassdale Estate on 26 March 1921.

Clyde Company/Russell, G.[8]

George Russell was the manager and then partner of the Clyde Company and later operated the Golf Hill station at Shelford near Geelong in his own right until his death. He was born on 18 June 1812 at Mains of Clunie farm, Fife, Scotland to Philip Russell, a tenant farmer, and Anne, nee Carstairs. George Russell attended various schools and at the age of 15 years went to work as a ploughman at Mains of Clunie farm. In 1830, he went to Edinburgh to attend some classes on chemistry, and on arithmetic, mathematics and bookkeeping. After attending these classes conducted at the University of Edinburgh for about six weeks, he sailed to Van Diemen's Land to join his elder half-brother, Philip Russell, who had gone to the colony in 1821 as manager of Captain Patrick Wood's pastoral concerns. George Russell gained colonial pastoral experience while under Philip Russell's supervision during 1831-36. In March 1836, George Russell followed John Batman to Port Phillip and found land suitable for pastoral operations on the Leigh River. This land was settled by a co-partnership formed in Scotland comprising Captain Wood, then of Scotland, several other British investors and Philip Russell as resident Australian partner.[9] The holding became known as Golf Hill. George Russell was appointed manager of this partnership which afterwards became known as the Clyde Company.

George Russell had became managing partner of the Clyde Company by 1844 when Philip Russell died. From 1844, the Clyde Company was dominated by the Dennistoun family of Golf Hill, Glasgow. In 1846, the Clyde Company acquired Terinallum station near Mt. Elephant. By 1848, the Clyde Company held over 72,000 acres at Golf Hill station of which 7,000 were freehold and also 57,000 acres at Terinallum. The Clyde Company was dissolved in 1857-58 when George Russell's interest in the partnership amounted to a one-sixth share. On dissolution, George Russell acquired the central Golf Hill freehold of 8,500 acres which he eventually enlarged to 28,000 acres. He held other stations including Elderslie, Leslie Manor (formerly Punpundhal) and Strathvean but resided at Golf Hill. While in Scotland in 1852, he married his cousin Euphemia Leslie, nee Carstairs, who died in 1867. He was a councillor of the Leigh Shire Council in 1862 and during 1865-66, 1868-73 and 1877-80 and served as President during 1869-71. George Russell died at Golf Hill on 3 November 1888 leaving seven daughters and an only son and net assets valued for probate purposes at £361,856. Philip, the only son, inherited Golf Hill but arranged, prior to his death in 1898, for his sister, Janet Russell (1866-1954) to take over the station. Janet married Commander John Biddlecombe in 1900 and the couple carried on Golf Hill until John Biddlecombe's death in 1929 when Janet took control of the station again. George Russell had been a magistrate from the early days at Port Phillip and was highly regarded as a methodical pastoralist and helpful adviser.[10]

Corney[11]

Born in London on 3 February 1816, William Corney came to Van Diemen's Land in 1821 with his parents to settle on the land. His father, Robert Corney, was formerly engaged in the shipping industry. After remaining on the family farm for 19 years, William Corney arrived in the Western District and settled on Wando Vale B, or as it was better known, Wando station in October 1840. Around 1846, he married Stephan Rowan, nee Robertson, a sister of John G. Robertson of the nearby Wando Vale station and had issue an only son, Robert William Corney. William Corney sold Wando station in March 1954 and visited England with his family. The Corney family returned to Portland in 1856. William Corney first became a member of the Portland Borough Councillor in 1859 and served several terms including a term as Mayor during 1869-71. He was also a Justice of the Peace. William Corney died at Portland on 27 January 1898 leaving his wife and son and net assets valued for probate purposes at £20,599.[12]

Robert William Corney was born at Wando station on 12 December 1847. He was educated at Scotch College, Melbourne on the family's return from England. Owing to ill-health, his education was completed at Portland under a private tutor. He purchased Tulse Hill station near Casterton in 1871 after gaining pastoral experience on the nearby Warrock station. On 24 August 1882, Robert William Corney married Eliza Mary, daughter of William Tulloh, Actuary, and Eliza Mary Tulloh of Portland. He operated Tulse Hill until his death on 21 June 1913. He left his wife, three children all of whom were educated at private schools, and net assets valued for probate purposes at £36,564.

Cumming[13]

John Cumming was born at Aberdeen, Scotland in 1796. In November 1829, he married Anne, nee Forrest, whose father was a farmer with land at Old Deer near Aberdeen. John and Anne Cumming came to Port Phillip in April 1838 after arriving in Van Diemen's Land from London in 1833. A master builder by trade, John Cumming became interested in pastoral pursuits in the late 1840s and was keen to place his four sons on the land. In 1856, John Cumming purchased Mt. Fyans station for his sons, George and William. George and William Cumming, the second and third born sons, were born in Tasmania on 5 February 1835 and 20 June 1837 respectively.[14] They were possibly both educated at a private school in Melbourne run by Robert Lawson who subsequently became the foundation rector of Scotch College in 1851. After their schooling and prior to 1856, the two brothers gained pastoral experience at Stony Point station, near Darlington, a property purchased by their father in March 1849 and subsequently gifted to Thomas Forrest Cumming, the youngest of the four sons, who was born in Melbourne on 26 September 1842. George and William Cumming operated Mt. Fyans in partnership until 1860 when the property was divided and George took the portion which became known as Mt. Violet station. In 1860, William Cumming married Catherine, daughter of William Burrow J.P., who was a Mayor of Geelong. In 1868, William Cumming increased his pastoral holdings by purchasing Stonehenge Estate, near Mt. Elephant. William Cumming was a councillor of the

Mortlake Shire Council from 1866-75 and served as President for one term. He also had various involvements with pastoral societies.

William Cumming died at Mt. Fyans on 7 May 1898 leaving his wife, seven of eight children and net assets valued for probate purposes at £124,903. His eldest son, William Burrow Cumming, was born at Mt. Fyans on 6 July 1861 and was educated at Geelong College and Scotch College. After his schooling, William Burrow Cumming immediately returned to Mt. Fyans to engage in pastoral pursuits and managed the station for almost 20 years prior to his father's death. On 8 March 1885, he married Ada, daughter of James Affleck who owned pastoral stations in South Australia. At public auction in 1899, he purchased a portion of Mt. Fyans including the homestead from the Estate of William Cumming. William Burrow Cumming also served on the Mortlake Shire Council. He was a councillor from 1886-1915 and served as President for two terms. He also had various involvements in pastoral societies. William Burrow Cumming died at Mt. Fyans on 16 June 1932.

Currie[15]

John Lang Currie was born on 17 November 1818 at Howford, Ettrick, Selkirkshire, Scotland to William Currie, a tenant farmer, and Henrietta, nee Lang. John Lang Currie was educated at Selkirkshire Grammar School and gained sheep breeding experience in Scotland before setting sail to Australia to join his cousins, Thomas and William Lang, who had arrived at Port Phillip in 1839. He arrived at Port Phillip in early 1841 and soon began to build his pastoral empire. In partnership with an old school friend, Thomas Anderson, John Lang Currie acquired Larra station, near Lismore in 1844. This partnership was terminated in March 1848 when John Lang Currie became the sole owner of the station. Around 1850, he acquired the Mt. Elephant station and purchased Titanga and Gala stations in 1886 and 1889 respectively. He also held pastoral interests in New South Wales and Queensland.

John Lang Currie had various other business and community involvements. He was a shareholder and chairman of the Victorian Woollen and Cloth Manufacturing Co. formed in 1865. During 1866-83, he was a Local Director of the National Bank of Australasia at Geelong. In 1879, he became director of the Australian Frozen Meat Export Co., the first company formed for the purpose of exporting meat to England. He was also a director of the Australasian Mortgage and Agency Co. In 1863, he became a member of the Hampden Shire Council after having previously been a member of the Hampden and Heytesbury District Roads Board from its formation in 1857. In 1871, John Lang Currie built "Eildon" in St. Kilda and used this property as his city residence after having resided at Osborne House in Geelong. On 14 May 1852, he married Louise, nee Johnston, daughter of James Stewart Johnston who represented the City of Melbourne in the Victorian Legislative Council during 1851-52 and also St. Kilda in the Victorian Legislative Assembly during 1859-64. They had issue seven sons and four daughters.

John Lang Currie died at Eildon on 11 March 1898, leaving his wife, five sons and three daughters, and net assets, valued for probate purposes, of £479,346 in Victoria and £66,767 in New South Wales. For some time before his death, Larra had been leased to Currie's second son, John Lang Currie the younger and Patrick Sellar Lang. Patrick Sellar Lang was married to Henrietta, the eldest daughter of John Lang Currie. From the time of their purchase, Titanga and Gala were under the management of Currie's fourth son, Edwin Currie, who subsequently, in conjunction with his brother Henry Alan (later Sir), leased Gala from his father. John Lang Currie's properties were left to various members of the family. Unlike the other properties that were left to sons, Titanga was left to Henrietta Lang and was operated by Patrick Sellar Lang from 1 June 1898 until his death on 13 April 1909. Of the 11 children of John Lang Currie, at least all of the sons attended private schools, principally Geelong College and the Melbourne Church of England Grammar School. His eldest son, William John Currie, also attended Cirencester College, England. Two other sons, Charles Sibbald and Henry Alan Currie, were educated at the University of Melbourne and Charles Sibbald also studied at Brasenose College, Oxford.

Dennis[16]

Alexander Dennis was born on 29 September 1811 at Trembath, in Penzance, Cornwall, England. He was the eldest son of Richard Dennis and Elizabeth, nee Vinicombe. His father was a farmer and his grandfather was a farmer and miller. Alexander Dennis received a formal education and was trained in farm work. After marrying Emma Williams, nee Tregurtha, daughter of Captain Edward Primrose Tregurtha, R.N., in December 1837, he decided to settle in Port Phillip and arrived in January 1840 with his wife and daughter, his two brothers, John and William Dennis, together with two male servants and two maids who accompanied the family on the voyage. Prior to settling permanently in Port Phillip, Alexander Dennis and his wife and child went to George Town, Van Diemen's Land where stock and implements were obtained for transportation to Port Phillip. Alexander Dennis returned to Port Phillip around April 1840 with the stock and implements and was met at Point Henry by his two brothers. The stock were ultimately driven to Keerangeballort station near Birregurra which was purchased by the three Dennis brothers from the Matson brothers around August 1840. In September 1840, Alexander Dennis brought his wife and two children to the station which was renamed Tarndwarncoort in 1848. Emma Williams Dennis was one of only three squatters' wives between Colac and Port Fairy.[17] In 1842, the Dennis brothers acquired the Poliah station on Lake Corangamite and in May 1848 they purchased Robertson's station on the Richardson River near Navarre. In August 1853, the brothers took up Carr's Plains station adjoining Robertson's station and these two stations were amalgamated. In 1861, the "Dennis Bros." partnership of 21 years was dissolved and in 1867 Alexander Dennis purchased the Eeyeuk station. John and William Dennis returned to Cornwell. Eeyeuk was leased to Richard Vinicombe and Alexander Dennis the younger, the only sons of Alexander Dennis, until 1872 when Alexander purchased the station from his father.

Alexander Dennis had a strong interest in local community affairs. In 1849, he was appointed a magistrate on the local Bench in nearby Colac and in 1859 was one of the foundation members of the Colac District Roads Board. He also was a councillor of the Colac Shire Council during 1868-73 and served as President during 1869-70. Alexander Dennis was also a foundation member of the first agricultural society in the Colac area and was appointed an honorary correspondent to the Board for the Protection of the Aborigines, a role he held for 12 years. Alexander Dennis died at Tarndwarncoort on 12 April 1892, leaving his wife, two sons and six daughters. His net assets were valued for probate purposes at £60,890. Later, Carr's Plains was sold to H.H. Wettenhall.

Richard Vinicombe Dennis was born at Keerangeballort on 12 February 1842. As a result of a childhood woolshed accident which crippled him for life, his education was received from a governess at Tarndwarncoort but he later attended Scotch College for a short period. He partnered his brother, Alexander, in operating Eeyeuk until 1872 and in 1880 took an interest with his brother and their cousin, William Dennis, in "William Dennis & Co." which operated Barenya station near Hughenden, Queensland until 1896 when the station was sold. Around 1882, he married Ada Caroline, daughter of Dr. O.V. Lawrence of Melbourne, and had issue three sons and two daughters. Richard Vinicombe Dennis acquired Tarndwarncoort after his father's death and died there on 13 November 1912.

French[18]

Archeson Jeremiah French was a colourful Western District identity. He was born at Monivae Castle, Galway in 1812 and was educated at the Royal School, Banagher and subsequently at Trinity College, Dublin where he took his B.A. degree. As the second son of Robert French, a High Sheriff, he was originally intended for the church but sought an alternative career when a change in religious beliefs brought him close to atheism. Around 1840, Archeson Jeremiah French arrived in Port Phillip and almost immediately began to combine a career as a pastoralist and a civil servant in the Western District. In 1841, he squatted on land near The Grange (subsequently Hamilton), which became known as the Monivae station and was appointed the first Police Magistrate of The Grange effective from 1 January 1842. At Werribee in February 1842 he married Anna Clark, daughter of Dr John Watton of London. Their first of 12 children, Amy, was born at The Grange on 4 September 1843. Amy was claimed to be the first child born in the township. By the end of December 1843, The Grange magistracy was abolished. Archeson Jeremiah French thereafter devoted more of his energies to developing Monivae, although he remained interested in community affairs.

Archeson Jeremiah French died intestate on 29 January 1870 after diving into shallow sea water at baths in St. Kilda. He dislocated his neck and expired five minutes later. Subsequently, the French family was required to dispose of the 13,004 acre Monivae station in order to clear debts incurred of approximately £20,000.[19] Archeson Jeremiah French was a strong advocate of religious freedom and toleration, views which were regarded as peculiar by his contemporaries.

Hood[20]

Born on 12 February 1821 at Longformacus, Berwickshire, Scotland, Robert Hood was the sixth son of William Hood, a tenant farmer, and Martha, nee Bertram. Robert Hood came to Victoria in January 1854 with his daughter and two sons after his wife Margaret, nee Weatherly, whom he married on 22 July 1843, died in 1849. In April 1854, Robert Hood purchased the Bolac Plains station from Robert Anderson and in December 1856 he acquired the Merrang station on the Hopkins River near Hexham from the executors of the Estate of Adolphus Sceales. On 30 December 1856, he married Jane Sceales, the Scottish-born widow of Adolphus. The Bolac Plains station was sold to Robert Jamieson in January 1859, allowing Robert Hood to concentrate on the development of Merrang.[21]

Robert Hood took an active role in local community and pastoral association affairs. He was a councillor of the Warrnambool Shire Council in 1874-83 and served as President in 1876. He was also a member of the Mortlake Shire Council from 1883-91. As a breeder of Lincoln sheep, Robert Hood was a founder of the Long-woolled Sheep Association and was President of the first Lincoln Sheep Show that was held at Hexham in 1873. He also served as Vice-president and President of the Australian Sheep Breeders' Association. Robert Hood was also Chairman of Directors of the Warrnambool Woollen Mill which started in 1874 but went into liquidation in 1876. The mill was carried on thereafter by Robert Hood in a private capacity until a fire destroyed the plant and building and caused the venture to fail.

Robert Alexander David Hood was born at Merrang on 8 August 1863. He attended the Geelong Church of England Grammar School and gained pastoral experience at Burenda station in Queensland. Robert Alexander David Hood leased Merrang from his father from January 1881. Robert Hood died at Warrnambool on 30 October 1891. His net assets were valued for probate purposes at £34,560. Robert Alexander David Hood bought Merrang from the Estate of Robert Hood and continued his father's sheep breeding policies. He also bred racehorses and polo ponies. Like his father, he was involved in local government and served on the Mortlake Shire Council from 1891-1934 and was President for three terms. On 18 July 1906, Robert Alexander David Hood married Edith Mary, daughter of Robert Calvert of Yan-Yan-Gurt station. She died in 1907 and on 24 June 1909, he married Georgina Martha McCall, nee Anderson, and had issue four children. He died at Merrang on 10 April 1934.

Hope[22]

The Hopes were an old Roxburghshire landed family. The Hope brothers, James, Robert Culbertson and George were born at Temple Hall, Morebattle, Roxburghshire, Scotland to Robert Hope and Joan, daughter of Rev. Robert Culbertson. The youngest of the three brothers, George Hope, was born on 20 September 1814, and decided to settle in Australia with his two elder brothers and sister Isobella after he attended the University of Edinburgh for a short period and following a visit to Canada. He arrived in Sydney in January 1839. George Hope soon after travelled overland to Port Phillip and, in partnership with his brothers, settled on land at Sutherlands Creek in 1840 which became known as Darriwill station. He was also a partner with his brother Robert Culbertson in Barwonleigh station and held an interest in Lake Wallace station near Edenhope, firstly with his brother James and subsequently with his other brother, Robert Culbertson. Later Barwonleigh and Darriwill went to Robert Culbertson Hope and George Hope respectively. In partnership with Robert Scott, George Hope held an interest in Toogimbie station on the Murrumbidgee, New South Wales during 1862-75. Later this partnership acquired interests in Beemery and Belalie stations, near Bourke, New South Wales. The partnership was dissolved in 1877 when George Hope took over

Beemery. In 1852, George Hope married Marianne, nee Hassall, third daughter of Rev. Thomas Hassall of Cobbity, New South Wales, and had issue seven sons and two daughters. In 1861, George Hope was a foundation member of the committee of management of Geelong College. George Hope died at Darriwill on 25 April 1884 leaving his wife, six children, and net assets, valued for probate purposes, of £118,072 in Victoria and £26,113 in New South Wales.

In January 1884, George Hope financed the purchase of Gnotuk Station by his second and fourth born sons, James Hassall and George Rowland respectively. James Hassall and George Rowland Hope were born at Darriwill on 3 August 1856 and 16 October 1861 respectively. James Hassall Hope was educated at Geelong College and the University of Melbourne. George Rowland Hope was also educated at Geelong College and also at Scotch College. After their schooling, James Hassall Hope managed Beemery station until 1882 and George Rowland Hope became prominently involved with the development of the dairying industry around Camperdown. In 1882, James Hassall Hope married Emily, daughter of Rev. Barcroft Boake of Melbourne, and had issue three children. In 1894, George Rowland Hope married Agnes Gray, daughter of Rev. W.C. Wallace, who was a Moderator of the Presbyterian Church in Victoria, and had issue four children. James Hassall Hope died at Darriwill on 27 March 1903 and George Rowland Hope died at Gnotuk on 30 July 1920.

Jamieson[23]

Robert Jamieson was born on 4 August 1812 at Farm House, Castlemaddie in the parish of Carsphairn, Kirkcudbrightshire, Scotland. He was the fifth child of Robert Jamieson, snr., tenant farmer, and Mary, nee Wallace. Robert Jamieson arrived at Port Phillip on 3 April 1841 following his younger brother William who emigrated to Australia in 1838. In June 1841, Robert and William Jamieson bought cattle in Melbourne and headed 150 miles into the country to around the Port Fairy area in the Western District. In the early 1840's, William Jamieson was involved in a partnership with C.D.H. Aplin and George Carmichael operating a run known as Union. Robert Jamieson was possibly associated with this venture. On 12 October 1843, a licence was issued to Robert and William Jamieson for a run on Darlot's Creek which became known as Castlemaddie. The brothers disposed of Castlemaddie in 1849 and moved to Geelong buying land there in June 1849. They built a flour mill near Buckley's Falls on the Barwon River which they operated until early in 1851 when the mill and all water rights were sold to a Mr. Highett. Robert and William Jamieson returned to the pastoral industry in 1851 when they acquired Eumeralla West station near Macarthur.

In 1854, Robert Jamieson left for Scotland leaving William Jamieson in charge. While in Scotland in 1855, Robert Jamieson married Johanna Douglas, daughter of William Black, town clerk, of Stranraer, Wigtonshire and returned to Australia with his wife in January 1856. Soon after William Jamieson dropped out of the partnership and Robert Jamieson carried on alone. By 1857 Robert Jamieson was looking for a suitable sheep run in preference to a cattle station and sold Eumeralla West in 1858. In February 1859, Robert Jamieson acquired Bolac Plains station from Robert Hood and subsequently concentrated on sheep operations. In 1881, Robert Jamieson purchased Stony Point station, near Darlington, from Thomas Forrest Cumming. Robert Jamieson took an interest in the affairs of the region and served as a member of the Mortlake Shire Council from April 1882 to August 1886. Robert Jamieson died at Stony Point on 8 November 1894 leaving his wife, son Robert and daughter Mary, and net assets valued for probate purposes at £58,001.

Robert Jamieson the younger was born at Bolac Plains, Woorndoo on 15 October 1863. He was educated at a private school in Edinburgh during a two year visit by the family to Scotland and, on returning to Victoria, completed his education at the Geelong Church of England Grammar School. At school in Geelong, Robert Jamieson was a champion gymnast and a bright scholar having won prizes for French, Bookkeeping, Divinity, Latin and English. Robert Jamieson left school in 1881 and immediately returned to Western District station life to be tutored in pastoral station operations by his father. On his father's death in 1894, Robert Jamieson became the manager of Bolac Plains and Stony Point. In 1899, he became the proprietor of both stations when his father's estate was settled. Robert Jamieson was also involved in local community affairs and served as a member of the Mortlake Shire Council for 13 years, from 1898 to 1910. He was President of the Council during 1907-09. In 1901, Robert Jamieson married Florence Jane, nee Usher, and had issue three children. He died at Stony Point on 22 April 1946.

Kininmonth[24]

James Leonard Kininmonth was born at Invertiel, Fifeshire, Scotland on 4 October 1834. He was the second son of James Kininmonth, a tenant farmer, and Elizabeth, nee McGlashon. He was educated at Kirkcaldy and later at the Edinburgh Institute of Languages and Mathematics. His scholarship was rewarded with prizes for French and Arithmetic in 1847 and 1849 respectively. As the second son, he was originally intended to join the clergy. However, he returned to Invertiel after his schooling and gained farming experience. At 18 years of age, James Leonard Kininmonth sailed to Australia to take up his appointment with Phillip and Thomas Russell and John Simson as manager and stud master of Barunah Plains station near Shelford. He arrived at Port Phillip on 26 August 1852 and, in 1859, became a partner holding an eleventh share in the Barunah Plains station. In 1881, he returned to Scotland for a holiday. He married Euphemia Russell, nee Carstairs, of Balwearie, Fifeshire, on 2 February 1882 and returned to Barunah Plains with his wife in June of that year. James Leonard Kininmonth soon after sold his interest in Barunah Plains and purchased the Mt. Hesse station near Winchelsea at public auction on 16 November 1882. He operated Mt. Hesse until his death on 14 December 1896. His net assets were valued for probate purposes at £28,445.

James Leonard Kininmonth took an interest in local community affairs and was a member of the Leigh, Winchelsea and Colac Shire Councils at various times. He was twice President of the Leigh Shire Council, once President of the Winchelsea Shire Council and was President of the Colac Shire Council in 1893. He also served as President of the Winchelsea Tennis Club and the Winchelsea Cricket Club. The trustees of the Estate of James Leonard Kininmonth still operate Mt. Hesse station which continues to be managed by the Kininmonth family.

Mackinnon[25]

Daniel Mackinnon was born in 1818 at Lagg, on the Isle of Arran, Scotland. He was the eldest son of John Mackinnon, a farmer in the parish of Kilmory in Argyllshire. Daniel Mackinnon studied theology at the University of Glasgow with a view to entering the Ministry of the Church of Scotland. He did not take a degree and, at the age of 21 years, he decided to settle in Australia, arriving at Port Phillip on 18 September 1839. After gaining pastoral industry experience at Sunbury and at Mordialloc, he joined his uncle, Dr. Daniel Curdie, in a venture to settle on land in the Western District. In 1840, they took up a run south of Purrumbete station. The partnership was dissolved in 1843 when Dr. Curdie took the portion of the run known as Tandarook and Daniel Mackinnon, in partnership with Hugh Scott, took over the Jancourt portion. In 1853, the Marida Yallock station, near Camperdown, was acquired by Daniel Mackinnon and Hugh Scott from Stephen Ewen. In March 1854, the partnership was dissolved and Hugh Scott took over Jancourt and Daniel Mackinnon accepted Marida Yallock. In 1876, Daniel Mackinnon acquired Marion Downs station in

Queensland in partnership with Andrew Tobin. Andrew Tobin subsequently left the partnership and Daniel Mackinnon became the sole owner, later handing it over to his sons, William Kinross, James Curdie and Kenneth John.

Daniel Mackinnon was involved in local community affairs. He was a member of the Hampden and Heytesbury District Roads Board and later the Hampden Shire Council and was an honorary magistrate in the district. He was President of the Camperdown Railway League and an advocate for railway extension westward from Geelong. On a visit to Scotland in 1858, he married Jane, nee Kinross, daughter of an Ayrshire merchant, and had issue five sons and two daughters. William Kinross Mackinnon, the second son of the marriage, took over the running of Marida Yallock in 1884. Daniel Mackinnon died at Marida Yallock on 19 February 1889 leaving his wife and six children. His net assets were valued for probate purposes at £123,993. His eldest son, Donald Mackinnon, inherited Marida Yallock.

Donald Mackinnon was born at Marida Yallock on 29 September 1859. In Australia, he was educated at Geelong Church of England Grammar School and Trinity College, University of Melbourne. He attended New College, Oxford and studied classics and jurisprudence. He graduated from Oxford in 1883 and was called to the Bar at Middle Temple. In the following year, he was admitted to the Victorian Bar. In 1889, he was chosen by Chief Justice George Higinbotham to assist in the intricate and laborious consolidation of the Victorian statutes. In 1900, Donald Mackinnon entered the Victorian Legislative Assembly as member for Prahran, a seat he held for 21 years. During his parliamentary career, he held various posts including Leader of the Opposition, Attorney-General, Solicitor-General, and Minister for Railways. In June 1923, he was Australian Commissioner in the USA, a post he held for almost 18 months. In 1922, he became chairman of the Geelong Church of England Grammar School Council after having been a member of the Council since 1909. Among various other posts, he was chairman of directors of Equity Trustees, Executors and Agency Co., and Victorian Insurance Co. In 1892, Donald Mackinnon married Hilda Eleanor Marie, daughter of Judge B.F. Bunny of Melbourne. Although Donald Mackinnon owned Marida Yallock from 1889 to his death in Melbourne on 25 April 1932, the station was managed for this entire period by his brother William Kinross. William Kinross Mackinnon was born at Marida Yallock on 13 August 1861 and educated at Geelong Church of England Grammar School and Ormond College, University of Melbourne. He gained pastoral industry experience at Wingadee station, New South Wales in the early 1880s.

Macknight and Irvine[26]

Charles Hamilton Macknight was born in Edinburgh, Scotland in 1819 to Rev. Dr. Thomas and his wife Christian Crawfurd, nee Macknight, a cousin. He was educated at the Edinburgh High School and the University of Edinburgh and attended the Scottish Naval and Military Academy before deciding to sail for Port Phillip in 1840. Before leaving Scotland, Charles Hamilton Macknight arranged a partnership with two old school friends, James Hamilton Irvine and William Campbell to enter into pastoral pursuits in Port Phillip. The three men arrived in Port Phillip on 1 March 1841 together with several young Scottish farmers to assist the partnership in developing pastoral operations. The partners operated runs near Castlemaine in the Western Port district until 1842 when a run between Macarthur and Belfast (later Port Fairy) in the Western District was taken up which they named Dunmore. William Campbell did not enjoy colonial life and sold his interest in Dunmore to the other two partners in 1847 before returning to Scotland. Charles Hamilton Macknight married Everina Isabella, nee Heatley, in 1856. In 1863, Dunmore was divided and Dunmore West was acquired by the Trust and Agency Co. The Dunmore portion was retained by Charles Hamilton Macknight and James Hamilton Irvine.[27] Charles Hamilton Macknight met his accidental death caused by a falling tree during a bush fire. He died on 9 March 1873 at which time the firm of Macknight and Irvine was carrying heavy secured debts on Dunmore to the order of £40,540. He left his wife, six young children, and net assets valued for probate purposes at £12,918, including his half-share in Dunmore which was valued at £9,604.

Charles Hamilton Macknight was involved in community affairs. He was a member of the Belfast Borough Council. He was also a magistrate for the Belfast General Sessions District and a member of the committee of management of the Belfast Hospital and Benevolent Asylum. As a scholar, he took a keen interest in the educational facilities in the Colony and delivered lectures on literacy and scientific subjects to various societies in the Western District. He was also a frequent contributor of letters and articles to Victorian newspapers on pastoral affairs. The Macknight family left Dunmore when the station was sold shortly after the death of Charles Hamilton Macknight.

McIntyre[28]

Duncan McIntyre was born at Ardachy, Loch Etive, Argyllshire, Scotland on 3 January 1814 to Peter McIntyre, a tenant farmer, and Isabel, nee McIntyre. Duncan McIntyre was educated at a local church school and later decided to join a friend, Edward McCallum, who was sailing for Australia to act for a syndicate of investors. They sailed from

Greenock and arrived at Hobart Town, Van Diemen's Land on 12 August 1837. Duncan McIntyre worked on stations at Jericho on the Jordan River and took up a position as overseer of shepherds at Malahide in the Fingal Valley. Having heard about pastoral opportunities in Port Phillip, he left Malahide and had arrived at Geelong by 5 May 1840. He held the position as Thomas Rickett's overseer at Clunie station near Harrow until April 1843, when Rickett became insolvent. Duncan McIntyre was owed a considerable sum of back wages by Thomas Rickett. In a deal with George Claridge, a merchant who was also owed a considerable amount by Thomas Rickett, Duncan McIntyre obtained the right to a run near Branxholme in 1843. Duncan McIntyre renamed the run Ardachy after his family home in Scotland. He also held the Narrawong station adjoining Ardachy in 1847-49. In September 1849, Ardachy was divided into two stations, Ardgarton and the new Ardachy, and Ardgarton was sold to William Swan. Duncan McIntyre was accidentally killed in a fall from his horse at Branxholme on 16 February 1854. He left, Miriam, nee Best, whom he married in July 1846, and five children under the age of seven years. He also left a flawed will which caused much argument among his descendants to their considerable financial detriment.

Millear, Maidment and Austin/Millear[29]

Thomas Millear was born to Thomas Millear, snr., and Eliza, nee Norris, on Edgarley, the family's freehold estate, at Glastonbury, Somerset, England on 16 February 1834. He was educated at Queen's College, Taunton, Somerset, and in 1858 left the Glastonbury district for Australia together with Thomas Maidment and Josiah Austin. In the same year, they leased, in partnership, Greenvale station on the Hopkins River, Willaura, from James Austin. The partnership also leased other Western District properties including Avalon and Berrambool stations. James Austin eventually sold Greenvale to the partners. In 1877, the longstanding partnership in Greenvale was dissolved. The northern portion of the station was acquired by Thomas Millear which he named Edgarley station. Thomas Millear together with his brother-in-law, Albert Austin of Eilyer station, also operated stations in New South Wales. In 1878, this partnership purchased the Wanganella station near Deniliquin, New South Wales. In 1895, the partnership was dissolved and Wanganella was divided into Wanganella Estate and the new Wanganella. Thomas Millear took over Wanganella Estate where he died shortly after on 27 November 1895. Wanganella Estate was carried on by the executors of the Estate of Thomas Millear until 1912 when it was sold.

On 3 July 1862, Thomas Millear married Nancy, daughter of Joseph Gardner Mack, a pioneering pastoralist of Berrybank station near Cressy in the Western District, and had issue six children. In the same year, Thomas Millear was appointed a Territorial Magistrate. He died leaving net assets, valued for probate purposes, of £114,007 in Victoria and £59,905 in New South Wales. The only son of Thomas and Nancy Millear, Thomas Millear, inherited Edgarley. Thomas Millear the younger was born at Greenvale station on 24 April 1866 and was educated at Melbourne Church England of Grammar School. In 1890, he was appointed a Justice of the Peace to the Western Bailiwick of Victoria. He married Rosa Elizabeth, daughter of the Rev. Walter Fellows. In 1898, Thomas Millear the younger acquired a station at Deniliquin, New South Wales, which he named Stud Park. He was a Council member of the Ararat Shire Council from 1895-1914 and served as Shire President in 1903-04. He died at Willaura on 14 December 1940.

Miller and Tulloh[30]
Pieracle station on the Glenelg River near Dartmoor was acquired by Henry Miller in 1845. The partnership of Henry Miller and William France Tulloh operated Pieracle station from 1848 to 1864. Henry Miller dedicated himself to accumulating wealth thereby earning the nickname of "Money Miller". He was born on 31 December 1809 at Londonderry, Ireland to Henry Miller, snr., captain in the 40th Regiment and Jane, nee Morpeth and was educated in Paris and Glasgow. In 1824, Henry Miller's father took his family to Sydney with a detachment of the 40th Regiment in charge of convicts. The family first moved to Van Diemen's Land in 1826. Henry Miller travelled with his family to New South Wales and Van Diemen's Land. In 1828, he joined the Audit Office, Hobart as a clerk. He settled in Port Phillip around 1840 and began a career as a financier and, in 1845, as a merchant. Henry Miller developed numerous business and pastoral interests. He founded the Victorian Fire and Marine Insurance Co. in 1849 and was the leading promoter of the Bank of Victoria, established in 1852. He was chairman of directors of the Bank of Victoria from its incorporation until 1888. Although Henry Miller had a policy to not invest in mining companies, he bought and sold many pastoral holdings and city properties during his long and successful business career.

Henry Miller became a politician in the new Colony of Victoria in 1851 representing South Bourke, Evelyn and Mornington (one electoral division) in Victoria's first Legislative Council. He remained in colonial politics until 1866 when he failed to be re-elected. He had married Eliza, daughter of Captain Mattinson, in Hobart on 11 March 1834. Henry Miller died on 7 February 1888 at his thirty-acre property in Kew, Melbourne. His net assets were valued for probate purposes in New South Wales at £163,817 and at £1,456,680 in Victoria. Henry Miller truly earned his nickname.

William France Tulloh was born at Waterford, Ireland around 1819 to William Tulloh, a port captain and Mary, nee Reynell. He arrived in Port Phillip around 1839 and was active in Melbourne and Geelong as a land buyer and a provider of legal advice. He was evidently the managing partner in Pieracle station, during which time Henry Miller continued to develop a diversity of business and pastoral interests from Melbourne. After the partnership disposed of Pieracle in 1864, William France Tulloh managed property at Mt. Cotterill for Henry Miller. William France Tulloh was unmarried when he died at East Melbourne on 4 September 1869.

Officer[31]

The first recorded member of the pioneering Officer family is James Officer (1550-1611) who was a farmer of Nether Pitforthe, Scotland. Robert Officer (later Sir) was born on 3 October 1800 to Robert Officer, snr., and Isabella, nee Kerr, at Fettereso, near Montrose, Scotland. He was educated at Marischal College, Aberdeen where he earned an M.A., and also at the Royal College of Surgeons, England. Dr. Robert Officer arrived in Hobart Town, Van Diemen's Land on 1 March 1822 and married Jamima, nee Patterson, there on 25 October 1823. In August 1847, he acquired the Mt. Talbot station from J.M. Airey and appointed his eldest son, Robert Officer, to manage the station. Robert Officer the younger was born at New Norfolk, Van Diemen's Land on 14 March 1825 and was educated privately. Mt. Talbot was managed by Robert Officer the younger until about 1854 when he purchased Rocklands Estate near Balmoral. The running of Mt. Talbot was then assumed by Charles Myles and Suetonius Henry Officer, the second and third born sons respectively of Dr. Robert Officer. Charles Myles and Suetonius Henry Officer were also born at New Norfolk, Van Diemen's Land on 14 July 1827 and 4 January 1830 respectively. They had assisted their brother Robert Officer in running Mt. Talbot from about 1848 after they had completed their education abroad at the Edinburgh Academy. While assisting brother Robert at Mt. Talbot, Charles Myles and Suetonius Henry Officer acquired Lingmer station near Lake Clear from their father in 1849. The partnership also acquired Kallara station on the Darling River and Murray Downs station at Willakool near Swan Hill. In 1859, the brothers acquired Mt. Talbot and in 1862 Suetonius Henry left the station to manage the partnership's holdings in the Riverina.

The freehold of a smaller portion of the original station was gained after Mt. Talbot was thrown open for selection in 1866.[32] Land "sharks" had forced up the price of Mt. Talbot land which was central to operations on the station. Charles Myles Officer stayed at Mt. Talbot until 1873 when he moved his family permanently to Melbourne. He entered politics in 1883 on being elected the member for Dundas in the Victorian Legislative Assembly after an unsuccessful attempt to gain the seat in 1880. He held the seat until his retirement from colonial politics in 1895. Charles Myles Officer had various other business involvements. He was one of the first directors of the Australian Frozen Meat Export Co., and was a director of the Trustees and Executors' Association. He was also chairman of the Board of Advice of Dalgety and Co. during 1885-94. He also held various positions in the community including his treasurership of the Deaf and Dumb Asylum and his membership of the Central Board for the Protection of the Aborigines. He was also a councillor of the Zoological and Acclimatisation Society and its president in 1887. Due to the financial strain of operating his indebted pastoral holdings including those which were drought-stricken, Charles Myles Officer was declared bankrupt on 25 June 1897. His younger brother, Suetonius Henry, had died earlier at Toorak on 26 June 1883. Suetonius Henry Officer was an irrigation pioneer and a magistrate in the Swan Hill district. He married Mary Lillias Rigg, daughter of the Rev. Dr. Adam Cairns, on 13 December 1868. Suetonius Henry Officer died leaving net assets, valued for probate purposes, of £1,785 in Victoria and £91,079 in New South Wales.

Charles Myles Officer married Christiana Susannah, nee Robertson, on 24 January 1854 and had issue 11 children. A further eight children came from his second marriage to Ellen Agnes, nee Besnard, whom he married on 28 November 1876. He died at Brighton, Melbourne on 1 February 1904 and was survived by his second wife and 11 of his 19 children. His net assets were finally valued for probate purposes at £7,011 on 26 March 1909. After 1883, Charles Myles Officer's second born son, William Officer, became a partner in Mt. Talbot with his father and later acquired full ownership of the station.[33] William Officer was born at Mt. Talbot on 3 December 1858 and was educated at Wesley College, Hawthorn Grammar School and the University of Melbourne where he earned an LLB degree. In 1885, he married Alexa Katherine Rose, nee Wilson, and had issue two sons both of whom were educated at Melbourne Church of England Grammar

School. He operated Mt. Talbot until his death at the station on 29 June 1925.

Ritchie[34]

The Ritchie family have been involved with the Blackwood station, near Penshurst, since 1842. James and John Miller Ritchie held the licence to operate Blackwood in partnership with James Scales in the period 1842-44. James and John Miller Ritchie were the second and fourth sons respectively of James Ritchie, snr., a farmer whose father was a tenant farmer, and Lillias, nee Linton, of Blyth Bridge, Peeblesshire, Scotland. James Ritchie arrived at Port Phillip in April 1841 and was joined by John Miller Ritchie in 1842. The partnership with James Scales was dissolved in 1844 and Blackwood was divided into Woodhouse and the new Blackwood. James Ritchie took over Blackwood in partnership with his younger brother, John Miller. The family partnership in Blackwood was dissolved in 1846 when James Ritchie became the sole owner of the station. In June 1854, he acquired Woodhouse from Adolphus Sceales. James Ritchie died on 10 February 1857 as a result of falling from a horse. He was unmarried. In 1858, Daniel and Simon Ritchie held the licences to operate Blackwood and Woodhouse. Daniel and Simon Ritchie were the third and fifth sons of James, snr., and Lillias Ritchie of Scotland. Daniel Ritchie was born in 1816 and became a doctor of medicine after attending the University of Edinburgh during 1832-37. He served the Royal Navy as a surgeon for 19 years and came to Australia on the death of his brother, James Ritchie. Before leaving for Australia, Daniel Ritchie married Janet, nee Roy. They had issue five children. In 1860, the partnership of Daniel and Simon Ritchie was dissolved at which time Daniel took over Blackwood and Simon took control of Woodhouse. By 1860, Daniel Ritchie was a Justice of the Peace and was the Chairman of the Mount Rouse District Roads Board (1860-64) for the term of its existence and became the first President of the Mount Rouse Shire Council founded in 1864. He died during a visit to Scotland on 26 December 1865. John Miller Ritchie died at Melbourne on 5 February 1882 and Simon Ritchie died at Edinburgh on 4 September 1886.

From December 1865 to 1886, Blackwood was operated by the executors of the Estate of Daniel Ritchie under the charge of an unrelated John Ritchie until his death in 1883 and subsequently came under the charge of Alexander Garden. In 1886, Robert Blackwood Ritchie became the owner of Blackwood. Robert Blackwood Ritchie was born in 1861 and was the first born son of Daniel and Janet. He took possession of Blackwood after completing his education in Scotland. In 1893, he married Lillian Mary, daughter of William and

Janet Ross of the Gums station adjacent to Blackwood, and had issue nine children. He represented the Western Province as member of the Victorian Legislative Assembly in the period 1903-07. After 1907, Robert Blackwood Ritchie made protracted visits to Scotland and later made Scotland his permanent home and died there in 1937.

Robertson/Patterson[35]

George Robertson is best known for establishing Warrock, a unique station property featuring about 40 specific purpose buildings around the station homestead. He was born in Stirlingshire, Scotland in 1808 and was a cabinet maker by trade. He arrived at Port Phillip in early 1840 and appears to have soon after purchased sheep in Van Diemen's Land and subsequently returned to Portland. John G. Robertson, of Wando Vale station, purchased the nearby Warrock station on the Glenelg River for George Robertson, his cousin, in 1844. Warrock was one of the few original pastoral stations in Victoria which did not decline in acreage until at least the mid 1930s. The collection of buildings designed and constructed by George Robertson are an outstanding tribute to his architectural and carpentry skills. In 1850, he married his cousin, Mary, nee Robertson, a sister of John G. Robertson. George Robertson was a councillor of the Glenelg Shire Council during 1868-72. He died at Warrock on 15 January 1890 without issue. His net assets were valued for probate purposes at £87,427.

George Robertson Patterson, a nephew of George Robertson, inherited Warrock on the death of his uncle. George Robertson Patterson was born at "Leckie House", Glasgow, Scotland in 1841 and came to Port Phillip with his parents in 1848. He gained pastoral experience on Warrock and eventually managed the station. In 1875, he purchased Capaul station near Casterton. Around this time, he married Mary Grace, daughter of the Rev. Charles Simson of Roseneath station. She died on 21 June 1884 at Melbourne. George Robertson Patterson was a councillor of the Glenelg Shire Council from 1882-89 and took an interest in various bodies in the local community. His second marriage was to Sara, nee Kilbride, of New Zealand who died on 28 October 1908 without issue. George Robertson Patterson died at Warrock on 8 July 1912 leaving three sons and one daughter from his first marriage.

Russell, P.[36]

Philip Russell was born around 1822 to James Russell, a tenant of Kincraig Farm, Fife, Scotland and Elizabeth, nee Couper, and was the sixth son of fourteen children. He was a cousin of George Russell of the Clyde Company and had gained farming experience at Beanston East Lothian. Philip Russell and his cousin Robert Simson came to Hobart Town, Van Diemen's Land in late 1842. In 1843, they arrived at Port Phillip and acquired Carngham station, south of Lake Burrumbeet. In January 1851, Philip Russell, in partnership with his brother Thomas Russell and John Simson, acquired Long Water Holes station, renamed Barunah Plains, but in 1857 withdrew his investment. In 1851, Philip Russell married Annie, nee Lewis, of Scotland and Van Diemen's Land and Robert Simson also took a marriage partner. The pastoral partnership was short-lived from this time and was dissolved in 1853 when Philip Russell became the sole proprietor of Carngham. In 1859, Philip Russell purchased Langi Willi station near Skipton. His wife died in Melbourne on 22 June 1869 leaving two sons, James and George. In 1877, Philip Russell married a second time in Scotland but this marriage was brief as Mary Ann Carstairs, nee Drysdale, a distant cousin, died on 28 March 1878, a week after giving birth to their only son, Philip.

Philip Russell was a member of the Victorian Legislative Council during 1869-75 and was a Ripon Shire Council member in the period 1865-69. He re-entered Parliament in September 1880 and again served as Member for South-Western Province until 1886. He was the President of the Ballarat Agricultural and Pastoral Society for six years. Philip Russell died at Carngham on 14 July 1892 leaving net assets valued for probate purposes at £214,264. James and George Russell inherited Carngham and Langi Willi respectively. James Russell was born at Boglily, Scotland on 4 November 1852 and was educated at Jesus College, Cambridge. He married Blanche, daughter of John Ritchie of Aringa station near Port Fairy, and died in 1905. George Russell was born in 1857 and was a member for Grenville in the Victorian Legislative Assembly from 1892-1900. He died in 1914. Philip Russell the younger was killed in the Boer war in September 1901.

Russell, T. et al.[37]

Thomas Russell was born at Kincraig, Fife, Scotland in 1828 and was a younger brother of Philip Russell of Carngham and Langi Willi. He came to Port Phillip in 1850 accompanied by Robert Simson, who was returning to Carngham, and John Simson, Robert's brother. As mentioned earlier, in 1851 the partnership comprising brothers Thomas and Philip Russell and John Simson bought what became known as Barunah Plains station situated between Inverleigh and Cressy. Philip Russell and John Simson withdrew their investments in Barunah Plains around 1857 but other investors joined Thomas Russell as partners of

Barunah Plains in the firm Thomas Russell & Co. James Leonard Kininmonth, who was manager and stud master of Barunah Plains from 1853, became partner holding an eleventh share in Barunah Plains in 1859. Acquired in February 1857 from Crompton Ferrers, the Wardy Yalloc Chain of Ponds station became the headquarters of Thomas Russell and was renamed Wurrock. For approximately 15 years from 1 January 1862, the Thomas Russell & Co. partnership of Thomas Russell; William, James and George Russell of Britain; the trustees of William Russell of Dennistoun and James Leonard Kininmonth operated Barunah Plains.

Thomas Russell married Anna Louisa, nee Parsons, on 23 August 1860 at Berriedale, Tasmania. He was a Justice of the Peace and was elected the first President of the Leigh Shire Council in 1862. He was a councillor of the Leigh Shire Council from 1862-72 and served as President during 1862-64 and 1866-67. He was also the member for Grenville in the Victorian Legislative Assembly in 1868-73. In January 1873, Thomas and his family left the Colony for England, where his four sons of seven children were educated at Eton, but returned to Victoria in 1887 after having purchased Haremere Hall, Hurst Green, Sussex. He settled permanently in England at Haremere Hall around 1900 and died on 6 July 1920.

The partnership of Thomas Russell & Co. was dissolved in 1877 when George Russell, a brother of Thomas and Philip Russell, became the sole owner of Barunah Plains. George Russell, then of Kincraig, Fife, Scotland, was never to visit Australia but had sent his son, James Russell, then aged 18 years, to Barunah Plains to gain experience under James Leonard Kininmonth. James Leonard Kininmonth departed Barunah Plains in 1883 when he purchased the nearby Mt. Hesse station. About 1888, James Russell was joined at Barunah Plains by his younger brother Andrew Russell. Around this time, the brothers owned the station in partnership. This unhappy partnership ended in 1897 when Andrew Russell sold his interest to James Russell who became the sole owner of Barunah Plains. George Russell died in Scotland on 3 July 1891 while James Russell died in 1911.

General Observations

This section contains general observations of nineteenth century Western District pastoralism based on the specific backgrounds of the pastoralists connected with the 23 pastoral entities whose surviving business records comprise the research sample for this study. The discussion of these general observations occurs under the following headings: Origin and Occupation; Class; Marriage; Religion; Second Generation and Service to Community.

Origin and Occupation

Seventy per cent of the pioneering Western District pastoralists whose nineteenth century records comprise the research sample were Scots, with the balance being almost equally divided between English and Irish settlers.[38] This compares with the assessment of Kiddle (1961, p.14) who stated:

> In the generation after the ending of the Napoleonic Wars it was the Scots who were the spearhead of middle-class emigration to the other side of the world; first to the island of Van Diemen's Land, and then to the country which was to become the Western District of Victoria. Their numbers cannot be known precisely, but at least two-thirds of the pioneer settlers of the Western District were Scottish. Nearly all these were Lowland farmers.

Gillison (1958, p.11), Anderson (1969, p.3), Forth (1979, p.29), Garden (1984, p.29) and de Serville (1991, p.164) also pointed to the hardworking dour Scots of farming backgrounds as the main colonists in the Western District.

Of the 70 per cent Scottish majority found in this study, 88 per cent of the pioneering Scots were identified to be of farming backgrounds. Of these, at least 72 per cent were found to be of tenant farming backgrounds. Hence, in this study, at least 63 per cent of the pioneering Scots were of tenant farming backgrounds.

The Scottish farmers in particular had good reason to emigrate to Australia for pastoral pursuits. Following the end of the Napoleonic Wars in 1815, economic conditions bore heavily on Scottish farmers (Strachan, 1927, p.5; Kiddle, 1961, pp.17-22). As explained by Kiddle (1961, p.18):

> The bubble of prosperity was burst by the fall in prices after the war ended in 1815. The big farmer and the great landowner survived, but the small cultivator who lacked capital was gobbled up by his large neighbours. Many tenant farmers found conditions impossible. In spite of the fall in prices after the war the 'high' farmers determined to maintain rents at their high levels. In 1814 it was calculated that rents throughout England and Scotland had risen between one hundred and one hundred and fifty per cent during the preceding twenty to twenty five years. . . . 'The rental of an acre in the more fertile districts of England was from £1 to £2; in similar districts of Scotland it reached or exceeded £4. . . .'[39]

During these difficult times, many Scottish farmers, particularly tenant farmers or sons of tenant farmers, chose to establish themselves in Australia. Many went to Van Diemen's Land where tracts of land were granted to approved applicants but no assisted passages were available and no grants were provided to the colonizers to develop the land granted (Strachan, 1927, p.5). After 1831, when the sale of land at a minimum price per acre replaced a land grant scheme, there was an increased propensity for opportunities to be sought on the mainland (Anderson, 1969, p.4). After 1836, many came to Port Phillip as unauthorized squatters. Some earlier arrivals came to Port Phillip from Van Diemen's Land with their stock, supplies and servants. In this study, about 30 per cent of the Scottish pioneering pastoralists first went to Van Diemen's Land before moving to the Western District. The expanses of fertile Western District lands provided opportunities that were unavailable in Scotland (Forth, 1982, p.35).

The remaining 30 per cent of the research sample comprised English and Irish pastoral pioneers. With the exception of the Corney family, the other English settlers (Armytage; Dennis; Millear) were of farming backgrounds. The Irish settlers (Beggs; French; Miller and Tulloh) were of mixed backgrounds. Of the Beggs family settlers, at least Francis Beggs had farming experience. For the entire research sample, a total of 78 per cent of Western District pastoral pioneers were identified to be of farming backgrounds in the British Isles.[40]

Class

According to Kiddle (1961, p.20), the pioneering pastoralists in the Western District were of a different class from the great majority of immigrants. Those interested in occupation and settlement of new land were people who were possessed with either personal or family capital and, generally, with some education (Kiddle, 1961, p.20). Kiddle (1961, p.20) argued:

> They [the pioneering pastoralists] did not emigrate, as the great majority did, because they had nothing or next to nothing. They wished at least to restore or retain a way of life of some comfort which was threatened; most of them wished to improve it.

The specific background information presented earlier in this chapter tends to support Kiddle's assessment. The large majority of pioneering pastoralists whose records comprise the research sample invested either personal or family capital in speculative pastoral ventures in isolated territory. In the case of the Clyde Company, British investors were prepared to invest resources under the management of George Russell, a skilled and trusted Scottish tenant farmer.

Based on the research sample, this study also presents evidence that many Western District pastoral pioneers had received a formal education. Of the Scottish pioneers, George Hope, Charles Hamilton

Macknight and Daniel Ritchie attended the University of Edinburgh and Daniel Mackinnon studied at the University of Glasgow. Robert Officer studied at Marischal College, Aberdeen and the Royal College of Surgeons, England. John Lang Currie was educated at Selkirkshire Grammar School and James Leonard Kininmonth studied at the Edinburgh Institute of Languages and Mathematics. Of those from England, Thomas Millear was educated at Queen's College, Taunton and George Armytage studied engineering in London. Of the Irish pioneers, Francis Beggs and Archeson Jeremiah French both attended Trinity College, Dublin, and Henry Miller was educated at schools in Paris and Glasgow. Other pioneers such as George Russell of Golf Hill and Alexander Dennis attended educational establishments in Britain whose names are unknown. Those pioneering pastoralists who had received a formal education undoubtedly found their educational background to be a virtue in their new isolated environment. With respect to their lifestyle, most pastoral pioneers connected with the research sample appeared to substantially improve their quality of life in the Western District and among others formed the basis of a landed gentry in colonial Victoria (Kiddle, 1961, p.359; Cannon, 1973, p.178; Forth, 1982, p.34; de Serville, 1991, pp.198-204).

Marriage

Of the Western District pastoral pioneers connected with the 23 pastoral entities involved in this study, only Francis Beggs, John Cumming, Alexander Dennis and Daniel Ritchie were married and were accompanied by their wives on emigrating to Australia. With the exception of a few who did not marry, the other pioneering pastoralists either married in Australia, mostly in Victoria, or returned to Scotland to seek a wife. In the latter category were Robert Jamieson, James Leonard Kininmonth, Daniel Mackinnon, and George Russell of Golf Hill, all of whom married in Scotland in the 1850s (or later in the case of Kininmonth).[41] As the evidence reported in the previous section demonstrates, the pastoral pioneers generally either maintained or developed links with those of a similar class and had a propensity to marry the daughters or widows of lawyers, politicians, clergymen, doctors, military officers and other pastoralists. George Robertson, and George Russell of Golf Hill married their first cousins and Philip Russell of Carngham and Langi Willi took a distant cousin as his second spouse. A pastoralist's marriage to a woman whose background and antecedents were a known quantity was considered to be important in a colony which comprised a large number of convict descendants (Cannon, 1973, pp.179-180).

Religion

Kiddle (1961, p.109) and de Serville (1991, p.173) pointed out that most of the Scottish pastoral pioneers were Presbyterian in religion. According to Kiddle (1961, p.22):

> The stern Calvinist faith of the Scots strengthens their pride. The farmers, like their servants, believed that 'the seed of the righteous were not forced to beg their bread'. There is more than a hint in the writings and moralizings of these people that those who were poor deserved to be so; those who obeyed their Bible, worked and lived frugally must succeed. Material success was often considered a measure of virtue, and if it could not be won at home it might be found abroad.

Most of the pastoral pioneers whose backgrounds were addressed in the previous section were also foundation members and subsequently elders of the Presbyterian church in the Western District (Ross, 1901). According to obituary notices and other available records, many of them such as George Hope, Robert Jamieson, Daniel Mackinnon, George Robertson, George Russell of Golf Hill and Thomas Russell made substantial donations towards the construction of church buildings throughout the Western District.[42] Although there were large numbers of Anglicans in the Western District, Kiddle (1961, p.109) contended:

> . . . that the station hands who formed the bulk of the population of the district counted themselves as members of that church, or, when in doubt, the compilers of the statistics designated them as Anglicans.

There is no evidence to suggest that any of the pastoralists connected with the 23 pastoral entities which form the research sample for this study were Roman Catholic. Catholicism spread as Irish immigrants arrived to join the labour force (Kiddle, 1961, p.111).

Second Generation

The sons of pioneering Western District pastoralists were commonly educated at private boarding schools. As evidenced in the previous section, the main private schools involved were the Melbourne Church of England Grammar School, Scotch College, Geelong Church of England Grammar School and Geelong College. The Melbourne and Geelong Church of England Grammar schools were Anglican schools while Scotch College and Geelong College were Presbyterian schools. Founded in 1851, Scotch College was a prime choice for Scottish colonists but the Geelong Church of England Grammar School became the most attractive school for the education of Western District boys even after Geelong College was established (Kiddle, 1961, p.486; Bate, 1990, p.32; de Serville, 1991, p.173). Apart from other reasons given for the Geelong Church of England Grammar School's popularity with Western District pastoralists, Kiddle (1961, p.486) argued that "most intangible and perhaps most important there was an element of snobbery or rather something better than snobbery involved". The evidence presented in this study to 1900 suggests that the Geelong Church of England Grammar School became the most popular school but was closely followed in popularity by Scotch College which itself was closely followed by Geelong College. The Melbourne Church of England Grammar School was supported to a lesser degree by Western District pastoralists as the nineteenth century came to a close. By the 1930s only a minority of Scottish pastoral "dynasties" continued to send their sons to Presbyterian schools (de Serville, 1991, p.173). According to de Serville, "it mirrored a change in society with the adoption by Presbyterian colonists of Anglicanism. This suggests that the change in religion followed a growing worldliness attendant upon material success" (1991, p.173).

    As seen in certain cases in this study, the education of the second generation of Western District pastoralists also involved the dispatch of sons to English schools and to universities in Victoria and England. George Herbert and Harold Augustus Armytage attended Brighton College; William John Currie attended Cirencester College, and the sons of Thomas Russell were educated at Eton. In Victoria, Archibald John and Niel Walter Black, Charles Sibbald and Henry Alan Currie, James Hassall Hope, Donald and William Kinross Mackinnon, and William Officer all studied at the University of Melbourne. In England, Charles Sibbald Currie and Donald Mackinnon also studied at Oxford. Elsewhere, Archibald John, Steuart Gladstone and Niel Walter Black along with James Russell, son of Philip Russell of Carngham and Langi Willi, studied at Cambridge. All of these six who studied at English universities were the sons of Scots who evidently believed that English rather than Scottish universities were better suited for their sons' development. According to de Serville (1991, p.174) "the dispatch of sons to Oxford or Cambridge was one sign that the large landowners were grooming their sons to become English landed gentlemen". Notwithstanding, the education of offspring at exclusive schools "hastened the progress from squatter to landed gentlemen" (de Serville, 1991, p.172) and enhanced the sophistication of Western District society.

    The children of successful Western District pioneering pastoralists enjoyed the security of the elite status gained by their parents and commonly sought to maintain or enhance their position in the social order by marrying into leading families. This strong propensity for intermarriage between leading families is evident in the marriages outlined in an earlier section. Marriages into other pastoral families were common as occurred in the cases of Archibald John and Steuart Gladstone Black, William Burrow Cumming, Robert Alexander David Hood, George Robertson Patterson, Robert Blackwood Ritchie, and James Russell, son of Philip Russell of Carngham and Langi Willi. The advantage of such marriages was propinquity (Cannon, 1973, p.180; de Serville, 1991, p.167). Marriage into ecclesiastical circles was also common. According to de Serville (1991, p.32) "by the 1880s large ecclesiastical dynasties had grown up, along English lines". As mentioned earlier, George Hope and his sons James Hassall and George Rowland Hope, Thomas Millear the younger, George Robertson Patterson, and Suetonius Henry Officer all married the daughters of clergymen.

Service to Community

In their respective regional communities, the nineteenth century pastoralists were involved in community affairs. Municipal and shire service was considered to be a traditional duty of the English gentleman (de Serville, 1991, p.77). As evidenced in this study, this expectation was manifest in Western District pastoralism where there was a strong propensity for pastoralists to be represented on district roads boards and shire councils.[43] In the 1860s, the roads boards metamorphosed themselves into shire councils and became the local government authorities in Victoria. Kiddle (1961, p.439) argued that:

> The members of these councils controlled the affairs of the towns and shires, and at almost every inaugural meeting of the Roads Boards the squatters attempted to ride rough-shod over all newcomers. For a few years their local knowledge, financial standing and force of personality carried the day, until chiefly by virtue of their superior numbers the newcomers found themselves powerful.

Pastoralists such as Theodore Beggs, Archibald John and Steuart Gladstone Black, William and William Burrow Cumming, Robert and Robert Alexander David Hood, Robert Jamieson the younger, Thomas Millear the younger, George Russell of Golf Hill, Thomas Russell and John Smith served for long periods as shire councillors. Most of the pastoralists who served on roads boards and/or shire councils also held the office of President and often held this key leadership role in the local community for more than one term.

In Colonial public life, Western District pastoralists were
represented in both the Victorian Legislative Assembly and Legislative
Council.[44] As seen earlier, Donald Mackinnon, Charles Myles Officer,
George Russell of Langi Willi and Thomas Russell sat in the
Legislative Assembly. Henry Miller, and Philip Russell of Carngham
and Langi Willi were members of the Legislative Council. On
Federation, Donald Mackinnon remained as a member of the Legislative
Assembly in State politics. Subsequently, Theodore Beggs and Robert
Blackwood Ritchie became members of the Legislative Assembly and
Steuart Gladstone Black was elected to the Legislative Council.
Political influence was undoubtedly important to the pastoralists in a
society which underwent a rapid transformation from squatting days as
the size and diversity of the population expanded.

Conclusion

This chapter has elucidated the specific backgrounds of the nineteenth
century pastoralists connected with the 23 pastoral entities whose
surviving business records comprise the research sample for this study
and has provided a range of general observations of Western District
pastoralism for this group of pastoralists. The pertinent background
information presented in this chapter together with the review of the
pastoral industry and station environments presented in Chapter 3
provides necessary context in examining and interpreting the structure
and usage of accounting information prepared for these 23 pastoral
entities. An understanding of the organisational and social context
provides for a better appreciation of the relationships between surviving
business records and the individuals associated with those records. It
also assists in formulating interpretations about the environmental
influences on accounting during any particular examination period. The
examination on a case by case basis of the specific backgrounds of the
pastoralists involved in this study also complements the reporting of
the research findings which follows in Chapter 6. Chapter 7 contains an
overview of the structure and usage of pastoral accounting information
based on the case observations presented.

NOTES

1. See Anon (1965); Billis and Kenyon (1974, pp.17, 209 & 253-254);
    Bride (1969, pp.171-176); Brown (1966); Henderson (1936, pp.1-18;
    1941, pp.302-314); Hone (1969a); Smith (1987); Armytage
    Collection (La Trobe Library, Melbourne); Blake and Riggall
    Collection: Fairbairn George, and Fairbairn Pastoral Company

(University of Melbourne Archives); Estate of Charles Henry Armytage papers held by Caroline Shepherd, Melbourne.

2. Henderson (1936, p.1) and Smith (1987, p.8) reported that George Armytage was born in 1794 while Henderson (1941, p.302), Brown (1966, p.27) and Billis and Kenyon (1974, p.17) recorded that he was born in 1795.

3. Billis and Kenyon (1974, pp.253-254) incorrectly recorded that Mt. Sturgeon was acquired by Charles Henry Armytage and George Fairbairn in 1865. According to the contract of sale, Mt. Sturgeon was purchased from Hugh Glass by Charles Henry Armytage and George Fairbairn on 9 May 1863 (Armytage Collection, La Trobe Library, Melbourne, Box 15/1).

4. See Anderson (1969, pp.77 & 246-247); Billis and Kenyon (1974, p.206); Burtchaell and Sadleir (1935, p.55); Henderson (1936, pp.249-257); *Riponshire Advocate*, 25 January 1879 and 31 December 1880; Beggs Collection (Gold Museum, Ballarat); Probate and Administration papers, Victoria (Public Records Office, Laverton); Shire of Ripon Archives, Beaufort.

5. Billis and Kenyon (1974, p.206) contained no mention of the partnership of George Beggs and Humphrey Gratton. However, Henderson (1936, p.252) reported upon the existence of the partnership while ledgers in the Beggs Collection for Eurambeen date from September 1855.

6. Henderson (1936, p.250) implied that the Beggs Brothers' partnership began around 1883. However, ledger records at the Gold Museum, Ballarat indicated that the partnership commenced on 30 December 1886.

7. See Billis and Kenyon (1974, pp.28, 214 & 277); Carnegie, (1991b); Henderson (1936, pp.70-72; 1941, pp.319 & 321); Kiddle (1961); Pastoral Review Pty Ltd (1910); Sutherland (1977b, p.80); Ward (1969); *Warrnambool Standard*, 18 May 1880; Niel Black & Co. and Smith Collections (La Trobe Library, Melbourne); Probate and Administration papers, Victoria (Public Records Office, Laverton); Shire of Mortlake Archives, Mortlake; Smith papers (Grassdale Estate, Branxholme). Sutherland (1977b) was first published in 1888.

8. See *The Australian Encyclopaedia* (1963, Vol.2, p.423; 1963, Vol.7, pp.521-522); Brown (1935, 1941, 1952, 1958, 1959, 1963, 1967, 1968, 1971); Kiddle (1961); Sutherland (1977b, p.206); Clyde Company Collection (La Trobe Library, Melbourne); Probate and Administration papers, Victoria (Public Records Office, Laverton); Shire of Leigh Archives, Rokewood.

9. The other partners were: Theodore Walrond of Calder Park, Lanark; Frederick Adamson, a merchant of Glasgow; John Stewart Wood of Edinburgh; William Wood, a merchant of Liverpool and John Cross Buchanan of Auchintoshan, Dumbarton. The first partnership agreement (described as Contract of Copartnery) was dated 26 and 29 September and also 1 and 4 October 1836 (Brown, 1935, p.107).

10. In his later years, George Russell methodically arranged and read his papers and letters and worked through his diaries to construct his "Narrative" which was later edited and published (Brown, 1935).

11. See Billis and Kenyon (1974, pp.50 & 296); Commonwealth of Australia (1921, pp.58-59); Henderson (1936, pp.529-534); Palmer (1973, p.22); Sutherland (1977b, p.53); *Sydney Gazette, and New South Wales Advertiser*, 30 June 1821; City of Portland Archives, Portland; Corney papers (Tulse Hill, Nareen); Probate and Administration papers, Victoria (Public Records Office, Laverton).

12. Henderson (1936, p.530) incorrectly reported that William Corney died on 27 June 1898.

13. See Billis and Kenyon (1974, pp.53 & 250); Henderson (1936, pp.494-499 & 552); Keith (1961, p.177); Power (1977, pp.9 & 37); Cumming Collections (La Trobe Library, Melbourne; University of Melbourne Archives); Cumming papers (Myrngrong, Darlington); Cumming, W.H., unpublished biographies of John and Anne Cumming, William Cumming and William Burrow Cumming (prepared for publication in the forthcoming *Western District Dictionary of Biography)*; Probate and Administration papers, Victoria (Public Records Office, Laverton); Shire of Mortlake Archives, Mortlake.

14. Billis and Kenyon (1974, p.250) reported that Mt. Fyans was acquired by John Cumming in January 1858. However, the ledgers of the Cumming family for Mt. Fyans date from March 1856. Papers in the Cumming Collection (La Trobe Library, Melbourne) also confirm that Mt. Fyans came under the control of the Cumming family in March 1856.

15. See Billis and Kenyon (1974, pp.54, 210 & 249); Brownhill (1990, p.316); Henderson (1941, pp.168-174); Hetherington (1964, pp.26-31); Hone (1969b); McAlpine (1982, p.6); Oman and Lang (1980, pp.5-35); Pastoral Review Pty Ltd (1910); Southall (1950, pp.24-26); Woods (1972); *Australasian*, 19 March 1898; *Pastoralists' Review*, May 1909; Currie Collection (La Trobe Library, Melbourne); Lang papers (Titanga, Lismore); National Australia Bank Ltd Group Archives, Melbourne; Probate and Administration papers, Victoria (Public Records Office, Laverton); Supreme Court of New South Wales (Probate Division, Sydney); The City of St. Kilda Archives, Victoria. Brownhill (1990) was first published in 1955.

16. See Billis and Kenyon (1974, pp.57, 189, 226-227 & 272); Denholm (1967); Dennis (1963); Hebb (1970, p.60); Henderson (1936, pp.49-59 & 60-61); Hone (1972); Sutherland (1977b, p.82); *Colac Herald*, 15 April 1892; Dennis papers (Tarnwarncoort, Warncoort); Probate and Administration papers, Victoria (Public Records Office, Laverton).

17. According to Hebb (1970, p.60) the other two squatter's wives were Mrs H. Murray and Mrs T. Manifold. Hebb (1970) was first published as a series in the *Colac Herald* in 1888.

18. See Billis and Kenyon (1974, pp.69 & 245); Burke (1958, p.273); Burtchaell and Sadleir (1935, p.308); Garden (1984), Kiddle (1961, p.274); Pine (1958, p.273); *Hamilton Spectator*, 17 July 1863 and 2

February 1870; *Port Phillip Gazette*, 16 September 1843; French Collection (La Trobe Library, Melbourne); Probate and Administration papers (Public Records Office, Laverton).

19. Kiddle (1961, p.274) referred to correspondence from Niel Black to T.S. Gladstone of 24 March 1870 which stated that Archeson Jeremiah French held 20,000 acres on his death while Garden (1984, p.104) refers to Monivae being of 16,200 acres when the last 4,400 acres were acquired under the Duffy Act.

20. See Billis and Kenyon (1974, pp.176 & 229); Geelong Church of England Grammar School (1907); Hood (1991); Pastoral Review Pty Ltd (1910); de Serville (1983; 1991, p.523); Sutherland (1977b, p.64); Hood papers (Merrang, Hexham); Probate and Administration papers, Victoria (Public Records Office, Laverton); Shire of Mortlake Archives, Mortlake.

21. Although Billis and Kenyon (1974, p.176) reported that Bolac Plains was held by Robert Hood until February 1861, the surviving business records of the Jamieson family indicate that Bolac Plains was controlled by Robert Jamieson from 17 January 1859.

22. See Billis and Kenyon (1974, pp.84, 198 & 233); Henderson (1941, pp.267-274); Keith (1961, p.3); Sutherland (1977b, p.164); Hope papers (Darriwill North, Moorabool); Probate and Administration papers, Victoria (Public Records Office, Laverton); Supreme Court of New South Wales (Probate Division, Sydney).

23. See Billis and Kenyon (1974, pp.88-89); Brownhill (1990, p.322); Carnegie (1990-91); Henderson (1936, pp.206-208); Martindale (n.d.); Pastoral Review Pty Ltd (1910); Sutherland (1977b, p.83); *Camperdown Chronicle*, 10 November 1894; Australian Mercantile Land and Finance Co. Ltd Collection (The Noel Butlin Archives Centre, Australian National University, Canberra); Geelong Church of England Grammar School Archives, Corio; Jamieson papers (Stony Point, Darlington); Probate and Administration papers, Victoria (Public Records Office, Victoria); Shire of Mortlake Archives, Mortlake.

24. See Gregory, Gregory and Koenig (1985, p.28); Henderson (1936, p.192); Kininmonth and Kininmonth (1987); Kininmonth papers (Mt. Hesse, Ombersley); Probate and Administration papers, Victoria (Public Records Office, Laverton).

25. See Billis and Kenyon (1974, p.106); Henderson (1936, pp.325-329); Kiddle (1961, pp.490 & 492); Serle (1986); Sutherland (1977b, p.86); Mackinnon Collection (La Trobe Library, Melbourne); Probate and Administration papers, Victoria (Public Records Office, Laverton); University of Glasgow Archives, Glasgow.

26. See Billis and Kenyon (1974, pp.106 & 202); Carnegie (1991a); Henderson (1941, pp.372-379); Hone (1974a); Kiddle (1961, pp.274 & 397); Powling (1980, pp.43-45); *Australasian*, 10 May, 1873; Macknight papers held by Dame Ella and Helen Macknight, Melbourne; Probate and Administration papers, Victoria (Public Records Office, Laverton).

27. Charles Hamilton Macknight was evidently the senior partner in the firm of Macknight and Irvine and also the manager of affairs on Dunmore. James Hamilton Irvine was the son of the Laird of Castle Drum, Aberdeenshire (Henderson, 1941, p.372). However, unlike the case of Charles Hamilton Macknight, Western District historians have evidently not showed any significant interest in the life of James Hamilton Irvine. In 1879, James Hamilton Irvine was a partner with Thomas Macknight Hamilton in a 1690 acre property at Ballangeich (de Serville, 1991, p.498).

28. See Billis and Kenyon (1974, pp.167 & 258); Gregory, Gregory and Koenig (1985, p.27); Henderson (1941, p.319); *Portland Guardian & Normanby General Advertiser*, 23 February 1854; McIntyre papers held by the McIntyre family, Geelong.

29. See Gibbney and Smith (1987, p.104); Henderson (1936, pp.156-159); Kiddle (1961, pp.212 & 379); Pastoral Review Pty Ltd (1910); The Pastoral and Agricultural Society of Deniliquin (1979, pp.26-27); Millear Collection (La Trobe Library, Melbourne); Probate and Administration papers, Victoria (Public Records Office, Laverton), Shire of Ararat Archives, Ararat; Supreme Court of New South Wales (Probate Division, Sydney).

30. See *The Australian Encyclopaedia* (1963, Vol.6, p.85); Billis and Kenyon (1974, pp.114 & 264); Mellor (1974); Mennell (1892, pp.323-324); *West Bourke & South Grant Guardian*, 11 September 1869; Probate and Administration papers, Victoria (Public Records Office, Laverton); William France Tulloh Collection (University of Melbourne Archives).

31. See *Australian Encyclopaedia* (1963, Vol.6, pp.388-389); Billis and Kenyon (1974, pp.121 & 254); Henderson (1936, pp.515-527); Hone (1974b); Mowle (1948, pp.129-132); Sutherland (1977b, p.57); Officer papers (Mt. Talbot, Toolondo); Probate and Administration papers, Victoria (Public Records Office, Laverton); Stamp Duties Office-Deceased Estates File (Archives Office of New South Wales, Sydney).

32. Hone (1974b, p.357) reported that Charles Myles Officer "finally gained [Mt. Talbot] freehold of 16,756 acres". However, the statement of assets and liabilities prepared for probate purposes as at 26 July 1883, the date of death of Suetonius Henry Officer, indicated that Mt. Talbot of 16,773 acres was held by Charles Myles and Suetonius Henry Officer as equal partners.

33. Sutherland (1977b, p.57) indicated that Mt. Talbot of 16,756 acres was held at the time by "Mr Charles Myles Officer, M.L.A., Balmoral, and the executors of the late Suetonius Henry Officer".

34. See Billis and Kenyon (1974, pp.130, 176 & 302); Kiddle (1961, p.139); de Serville (1991, pp.332 & 484); Mount Rouse Shire Council Archives, Penshurst; Ritchie Collection (University of Melbourne Archives); Ritchie family history notes held by John L. Ritchie, Benalla.

35. See Billis and Kenyon (1974, pp.131 & 298); Bride (1969, p.158); Henderson (1936, pp.380-382; 1941, p.357); Hetherington (1964, pp.19-25); Palmer (1973, pp.22, 33 & 80); Shire of Glenelg (1963, p.11); Probate and Administration papers, Victoria (Public Records Office, Laverton); Robertson/Patterson papers (Warrock, Casterton).

36. See Anderson (1969); Billis and Kenyon (1974, pp.134-135 & 188); Brown (1974); Nunan (1971, pp.8-10); de Serville (1991, pp.330 & 333); *Ballarat Star*, 15 July 1892; Philip Russell Collections (Geelong Historical Records Centre; La Trobe Library, Melbourne); Philip Russell papers (Langi Willi, Skipton); Probate and Administration papers, Victoria (Public Records Office, Laverton); Shire of Ripon Archives, Beaufort.

37. See Billis and Kenyon (1974, pp.135 & 297); Brown (1935, p.219; 1974); Kininmonth and Kininmonth (1987); Pastoral Review Pty Ltd (1910); Sutherland (1977b, pp.206-207); Australian Mercantile Land and Finance Co. Ltd Collection (The Noel Butlin Archives Centre, Australian National University, Canberra); Russell papers held by Geordie Russell, Barwon Heads; Shire of Leigh Archives, Rokewood.

38. This Scottish majority reflects the proportion of pioneering Scots connected with the 23 sets of surviving business records which comprise the research sample. Of the 23 sets of records involved, 16 sets are linked to Scottish colonists while 4 and 3 sets are linked to English and Irish colonists respectively.

39. As reported by Halevy (1949, pp.230-231) who was quoting the Corn Laws Report (Report from the Select Committee . . ., 1814, pp.56 & 106-107).

40. Corney, French, Macknight and Irvine, Miller and Tulloh, and Robertson/Patterson were identified to be of occupational backgrounds in the British Isles other than farming.

41. These pastoralists spent many years developing their Western District pastoral interests and establishing themselves before seeking a marriage partner in Scotland (as identified in the following brackets): Robert Jamieson (14 years); James Leonard Kininmonth (29 years); Daniel Mackinnon (19 years) and George Russell (16 years). Niel Black also returned to Scotland in the 1850s where he married in 1857 (Henderson, 1936, p.71).

42. Cannon (1973, p.189) pointed out that when townships began to expand pastoralists often "paid the expense of bringing out clergymen from Britain".

43. As the first local government authorities in Victoria, the Roads Boards were not established until the late 1850s after the formation of the Board of Lands and Works (Kiddle, 1961, p.439).

44. According to de Serville, the term "public life" was widely used in the nineteenth century. However, in Victoria "municipal and shire service was not usually counted as public life in the colony" (1991, p.77).

CHAPTER 6
PASTORAL ACCOUNTING RECORDS IN REVIEW

This chapter presents the findings of detailed examinations of the surviving pre-Federation business records on a case by case basis for each of the 23 pastoral entities comprising the research sample. The discussion in each instance includes an outline of the nature of the accounting records examined and identifies, where possible, the factors which appeared to influence changes in the structure and usage of the accounting information observed. An overview of the findings is provided in the form of a summary in each case. Chapter 7 examines the structure and usage of accounting information in pre-Federation pastoralism based on the findings reported in this chapter for all of the 23 pastoral entities involved.

Financial records were examined for each of the 23 pastoral entities in the research sample. In three cases (Corney; Dennis; Miller and Tulloh), no pre-Federation volume records were found. In four other cases [Black Bros. (& Smith); Cumming; Hood; Hope], the surviving accounting records were identified during examination to be primarily of a financial nature. Hence, for 16 pastoral entities (70 per cent of the research sample), the discussion is balanced between financial and volume records.

Table 6.1 shows for each of the 23 pastoral entities involved the date of Western District pastoral occupation, the dates of the earliest surviving financial and volume records found and the lags, if any, from occupation to the dates of the earliest surviving financial and volume records.[1] The earliest surviving volume record was prepared after the date of the earliest surviving financial record in 13 of the 20 instances where both financial and volume records were available for examination. The earliest surviving volume record was prepared prior to the earliest surviving financial record in only four cases. In the other three cases, the earliest surviving financial and volume records were prepared in the same year. Table 6.1 also shows for both financial and volume records the mean and median availability lags from occupation. Both the mean and median lags are longer in the case of volume records. These results indicate that the financial records examined are generally of an earlier vintage than the volume records examined.

TABLE 6.1: Earliest Surviving Financial and Volume Records Found

Entity (23)	Western District Pastoral Occupation	Financial/Volume Records	Financial/Volume Records Lags (from Occupation)
Armytage	1857	1863/1863	6/6
Beggs	1855	1855/1860	-/5
Black Bros. (& Smith)	1885	1885/1887	-/2
Clyde Company/ Russell, G	1836	1836/1837	-/1
Corney	1840	1842/ -	2/-
Cumming	1856	1856/1860	-/4
Currie	1844	1876/1846	32/2
Dennis	1840	1840/ -	-/-
French	1841	1841/1849	-/8
Hood	1854	1854/1856	-/2
Hope	1840	1852/1878	12/38
Jamieson	1841	1842/1841	1/-
Kininmonth	1882	1882/1882	-/-
Mackinnon	1840[a]	1853/1872	13/32
Macknight and Irvine	1842	1847/1856	5/14
McIntyre	1843	1843/1843	-/-
Millear, Maidment and Austin/Millear	1858	1870/1862	12/4
Miller and Tulloh	1845	1848/ -	3/-
Officer	1847	1852/1857	5/10
Ritchie	1842	1855/1866	13/24
Robertson/ Patterson	1844	1876/1887	32/43
Russell, P	1843	1843/1870	-/27
Russell, T. *et al.*	1851	1897/1880	46/29

Mean and Median lags

Mean (years)[b]	8/12.6
Median (years)[b]	2/5.5

Notes:
(a) This date relates to the advent of the partnership of Daniel Curdie and Daniel Mackinnon
(b) These lags have been determined on the basis of 23 and 20 sets of records respectively for financial and volume records.

Notwithstanding, these findings do not suggest that non-financial operating information was subordinate to financial information in pre-Federation pastoral industry engagement. Instead, volume records, with their emphasis on operational statistics, were probably generally less treasured by the descendants of pastoral pioneers than early day books, ledgers and the like which, as will become apparent later, readily elucidated the human side of station establishment and development. As vignettes of the station community, financial records rather than volume records were probably generally seen to be more relevant in reflecting the history of the family, station, region, Colony and even the country. In addition, volume records such as stock books, shearing tally and wool books are more likely to be housed in shearing sheds than financial records such as ledgers which are more prone to be located in station homesteads. Homesteads generally provide better climatic conditions for record preservation and also better record security than station outbuildings.[2] Hence, a greater propensity appears to have existed for the destruction of volume records.[3]

The median availability lags determined for financial and volume records were two years and five and a half years respectively or 25 per cent and 43.7 per cent of the respective mean availability lags calculated for financial and volume records. These results were influenced by the tendency for pre-Federation financial and volume records to be generally available from the date of Western District pastoral occupation or shortly after this time in many instances as shown in the table. The research findings on a case by case basis are detailed in what follows.

Armytage[4]

The only available accounting records relating to the period May 1863 to the death of Charles Henry Armytage on 26 April 1876 are records pertaining to Mt. Sturgeon. The Mt. Sturgeon ledgers spanning this period were structured primarily on a personified basis and provide evidence of bookkeeping barter.[5] The only non-personal accounts in these ledgers were for carriage, station expenses and incidentals (A.C. W/2-4).[6] Double entry bookkeeping was not adopted in entering the ledgers. Day books dating from 1869 recorded cheque payments and details of issues of stores, while another book recorded cash payments from 1870 (A.C. A/1a & 1 and A.C. M/1). For the period to February 1865, a separate stores book was used to record issues of stores that were costed and posted to personal ledger accounts (A.C. SB/1). Shearing records (1873-75) indicated the total sheep shorn by each shearer and the consideration due to each shearer based on their performance (A.C. M/1). There is no evidence of the preparation of profit and loss accounts or balance sheets for operations on Mt. Sturgeon or Fulham in the period to 1876.

The available evidence indicates that William Henry Tuckett, a Melbourne accountant, began to provide accounting services to the

Armytage family approximately four months after the death of Charles Henry Armytage on 26 April 1876.[7] The station managers of both Mt. Sturgeon and Fulham stations submitted periodic financial and non-financial operating information to William Henry Tuckett from this date (A.C. M/2 & 3).[8] From 1876, the ledgers maintained by the respective station managers remained substantially personified although specific accounts in the Mt. Sturgeon ledgers were entered for: carriage, travelling expenses, stamps, improvements, stock and plant, land, stores, and the Afton Downs station in Queensland (A.C. A/2). The only non-personal account entered in the Fulham ledger was for incidentals (A.C. W/6). Despite the involvement of an accounting firm, the ledgers for both stations were not entered under the double entry bookkeeping approach. Station day books continued to be maintained on a similar basis to that which applied pre-1876 (A.C. A/3, 4, 8 & 9). Financial information reported periodically to William Henry Tuckett included a list of cheques drawn (in cheque number order) and an "abstract" list of cheques which detailed the cheques drawn in the period for specific categories of expenditure. The abstracts were evidently prepared from the cheques listing rather than the station ledgers. A detailed summary of cash transactions was also provided to William Henry Tuckett together with an inventory report encompassing stock, goods and iron in store on a periodic basis.

William Henry Tuckett prepared the accounts of the Estate of Charles Henry Armytage and entered various financial statements in a specific account book on the annual periodic basis after an initial time when the accounting period was shorter. This book included the executors' account of receipts and reimbursements, income account, balance sheet along with the income accounts of beneficiaries and the corpus account. Although not any journals or ledgers for the Estate appear to have survived, the comprehensive and detailed nature of the surviving financial statements would suggest strongly that they were prepared under a double entry bookkeeping system. The accounts/statements in the account book were audited by J. Wemyss Syme from 26 April 1876 to 31 January 1881. For the year ended 31 January 1882, the accounts were audited by James Knight Bickerton. J.Wemyss Syme attested to the accounts using the statement "audited and found correct" while James Knight Bickerton used the certification "examined and found correct". There is no evidence of the accounts being audited after 1882 and no explanation can be made from the available evidence for this apparent cessation.

Unlike for the period to 26 April 1876, profit and loss account and balance sheet information is available for operations on both Mt. Sturgeon and Fulham throughout the remaining pre-Federation period.

The income account showed the combined profit of the Mt. Sturgeon and Fulham operations and provides evidence of a regard for accrual accounting. Sales of stock were recorded for each station while the total wool clip revenue was disclosed as a single item for both stations. Based on the total clip, wool clip revenue was estimated on the basis of expected selling prices and adjustments were made in the subsequent year for variations on receipt of the proceeds from wool sales. Expenses were classified and itemized separately for each station. A separate report titled "Statement showing average Profits for the seven years ending Jan. 31st 1894" disclosed "income receipts" and "working expenses" for each station on an annual basis over these years. The report also showed the seven-year totals of income receipts, working expenses and profit for each station together with average per annum figures for each of these items over the same period. The executors' regard for return on investment (assets) with respect to both stations is evident as, based on these average per annum profits, overall returns expressed in percentage terms were determined using the station values shown in the balance sheet.

The balance sheet values for assets and liabilities recorded in the account book as at 26 April 1876 were exactly those as contained in the statement of assets and liabilities dated 4 August 1876 and lodged with the Master-in-Equity of the Supreme Court of Victoria for death duty determination purposes.[9] Many of these stated asset valuations remained unchanged to Federation. The valuations attributed to livestock in 1876 remained virtually unchanged to 1900 indicating that the stated livestock values during this period were not based on the reports of stock numbers supplied periodically to William Henry Tuckett or on the prevailing market prices (per head) at each balance date for livestock. Further, the values assigned to station real estate in 1876 changed only by virtue of the subsequent purchase or sale of station land. During 1876 to 1900, the costs of improvements and plant were capitalized as assets but were not subject to depreciation. The 1876 valuations for other real estate, including the Melbourne residence Como, remained unchanged to 1900 while furniture at Como was shown in 1900 at its 1876 valuation. The annual wool clip shipped to London for sale was shown as an asset while the amount advanced on the clip was deducted from the wool clip valuation until 1885 when the advance payment was thereafter shown under liabilities. Stores was recorded as an asset in balance sheets to 30 April 1877 but not thereafter.

There is a wide range of volume records available for the post-1876 period which indicate the existence of control systems for stock and stores and the determination of performance measures for annual lambing and wool production. Stock books date from 1877 for Mt.

Sturgeon and from 1876 for Fulham (A.C. S/6 & 7 and A.C. S/1 & 2). These stock books confirm the adoption of a perpetual inventory system as sheep numbers were related to specific paddock locations and movements of sheep were recorded together with the deficiency or surplus in each paddock arising on the periodic counting of sheep. Based on the total number of sheep shorn as per "shearers tallies book", an annual summary of total sheep depasturing on Fulham was prepared. The total deficiency of sheep shown in this statement was reconciled with the sum of the discrepancy figures determined for each paddock. From 1881, the annual sheep summary prepared for Fulham also showed the lambing productivity rates of ewes in each paddock. A surviving "lambing" record book recorded such information from 1899 for Mt. Sturgeon (A.C. S/10). Evidence of a perpetual inventory system for stores held on Fulham dates from June 1876 (A.C. SB/2). Both stores received and issued were recorded in this surviving stores book, while periodic counting of stores occurred and deficiencies were recorded for the different types of stores under control (sugar, tea, flour, tobacco and soap).

The finalisation of the sale of the wool clip in London resulted in the calculation of performance measures relative to the annual wool production. The account book of the Estate of Charles Henry Armytage maintained by William Henry Tuckett shows from 1886 (based on the 1885 clip) the gross proceeds, expenses (shed charges and selling costs) and net proceeds of the wool clip for each station. Also recorded for each station were the average gross and net proceeds per pound of wool sold. The shed and Melbourne charges along with the London charges were also recorded and the totals of each were also expressed on the average per pound sold basis. Evidence of the comparison of these performance measures against the outcomes for both stations in preceding years is available (Box 15/16). At the station level, other wool performance measures were determined. The Mt. Sturgeon lambing book shows the average weights of wool per head for both sheep and lambs (1899 to 1900) and the average gross and net proceeds per pound for both sheep and lambs for 1899 (A.C. S/10). Further, a surviving bale book for Fulham shows particulars of bales sold including the individual bale weights; details of wool type (for example, fleece, lambs, pieces and broken); the average weight per bale and the prices per pound for different types of wool commencing with the 1875 clip (A.C. S/5).

Evidence shows that there was a regard, at least by station managers, for the projection of expenditure, as a statement described as "Estimate of Expenditure" for the period 1 November 1882 to 31 October 1883 was prepared for both Mt. Sturgeon and Fulham (Box 5/3(d) & (e)). The estimated expenses shown were classified into categories including improvements, maintenance of station (including the remuneration of station hands and house servants), sheepwashing, shearing, freight, and rates and taxes.[10] The financial year of the Estate of Charles Henry Armytage closed on 31 January from 1879 which is at variance with the budgeted period, although the Mt. Sturgeon and Fulham station managers were probably more concerned with production cycles which began around November on the shearing of the flock (A.C. S/2).

Summary

The ledger records available both before and after 26 April 1876 are structured primarily on the personified basis although in the case of Mt. Sturgeon the ledgers prepared after 26 April 1876 included more non-personal accounts. The periodic financial information forwarded to William Henry Tuckett was prepared on the cash basis of accounting. Double entry accounting was not adopted at the station level during the period to 1900. In contrast, the periodic financial statements prepared by William Henry Tuckett for the Estate of Charles Henry Armytage included a profit and loss account and balance sheet and indicate a regard for accrual accounting in recording wool sales. These statements were most probably prepared under a double entry bookkeeping system. There is evidence of the practice of budgeting for expenditure in 1882-83. The surviving volume records examined primarily relate to the period after 26 April 1876. These post-26 April 1876 records indicate the adoption of perpetual inventory systems for control over livestock and stores and there is evidence of the use of performance measures for production of lambs and wool. Various wool performance measures were embraced including the determination of performance on a per pound of wool sold basis and a weight per head basis. Lamb performance records indicated lambing productivity on a per paddock basis.

Beggs[11]

The earliest surviving financial records found for Eurambeen date from September 1855 when George Beggs purchased the station in partnership with Humphrey Gratton. The surviving volume records pertaining to Eurambeen date from October 1860 and are of various kinds. The earliest ledger covered the period September 1855 to January 1862 and hence continued in use after Francis Beggs acquired Humphrey Gratton's interest in the station in 1859. Other ledgers of G. & F. Beggs spanned the period from January 1862 to 17 January 1879 when George Beggs died and the balances in the then existing ledger were ruled off. The ledgers maintained during 1855-79 were structured primarily on the personified basis and provide evidence of bookkeeping barter. They were not prepared on the double entry basis. The earliest ledger included a sundries account which ceased to be used in 1859. The sundries account appeared to be mainly used to record stock sales and purchases. Personal accounts were maintained in the names of the partners, G. & F. Beggs, and evidence of the periodic settling-up of respective contributions was found. Apart from these ledgers, no other financial records were found for the period to 1879.

The next oldest surviving ledger of the Beggs family begins on 29 December 1880, the date of death of Francis Beggs. At the commencement of this ledger the assets and liabilities of Francis Beggs as at 29 December 1880 were listed at values that were taken from the statement of assets and liabilities prepared by Taylor, Buckland and Gates (then a Geelong legal firm) using particulars supplied by the family and lodged with the Master-in-Equity. However, specific ledger accounts for these assets and liabilities were not entered in the ledger. Instead, the ledger contained a mixture of personal accounts and certain expense/capital accounts. Expense accounts included shire rates, land tax and interest paid while capital accounts included stock and produce sold on account of the executors (being part of capital at date of death) and division fence. The emphasis in accounting evident from an examination of this ledger was the recording of receipts and disbursements on both income and capital accounts under the cash basis of accounting. Both single and double entry bookkeeping was adopted in this ledger. A personal ledger account provides details about who prepared the books of the Estate of Francis Beggs for the period of six and a half years from 29 December 1880. The accountant, as described in the surviving records, was Thomas Edward White, who worked from 7 June to 13 July 1887 to post the ledger and prepare the respective annual accounts of the estate for the period 29 December 1880 to 29 June 1887. Evidently, there was not any periodic accounting for the estate throughout this extended period. For each of the six years to 29 December 1886 and for the six months to 29 June 1887, Thomas Edward White determined the total receipts and disbursements for both the income and capital accounts and rendered a summary of the income and capital account balances over this entire period. No balance sheets were prepared in the ledger or found for this period and there is no evidence of the involvement of any auditor. Although this ledger was maintained to 29 December 1898, the date when the Estate of Francis Beggs was settled, no further mention of Thomas Edward White was made after July 1887.

Another surviving pre-Federation ledger of the Beggs family is that of the Beggs Brothers partnership which leased Eurambeen from 30

December 1886. This personalized ledger spans the period 1893-1897 and also provides evidence of the adoption of both single and double entry bookkeeping. The periodic listing of receipts and expenditure was a separate recording function as these were not able to be extracted by means of the periodic balancing of personal ledger accounts. There was a regard for accrual accounting as both debtors and creditors amounts were included in the annual determination of total receipts and total expenditure respectively. Opening entries were made to ensure that such amounts were not double-counted when collected or paid in the following period.[12] No evidence of the involvement of any professional accountant in the preparation of this ledger was found. For each calendar year, a determination of profit/loss occurred based on the subtraction of total expenditure from total receipts. The ledger does not contain any evidence of cost aggregation by expense type except in one instance where items marked with an "X" in the 1896 listing of expenditure were to be aggregated under the heading of general expenses on the 1896 income tax return. No balance sheets of the Beggs Brothers partnership were sighted. A surviving Beggs Brothers day book (1886-89) recorded cash payments and details of issues of stores along with sheep counts and particulars of transfers of sheep.

Stock books as variously described are available for the period 1860-92. These stock books provide evidence of the adoption of a perpetual inventory system for sheep and cattle. Sheep numbers were seemingly related to specific paddock locations from 1860 and movements of sheep were recorded along with the deficiency or surplus in each paddock arising on the periodic counting of sheep. Detailed reconciliations were found of opening and closing livestock totals and these provide evidence of the exercise of control over livestock resources. Stock books also showed the classification by age of total sheep numbers.

The surviving stock books also contained a range of other information including records of productivity. During 1866-68, the lambs tailed records indicated the losses observed upon shearing sheep that were tailed in 1865. Such records expressed the stock losses in percentage terms based on total lambs born in 1865. The rates of lambing productivity of ewes in each paddock were found to be first recorded in 1868. Wool productivity records were also found in stock books for 1866-82. The key wool performance measures determined were as follows: the average weight of wool per head (and per lamb and per sheep); the average net proceeds (price) per pound and the average net proceeds per head (and per lamb and per sheep). Evidence was found of the comparison of wool performance measures determined for Eurambeen with those derived for nearby pastoral stations. During

1877-78, the average weight of wool per head and the average net proceeds per head were compared with those ascertained for Carngham station and in 1879 the average net proceeds per head was compared with that ascertained for Stoneleigh station.

Other volume records related to the period from 30 December 1886 and consisted of a store book and a ram sales book. The store book included a store account which was a record of stores as at 30 December 1886 and of additions to and issues from the store. The store comprised food items such as flour, sugar, tea and potatoes and these were counted periodically. At stocktake, the closing quantities of these items were recorded along with any quantities identified to be missing. This book provides evidence of the adoption of a perpetual inventory system for stores. The store book also recorded the details of sheep issued to station hands, huts and the homestead. The ram sales book showed the details of the number of rams sold during each year and the average sales price of the rams sold.

Summary

The surviving ledger records for Eurambeen are generally structured on the personified basis. The ledger identified as having been prepared belatedly for the Estate of Francis Beggs by accountant Thomas Edward White shows some variation and demonstrates a dichotomy of receipts and disbursements to capital and income accounts. The Beggs Brothers adopted a form of accrual accounting in recording periodic receipts and expenditure after allowing for debtors and creditors. The surviving Eurambeen volume records demonstrate a regard for control over livestock and stores and contain a variety of information that was used to periodically determine measures of station performance. Key performance measures were derived for lamb and wool production. There is also evidence of the comparison of wool performance measures with those determined for nearby stations. The periodic determination of key performance measures as occurred in the surviving Eurambeen records was integral to inter and intra station comparisons of outputs.

Black Bros. (& Smith)[13]

The surviving pre-Federation accounting records of the "Black Bros." partnership in the stations formerly owned by their father, Niel Black, date from the apparent dissolution of the Estate of Niel Black which seems to be occurred on or around 13 June 1887.[14] These records consist of duplicate sets of financial statements spanning the period to 31 December 1899 that were prepared by Joshua Edward Vines (Box 57(b)) and also a stock book (Box 58(e)). Joshua Edward Vines became assistant bookkeeper at the Black family's Mt. Noorat station in 1884 and subsequently became the manager of the Mt. Noorat and Glenormiston stations.[15] The partnership's financial statements comprised a monthly statement of expenditure to 31 December 1890 and subsequently a monthly statement of receipts and expenditure; an annual profit and loss statement and balance sheet and a separate report titled "Stock Valuations" which was effectively a note to the annual accounts that showed details of the bases of valuing livestock and wool. These statements show the adoption of accrual accounting for the partnership. The surviving balance sheets show the capitalisation of the costs of improvements and the inclusion of such costs in station real estate valuations which otherwise generally remained stable except in years where additional land was acquired. Livestock was valued on a per head basis at different amounts for each class of livestock based on stock numbers at each balance date. The per head valuations applied in 1887 remained stable to 1893 for cattle and horses and to 1895 for sheep. Depreciation was charged on both plant and improvements throughout the period to 1899. Wool (unsold) was shown as an asset throughout this period. No audit certification appeared in the pre-Federation financial statements of the partnership and there is no evidence to suggest that these financial statements were audited. The surviving stock records (1887-98) provide evidence of the adoption of a perpetual inventory system for livestock. These records reflected overall stock numbers for sheep, cattle and horses along with movements within each class of livestock. Stock were not identified in this surviving record with specific paddock locations.

The surviving nineteenth century accounting records of the "Black Bros. & Smith" partnership for Grassdale Estate consist of financial statements only (Box 2718/4-5).[16] The earliest financial statement is a statement of receipts and disbursements for the period 11 December 1885 to 1 April 1886. The financial statements show the adoption of accrual accounting from 1 April 1886 and they were prepared annually from 14 January 1887. For the period ended 14 January 1887 and year ended 14 January 1888, the financial statements were prepared by W.H. Foley, a Melbourne accountant.[17] For the year ended 14 January 1889 to Federation, the financial statements of the partnership were prepared by Joshua Edward Vines.[18] The partnership's financial statements comprised a profit and loss account and balance sheet and, from 1891, a separate report titled "stock valuations". The balance sheets as at 14 January 1887 and 1888 recorded real estate at cost as incremented by the costs of improvements and livestock was valued on a per head basis at different amounts for each class of livestock based on stock numbers at each balance date. The change in accounting personnel around 1889 brought the advent of depreciation of plant, and the treatment of the costs of books and stationery as a periodic expense rather than as an asset. From the year ended 14 January 1890, depreciation was also charged on improvements. Throughout the pre-Federation period, stores was recorded as an asset at varying valuations while wool (unsold) appeared as an asset at valuation from 1894. During the period 1889 to 1900, the per head livestock valuations remained virtually unaltered from those which applied during 1887-88 and they continued to be based on stock numbers at each balance date. Excluding improvements, the stated real estate valuations also remained stable during the period to 1900. As in the case of the financial statements of the Black Bros., no audit certification appeared in any of the surviving financial statements of the Black Bros. & Smith partnership.

Summary
The examination of the surviving pre-Federation accounting records of the Black Bros., and Black Bros. & Smith partnerships shows the involvement of persons with accounting skills in the preparation of periodic financial statements. These financial statements indicate the adoption of accrual accounting and, in the case of Black Bros. & Smith, provide evidence of certain changes in accounting practice on the change in accounting personnel around 1889. As a reflection of the influence of Joshua Edward Vines, the accounting policies adopted in preparing the annual financial statements of the respective partnerships during 1889-99 appeared to be generally consistent. Although not any journals or ledgers of the respective partnerships seem to have survived, the comprehensive and detailed nature of the surviving financial statements would suggest strongly they were the product of double entry bookkeeping systems. The surviving stock records of the Black Bros. partnership demonstrate a regard for control of livestock resources on an aggregated basis under a perpetual inventory system.

Clyde Company/Russell, G.[19]
As discussed in Chapter 5, the Clyde Company was substantially owned by investors based in Britain. The Clyde Company papers include periodic returns that were prepared by George Russell and forwarded to the firm of J. & A. Dennistoun of Glasgow who were agents of the Clyde Company in Scotland (Brown, 1935, p.107).[20] As manager of the Clyde Company's operations in Australia, George Russell was accountable to the partnership's investors and prepared increasingly comprehensive financial and non-financial operating information for them on a half-yearly basis from at least 1838. These returns were prepared as at 30 June and 31 December and were submitted on each occasion under a comprehensive covering letter which addressed

the progress and prospects of the Clyde Company. Despite calls from J. & A. Dennistoun's representative, William Cross, for more frequent communications, George Russell argued successfully that more frequent communications would amount to a repetition of the information provided on the half-yearly basis (Brown, 1952, pp.180 and 403; 1958, p.86). Commencing for the half-year ended 30 June 1840, printed (pro-forma) return forms were completed at the request of William Cross (Brown, 1952, pp.365 and 403).[21] Half-yearly reporting seemingly ceased in 1854 when George Russell advised that the preparation of bi-annual reports was too troublesome and proposed a system of annual reporting from 1 January 1854 (Brown, 1968, p.81). However, no returns from 1854 to 1858 when the Clyde Company ceased business appear to have survived (Brown, 1968, p.81).[22]

The earliest surviving half-yearly returns relate to 1838 (Brown, 1952, pp.185-186). These returns and all the surviving subsequent returns included detailed particulars of livestock (sheep, cattle and horses) numbers at balance date and explained movements in the size of flocks and herds during each six-monthly period. Remarks about the condition of livestock and details of expected or actual lamb and wool production were also provided. A detailed half-yearly statement of expenditure was also included which categorized expenditure into various categories including labour, stores (of various kinds), sheep-dressing, tools and implements, and travelling expenses. The returns from 1839 were expanded to include a labour account and a cash account. The labour account showed the half-yearly labour costs and the amounts settled (in cash or in kind) and the amount payable at balance date. The cash account represented a summary of the transactions on the partnership's bank account. From the half-yearly period ended 31 December 1843, a statement of receipts and expenditure was reported in lieu of the labour account. George Russell believed that this statement was "simply a copy of the Profit and Loss a/c of the Co." (Brown, 1958, p.387). The partners were advised of the nature of expenses incurred above the "ordinary" expenses for items such as the erection of a cottage and a shearing shed (Brown, 1959, pp.183 and 319).

The half-yearly returns from 1845 further increased in sophistication when, in response to a request from William Cross for the provision of a regular "stock" account, George Russell prepared a statement of "Receipts and Expenditure, Debts and Stock Account" (Brown, 1958, pp.457 and 583). William Cross sought a statement which showed the market value of each kind of property so as to "enable us [the investors] to see at a glance the real position of the Co, and the value of their property" (Brown, 1958, p.457).[23] The resultant statement included valuations of land, livestock, tools and implements,

wheat, oats, stores and wool (unsold) as at 30 June 1845 and showed
debts payable including amounts due for labour as at that date (Brown,
1958, p.583). Land (with improvements) and livestock were valued on a
per acre and per head basis respectively. George Russell expressed his
concerns to William Cross about the "uncertainty and difficulties" of
valuing property of any description in the Colony and stated "this
statement must only be considered an approximation of the truth"
(Brown, 1958, p.578). The surviving records show that a statement of
receipts and expenditure and balance sheet was prepared bi-annually until
1853. Throughout the period 1842-50 the half-yearly returns also
commonly included a summary of George Russell's own account with
the Clyde Company. The form and contents of the periodic reports did
not alter substantially during 1850-53 when William Lewis managed
the Clyde Company on account of George Russell's temporary residence
in Britain (Brown, 1935, p.256). During this period, William Lewis
incorporated a summary of his own account with the Clyde Company
in the half-yearly returns. During 1845-53, the stated values of land and
livestock were subject to variation. Stated land valuations increased as
additional land was purchased and as the per acre value of land rose.
Sharp rises in land and livestock values were recorded in the early 1850s
during the Victorian gold rush era.

The surviving station accounting records of the Clyde Company
(1836-58) and of George Russell (1858-88) represent a significant
collection of records of this nature. The Clyde Company ledgers provide
evidence of bookkeeping barter and show the adoption of periodic
accounting. The earliest ledger (1836-39) featured personal accounts and,
from 1 January 1838, a range of non-personal accounts for items of
stores and supplies which were costed as issued to either station workers
or outstations (huts) (List 3/1). It featured a mixture of single entry and
double entry bookkeeping from this date. Ledger accounts for goods
rendered to workers in lieu of cash such as tobacco, soap and slop
clothing were credited as goods were issued while the debit entries were
made in the specific personal accounts. Accounts for rations such as
flour, sugar and tea were also credited as issued while the debit entries
were made in accounts (effectively cost centres) such as upper, middle,
lower and home stations. This ledger provides evidence of the adoption
of a rigid system of control over stores and supplies under a perpetual
inventory system from 1838. From 1839, the Clyde Company ledgers
were prepared on the double entry basis. During 1839-50, the ledgers
featured non-personal accounts including an account for labour which
confirmed the adoption of accrual accounting and also show the
continued use of a perpetual inventory system for stores (List 3/2, 7, 18
& 43). Personal accounts were still maintained but were recorded

separately as evidenced in the surviving wages books.[24] A ledger dating from 1 January 1850 was maintained by William Lewis until around October 1853 and was structured primarily on a personalized basis (List 3/9). Subsequently, the Clyde Company ledger records and those of George Russell (1858-83) featured a renewed interest in non-personal accounts (List 3/21, 23, 25 & 45). From at least 1 January 1843, the double entry system of recording involved the maintenance of a general journal (List 3/5, 8, 20, 22, 24 & 26). Surviving day books (1840-87) incorporated details of various transactions including issues of rations, and purchases and sales (List 3/3, 4, 6 & 19). Cash books (1857-88) recorded receipts and disbursements (List 3/27 & 28).

Surviving annual profit and loss statements and balance sheets of George Russell pertain to the period 1859-77 (List 3/23 & 25). The expenses in the profit and loss statements included a write off of improvements (effectively depreciation) at the annual rate of 10 per cent on original cost. A notation in the improvements ledger account stated that the deduction was for "wear and tear" (List 3/23). The balance sheets also included valuations of livestock (sheep, cattle and horses), land, grain and hay, and carriage and harness which were generally stable over time. The stated sheep valuation did not alter during 1867-71 nor during 1873-77. The cattle valuation recorded during 1869-77 also remained unaltered. Notwithstanding, livestock numbers undoubtedly varied during these periods. The land valuation shown also remained unchanged in the period 1867-77. The policy of stating generally steady valuations in the balance sheet for real estate and livestock appears to be consistent with George Russell's concerns, as expressed to J. & A. Dennistoun in 1845, about the use of market values to value property of any description in the Colony. Neither wool (unsold) or stores were recorded as assets during 1859-77.

A range of Clyde Company volume records have survived. These include stock books, shearing tallies, bale records and annual wool productivity summaries. The earliest stock records date from 1 January 1837 and demonstrate the maintenance of control over specific flocks under a perpetual inventory system (List 3/1). Other stock records depict the maintenance of control over livestock resources during 1846-57 (List 3/44). Shearing tally records are available for the period 1847-57 which show the performance of each shearer with respect to each flock taken into the shed during the season (List 3/44). The total of each shearer's tally for the season was reconciled with the total of sheep shorn in all flocks. The amounts due to shearers based on their overall performance were also shown. Bale records (1846-56) indicated wool type details for each consecutively numbered bale (List 3/42 & 47). For 1846 and 1847, individual bale weights were also recorded while for

1846 the average bale weight was also shown. The total weight of the annual clip was recorded at least during 1846-48 and for 1850. A comparative statement of wool productivity for the years 1847-56 has survived (List 6/7(i)). For each year, this statement shows the total number of sheep shorn; bales shipped; average weight of wool per head; total net weight of wool (in London); net proceeds (price) per pound and the total wool proceeds. Although the average weight of wool per head measure was determined annually, neither the performance result itself nor any specific movements in the measure were reported to J. & A. Dennistoun. Rather, information on the total number of bales produced and the actual or expected overall weight of the annual clip was commonly reported to the partners (Brown, 1958, pp.201, 295 and 620; 1959, pp.77 and 423). Evidently, the performance measure was believed to be more relevant for George Russell's operational purposes while the overall wool clip particulars were considered to be more important for assessing the total wool proceeds based on expected selling prices in the London market. The earliest evidence of the determination of lambing productivity rates was found in the half-yearly return to 30 June 1840. In his remarks concerning livestock, George Russell reported the overall lambing productivity rates for all flocks and the upper range of productivity for some flocks (Brown, 1952, p.365).

The surviving records of George Russell include stores books from 1871 (List 3/31-33) and annual comparative reports for the period 1864-73 which showed key operational statistics and performance measures for Golf Hill and Leslie Manor (from 1867) and three other Western District stations which were operated by other parties (List 6/7(ii)).[25] The information recorded in these annual reports for each station (therein described as "run") included the number of sheep shorn; average weight of wool per head; average proceeds (price) per pound and the average proceeds per head; number of sheep sold; the average price of sheep sold; number of sheep shorn; size of station (in acres) and the receipts per acre. These reports indicate the nature of key operational statistics that were prepared from the volume records maintained by George Russell and those prepared for the other three pastoral entities during this period.

No evidence was found of the involvement of a professional accountant in the affairs of the Clyde Company or George Russell. Taylor, Buckland and Gates prepared an account of management (effectively a statement of receipts and expenditure) of Golf Hill on behalf of the executors of the Estate of George Russell for the twelve months period prior to the handing over of the station to Philip Russell on 3 November 1889 (List 7/4). A surviving statement of receipts and expenses for the period ended 3 May 1892 and a balance sheet as at that date for the Estate of George Russell does not indicate who prepared the statements (List 7/5). The balance sheet recorded valuations of real estate, livestock and unsold wool among other items while the costs incurred on improvements and plant were immediately written off as expenses. For the year ended 31 December 1896, James Gardener, an accountant of Geelong, prepared a statement of income and expenditure and a balance sheet as at 31 December 1896 on behalf of Janet Russell for Golf Hill (List 2/60). Land (with improvements) and livestock were valued in this balance sheet on a per acre and per head basis respectively while plant, furniture, stores and hay were also shown as assets. James Gardener's involvement around this time was related to the transfer of control of Golf Hill to Janet Russell from her brother, Philip. A James Gardener was Geelong manager of AML&F from at least 1881 to beyond 1900. Based on AML&F's long-standing involvement with Golf Hill and the dealings involving AML&F on the transfer of Golf Hill in December 1895 (as evidenced in the bills of costs (List 7/2) to Janet Russell from Taylor, Buckland and Gates of 15 April 1896), it is evident that James Gardener, the accountant, and James Gardener, the manager, were the same person.

Summary

The accounting records of the Clyde Company dating from 1836 are the earliest pastoral accounting records available for this study. As manager of the partnership, George Russell prepared meticulous financial and volume records and submitted detailed half-yearly reports to the non-resident partners. The partners were kept informed of numerous matters including livestock numbers and movements of livestock; the state of flocks and herds; lamb and production details; station expenditure and later receipts; valuations of assets and liabilities; cash movements and the state of George Russell's account with the Clyde Company. Profit and loss statements and balance sheets continued to be prepared by George Russell in the period after the Clyde Company had ceased operations. The surviving station accounting records of the Clyde Company and George Russell depict considerable skill in their preparation as evidenced by the early adoption of accrual accounting under a double entry system of recording and the determination of a range of performance measures. The average weight of wool per head performance measure determined during 1847-56 was evidently used for operational purposes only. The five station comparative reports prepared during 1864-73 did not feature station profitability even though profit and loss information was available in George Russell's case. The only available evidence which shows the involvement of professional advisers in station accounting relates to Golf Hill in the period following the death of George Russell.

Corney

The surviving pre-Federation accounting records of the Corney family comprise financial records only. The only surviving financial records of William Corney appear in a ledger prepared during August 1842 to January 1854 for operations on Wando. This ledger was prepared on the personified basis and shows evidence of bookkeeping barter. It was not prepared on the double entry basis. Most ledger accounts involved station hands or shearers. For each ledger account involving station hands or shearers, the amounts settled in cash or in kind were listed in a single column of figures on the ledger page. When an account was to be finalized the total amounts settled and the total consideration due were determined in order to arrive at the balance of the account for settlement. The wages due to station hands were evidently determined with reference to employment arrangements that were recorded at the front of the ledger and which indicated when workers commenced duties at the station and the respective agreed periods of employment. No evidence of specific cost control exists in this ledger and not any financial statements were found.

The surviving pre-Federation ledger of Robert William Corney of Tulse Hill covered the period from 1 December 1871 when the station was purchased to 31 December 1894. This ledger comprised a cash account for the period to 31 December 1891, a bank account and personal accounts which ceased to be maintained in this ledger from 1881. The cash account recorded receipts and expenditure (effectively disbursements). The purchase money for Tulse Hill paid on 1 December 1871 was included in total expenditure for 1871 (to 31 December). The difference between receipts and expenditure since 1 December 1871 was accumulated and carried forward into each calendar year. The personal accounts in this ledger related primarily to station hands and shearers and provide evidence of bookkeeping barter. Evidence of the adoption of a mix of single and double entry bookkeeping is found in this ledger. The ledger accounts were not ruled off on a periodic basis and there is no evidence of specific cost control in this ledger. From 1874 to 1906, Robert William Corney also recorded the annual proceeds of wool sold at the rear of this ledger.

The surviving pre-Federation financial records for the period 1 January 1895 to 31 December 1900 comprise a cash book. This cash book recorded receipts and expenditure from 1 January 1895 when a cash balance was brought forward. The practice adopted previously of carrying forward the accumulated difference between receipts and expenditure ceased on 31 December 1896. From 1 January 1897, annual totals for receipts and expenditure were determined and the balancing amount shown was a reflection of a cash surplus or deficit result. No balance sheets were sighted for the period from 1871 to 1900.

Summary

The surviving ledger records relating to Wando and Tulse Hill stations were structured on the personified basis and provide evidence of bookkeeping barter. Records of receipts and expenditure prepared for operations on Tulse Hill focused on the reporting of the cumulative cash result rather than the reflection on an annual surplus or deficit result during 1871-91 and 1895-96. The change in 1897 as observed could have been a consequence of the newly-introduced income tax legislation. There was no evidence found of the use by the Corney family of the services of a professional accountant throughout the pre-Federation period.

Cumming[26]

The surviving nineteenth century accounting records of the Cumming family of Mt. Fyans consist primarily of financial records. The earliest accounting record for Mt. Fyans is a ledger for the period March 1856 to 1860 (LS3/6/11). This ledger was structured primarily on a personified basis and provides evidence of bookkeeping barter. The only non-personal accounts in this ledger were those for carriers and sundries. This ledger was not systematically ruled off and there is no evidence of double entry bookkeeping. It also recorded the number of bales of particular wool types (fleece, hogget, pieces and locks) for each of 12 flocks and the total number of bales for all flocks in 1860, the year of the advent of the Mt. Fyans merino stud (Cumming, 1992, p.40). Another surviving ledger relates to 1883-84 (LS3/6/11). This ledger was also structured primarily on a personified basis but features additional non-personal accounts including accounts for cash, shire rates and land tax. Although this ledger is neater than the surviving predecessor, it was not prepared on the double entry basis and was not systematically ruled off. There is no evidence of the preparation of profit and loss accounts or balance sheets for operations on Mt. Fyans from March 1856 to 31 December 1894 and Stonehenge Estate from 1868 to 31 December 1894, and no volume records were found for these periods.

Peter Wares Tait, an accountant of Camperdown in the Western District, became involved on a professional basis with the Cumming family from at least 1895. William Cumming was an executor of the Estate of Robert Jamieson. Robert Jamieson died on 8 November 1894 and the executors appointed Peter Wares Tait to act for the estate. William Cumming may have been decided to appoint Peter Wares Tait as the family accountant following his observation of the accountant's work for the Jamieson family (see later discussion of Jamieson records). Peter Wares Tait was engaged by the Cumming family until his death on 29 March 1901.

A double entry bookkeeping system involving a general journal and ledger was established and maintained by Peter Wares Tait from 1 January 1895.[27] Accrual accounting was adopted by the accountant involving the recording of debtors and creditors. The first journal entry recorded the assets and liabilities of William Cumming as at 1 January 1895. This entry and others for the period to September 1895 seem to have been made on 28 September 1895, the date written in the journal by Peter Wares Tait where his initials appeared for the first time. An expense for this period was accounting fees of Peter Wares Tait as of 24 January 1895, indicating that the accountant might have provided professional services to William Cumming with respect to the 1894 calendar year. The Mt. Fyans and Stonehenge Estate lands were valued on a per acre basis at different amounts for each station while sheep, cattle and horses were valued on a per head basis at varying amounts for each class of livestock. A balance sheet as at 1 January 1895 was reported in the ledger. Balance sheets as at 1 January were prepared during 1896-98. The balance sheets as at 1 January 1895, 1896 and 1897 recorded a contingent liability determined as a fixed amount on shares in a company. The disclosure was in note form beneath the liabilities total and preceded the capital amount total. The per acre and per head valuations attributed to land and livestock respectively did not alter in the period to 1 January 1898 although the valuations of the different classes of livestock altered in line with movements in stock numbers. During this period, annual profit results were determined and recorded in the profit and loss account in the ledger. No separate profit and loss statements were found.

An entry in the journal detailed the assets and liabilities of William Cumming at his date of death on 7 May 1898. The values attributed to these items were exactly those as recorded in a statement of assets and liabilities lodged with the Master-in-Equity. Valuations of station real estate and livestock were made by Joseph Raleigh. The Stonehenge Estate valuation (per acre) and the sheep and horses valuations (per head) were recorded at different amounts from those which where shown in the accounts since 1 January 1895. The valuation (per acre) of the Mt. Fyans station and the valuation (per head) of cattle recorded as at 7 May 1898 were the same amounts as shown on 1 January 1895. The books of the Estate of William Cumming were ruled off on 7 May 1899 and

20 March 1900 in the period to Federation. Profit results were determined for each of these periods and balance sheets as at these dates were recorded in the journal.[28] The per acre and per head valuations attributed to land and livestock respectively as at 7 May 1899 were the same as those used as at 7 May 1898. Livestock valuations as at 7 May 1899 were based on stock numbers as at that date. By 20 March 1900, the executors of the Estate of William Cumming had disposed of the estate's pastoral land and livestock. As no separate financial statements for the estate were found, if indeed there were any, no definite conclusion can be drawn as to whether the accounts were audited.

Costs of improvements and a particular item of plant incurred during 1 January 1895 to 7 May 1898 were written off as expenses. Plant brought to account at valuation on 7 May 1898 was subject to depreciation from that date. No other assets were subject to depreciation during 1895 to Federation. The balance sheets prepared for this period did not record either wool (unsold) or stores as assets. The Mt. Fyans "working" results included the contribution of Stonehenge Estate and the overall net profit or loss was determined after deducting the items: interest, allowances and personal account items. The balance of the overall profit and loss account was transferred to the capital account at the end of each calendar year from 1895 to 1897 and on 7 May 1898. Subsequently, transfers were made to accounts in the names of family members. The wool account in the ledger also contained key operating particulars and performance measures. The details provided in the wool proceeds entry included the total number of bales sold; the total weight of wool sold; the total number of sheep shorn and the average weight of wool per head for each year during 1 January 1895 to 31 December 1899. For the years ended 31 December 1898 and 1899, the gross proceeds, expenses (shown as "all expenses") and net proceeds per head were also shown.

Evidence of the adoption of a dual system of accounting exists for the period 1 January 1897 to 6 May 1898. A station ledger spanning this period was structured primarily on a personified basis. Peter Wares Tait's involvement with this ledger came upon the death of William Cumming as entries in the accountant's handwriting as at 6 May 1898 were made for the purpose of ascertaining the amounts due to particular parties at that time. This ledger did not feature double entry bookkeeping and was maintained in addition to the double entry recording system maintained by Peter Wares Tait during the period.

According to a surviving ledger of William Burrow Cumming, Mt. Fyans came under his ownership on or around 22 December 1899.[29] This ledger was structured on the personified basis and does not provide any evidence of the involvement of Peter Wares Tait or any other

professional accountant during the period to 31 December 1900. If Peter
Wares Tait did not act for William Burrow Cumming, it was possibly
due to a perceived conflict of interest given the accountant's
involvement with the deceased estate.

Summary

The surviving ledger records for Mt. Fyans pertaining to the period
before 1 January 1895 were structured primarily on a personified basis.
Of the two ledgers available for this period, the later dated ledger
contained more non-personal accounts than the earlier ledger while the
earlier ledger recorded a statement of bales produced for each flock in
1860. The involvement of accountant Peter Wares Tait from at least
1895 brought the implementation of a double entry bookkeeping
system and the adoption of accrual accounting. The accountant produced
profit results and prepared balance sheets on a periodic basis for William
Cumming and then the Estate of William Cumming. A Mt. Fyans
station ledger maintained primarily on a personified basis in the period
leading to the death of William Cumming was found in addition to the
general journal and ledger prepared by the accountant thus indicating the
adoption of a dual system of accounting. The ledger prepared by Peter
Wares Tait featured key performance measures for wool production
comprising the average weight of wool per head (1895-99) and the
proceeds (gross and net) and expenses per head (1898-99). The surviving
ledger of William Burrow Cumming from 22 December 1899 is
structured on a personified basis and does not provide any indication of
the involvement of a professional accountant.

Currie[30]

The earliest surviving financial records pertaining to Larra consists of
cash books, journals and ledgers of John Lang Currie which spanned the
period 1 January 1876 to 31 December 1881 and show the adoption of
periodic accounting on the annual cycle (Box 824/4; 823/5; 825/4).[31]
These surviving books were prepared on the double entry basis and
show a regard for accrual accounting in the recognition of debtors and
creditors. The evidence also shows the involvement from 1 January
1876 of William M. Fergusson, a Camperdown stock and station agent,
as accountant who was paid a half-yearly allowance for his services. The
cash books separately recorded transactions on both the station and
private bank accounts of John Lang Currie thus showing a regard for
the separation of Larra from other business interests (Box 824/4). The
ledgers feature a combination of personal accounts, and non-personal
accounts including station expenses, labour and charges (Box 825/4).
For Larra, the lands ledger account contained balances as at 1 January

1876 for land and buildings respectively. Land was presumably valued on the per acre basis. Subsequently, the ledger account reported values for land and buildings combined. The valuation of this item remained virtually unaltered during 1876-81. The sheep, cattle and horses ledger accounts show the use of per head valuations that were different for each class of livestock but which remained stable throughout the period to 31 December 1881. The valuations of different classes of livestock moved in line with changes in stock numbers. Ledger accounts for station plant, and furniture recorded acquisitions of items during 1876 although transfers from the stock account (that is, capital account of John Lang Currie) were made on 31 December 1876 to recognize the respective plant and furniture on hand as at 1 January 1876. No depreciation was charged on either plant or furniture during 1876-81. An improvements ledger account was established in 1878. Costs of improvements were immediately written off as expenses in the profit and loss account. Unsold wool at balance date was not recorded as an asset; instead the woolbroker's advances on wool to be sold were included as revenue in the profit and loss account. Stores were also not recorded as an asset. The profit and loss account showed the annual profit results for Larra and other business interests combined; these amounts were transferred at each year end (31 December) to the stock account. Although the journals recorded a listing of ledger balances as at each 1 January, no balance sheets or separately written profit and loss statements were found for this period (Box 823/5).

Two financial statements of John Lang Currie, each described as a balance sheet, have survived (Box 822/5). These balance sheets were prepared as at 30 June 1894 and December 1897. However, the associated books of account do not appear to have survived. The balance sheet as at 30 June 1894 incorporated three columns: "Dr."; "Cr." and "Depreciation". The total of the depreciation column was equal to the amount of depreciation shown as a credit item in the balance sheet. Depreciation was adjusted against the capital account rather than debited against the individual asset accounts involved. Hence, the amounts shown in the depreciation column were deductions to be made against the book values of the respective assets including station real estate, livestock, improvements and company shares to arrive at their revalued amounts. The existence of a separate ledger account for depreciation was most probably a consequence of the impact of the early 1890s economic depression on asset valuations. The balance sheet as at December 1897 indicates a similar treatment for depreciation (which had not altered in amount since 30 June 1894) except that notations rather than a third column were used to identify the depreciation amounts relevant to individual assets. It is not known when William M. Fergusson ceased to act as accountant for John Lang Currie. However, Hugh M. Strachan of woolbrokers and stock and station agents Strachan, Bostock & Co. was the accountant and tax agent of John Lang Currie from at least 1896 until the pastoralist's death on 11 March 1898.[32]

For Titanga, there survives a cash book, petty cash book, journal and ledger spanning the period 1 January 1896 to 11 March 1898. These books were maintained by William Drinnin, the resident manager of Titanga from 1886. The ledger recorded a small number of non-personal accounts such as for station, supplies and produce and, in a separate section, a set of personal accounts. A system of double entry bookkeeping was adopted. Wages were recorded as expenses (debit entries) in the Station account on the accrual basis of accounting. The credit entries were recorded in the various personal accounts. Payments of wages were debited to the respective personal accounts. On 11 March 1898, all ledger accounts with balances were transferred to an account titled "trustees late J.L. Currie". Otherwise the ledger was balanced half-yearly on 30 June and 31 December. There is no evidence of the involvement of a professional accountant in the establishment and maintenance of this set of station books.

Although there appears to be no surviving pre-Federation books containing non-financial operating information for Larra, a record of shearing for 1846-79 and a statement of wool returns for 1883-94 have survived indicating that such books were maintained. The record of shearing at Larra is in both hand-written and a summarized type-written form. The hand-written copy contains information under the following headings: year; shearing commenced (date); number of days shearing; number of shearers; number of sheep shorn (categorized as washed, greasy and total); average shearing per day; average shearing per man per day; rate paid for shearing (per 100) and remarks. For 1844 and 1845, a note indicates that no record was maintained for these years. The key shearing performance measures derived from the volume records maintained were the average shearing per day and average shearing per man per day as reflections of productivity in the shed. The "Comparative Statement of Larra Wool Returns of 12 years: 1883-1894" report detailed various weights of wool per head under the following headings: sheep; lambs; sheep and lambs together; two tooths (ewes and wethers); four tooths (ewes and wethers). It also showed the average gross proceeds (price) per pound and the average net proceeds per bale sold. This report provides evidence of the maintenance of volume records for wool production and stock numbers. Both of these reports highlight the comparison of station performance over a number of years and the adoption of a range of performance measures.

Various records have survived for Titanga which contain non-financial operating information dating from 1886. The following account relates to the pre-11 March 1898 period. Livestock records were maintained during 1886-98 in a stock book which shows the adoption of a perpetual inventory system for control of livestock. Stock counts took place at shearing when "sheep shorn" were recorded as those on hand and discrepancies were identified. Cattle and horse numbers were usually recorded as at 30 June. During 1890-98, the average weights of wool per head were recorded for sheep, lambs, sheep and lambs and hoggets together with the annual station rainfall. The recording of the annual rainfall permitted the weather variable to be taken into account in the examination of shifts in average wool production per head. For rams, the individual fleece weights were recorded during 1896-98. Such a focus on individual ram fleece weights would have permitted the selection of rams with superior fleece weight as future sires. The lamb marking records maintained from 1887 showed the lamb productivity of ewes of different ages and the overall lamb productivity of breeding ewes. The annual rainfall was also shown in these records.

The executors of the Estate of John Lang Currie appointed Peter Wares Tait of Camperdown to act as auditor for the estate. So far as can be established, Peter Wares Tait did not provide professional accounting services to John Lang Currie himself. For a short period after 11 March 1898, Hugh M. Strachan kept the books of the Estate of John Lang Currie. An unsigned memorandum of 7 March 1899 expressed some concerns about the accuracy of the draft financial statements of the estate as prepared by Hugh M. Strachan (Box 847). The concerns related to the proportionment of items to the pre and post-11 March 1898 periods. Subsequently, Robert Gillespie, an executor of the Estate of John Lang Currie, kept the books of the estate.[33] Robert Gillespie was Manager of the National Bank of Australasia at Geelong during 1866-82 (National Australia Bank Ltd Group Archives, Melbourne), a period almost exactly coinciding with the term of John Lang Currie's (Geelong) directorship of the bank. Pre-Federation audited financial statements for the Estate of John Lang Currie are available for the year ended 11 March 1900 (Box 848). These consisted of the following: statement of income and distribution of income; balance sheet; capital account; statement of realized assets and an account of appropriated funds. The certification "examined and found correct" was written by Peter Wares Tait on most of these statements. The accountant acted for the Estate of John Lang Currie until his death on 29 March 1901.

A cash book for Titanga dating from 11 March 1898 confirms the involvement of Peter Wares Tait as accountant for the partnership of "Currie, Lang & Currie" in the period to 31 May 1898 and for "P.S.

Lang & Co." from 1 June 1898. Peter Wares Tait also prepared a record of "rents, loans and statistics" for P.S. Lang & Co. from May 1900. The stock, weights of wool and lamb marking records for Titanga pertaining to the period after 11 March 1898 were maintained on the same basis as those kept in the pre-11 March 1898 periods. However, additional volume records are available only from 1898. Shearing tally records indicated the numbers of sheep shorn per day by each shearer together with the totals of sheep shorn per day and sheep shorn by each shearer during the season. The total of sheep shorn during the season was reconciled with the total of the tallies of each shearer. A report titled "Abstract of Account Sales of Wool" dating from 1898 contained statistics of sheep shorn, bales of wool, net weights (pressed and sold) of the wool clip and the average weight of wool per head. The abstract also detailed gross proceeds, selling charges and net proceeds pertaining to the annual clip. Other performance measures for wool production recorded in the abstract are as follows: average net proceeds (price) per head (and per lamb and per sheep); average gross proceeds per pound and average net proceeds per bale sold. A further report also dating from 1898 titled "Tabulation of Expenses Connected with Wool from 'Sheeps' Back' to 'Value Received'" incorporated shearing and carriage (to Geelong) expenses in total expenses and recorded the average net proceeds per head and the average expenses per head based on total expenses. The abstract and the tabulation of expenses reports for Titanga also featured particular average wool production and expense figures respectively for Larra during the period 1892-96, thus enabling comparisons to be drawn with the earlier derived average results of another (nearby) station formerly owned by John Lang Currie.

Summary

The surviving financial records of John Lang Currie indicate the adoption of double entry bookkeeping from 1876 (1896 for Titanga) and the involvement of William M. Fergusson and subsequently Hugh M. Strachan as accountants for the pastoralist. Surviving balance sheets of John Lang Currie indicate the notion of depreciation as a valuation adjustment rather than as a process of cost allocation. Peter Wares Tait became the auditor of the Estate of John Lang Currie and the books of the estate were kept by Hugh M. Strachan for a short period and then by Robert Gillespie. Peter Wares Tait also had a professional involvement at Titanga after 11 March 1898. The surviving volume records maintained for Larra and Titanga permitted the production of a range of reports which featured the use of a range of information in the determination of various performance measures for wool and lamb production and for shearing. These reports are an exemplifier and indicate the comparison of station performance on a longitudinal basis and provide evidence of the comparison of certain key performance measures with those of another station (Larra). The surviving stock records for Titanga indicate the adoption of a perpetual inventory system for control of livestock. The accounting records of the Currie family are witness to the integral role of financial and non-financial operating information in successful pre-Federation pastoralism.

Dennis

The surviving pre-Federation accounting records of the Dennis family comprise financial records only. The earliest ledger dates from 21 February 1840 when the Dennis brothers opened a bank account and therein deposited their initial capital. This ledger consisted primarily of personal accounts but also contained non-personal accounts and spanned the period to 1852. It was not prepared on the double entry basis but provides evidence of bookkeeping barter. The non-personal ledger accounts in 1840 were as follows: bank; bullocks; sheep; expenses in fitting up station and horses. Personal accounts for each of the Dennis brothers appear to have recorded expenses of a personal nature such as for clothing and boots. The expenses in fitting up station ledger account became the expenses of sheep station account on the transfer of the account to another ledger page on 16 August 1841. The expenses of sheep station account was totalled during January 1842 and at the end of each December thereafter. The sheep ledger account recorded purchases and also sales of sheep and wool. This account was not ruled off as both the debit and credit balances were accumulated and carried forward throughout the period to 1852.[34] A Robertson's Station ledger account was established in May 1848. From this time, the expenses of sheep station account became the expenses of Colac station account (that is, Tarndwarncoort station). Hence, separate ledger accounts were maintained for different station operations. As a specific sheep account was not established for Robertson's station, the sales of sheep and wool were credited to the station account. Although the station expenses account was totalled annually from 1842, periodic accounting did not occur throughout the currency of this ledger.

Another surviving ledger is a continuation of the earliest ledger and spans the period to 1866. This ledger was kept on a similar basis to its predecessor. In this ledger the Colac station account rather than the sheep account was used to record sales of wool and certain sales of sheep. The sheep account and the Colac station account were generally totalled at the end of each December and periodic surpluses or deficits were either recorded or were able to be identified. The Robertson's Station account was totalled at varying times.[35] A day book for the period January 1861 to September 1864 has survived. This day book recorded various transactions such as stock acquisitions, details of goods supplied and payments and receipts and was a record of original entry for updating the ledger. A statement of assets and liabilities of Alexander and William Dennis as at September 1866 and a statement of assets of Alexander Dennis as at September 1874 were found. A note to the September 1866 report stated "balance [net assets] to be divided between Alexander and William Dennis".[36] This report was prepared independently of the surviving ledger as a discrete function.

A further surviving ledger pertained to Richard Vinicombe Dennis and dates from 1 July 1893. The ledger incorporates a bank account and personal accounts and was not prepared on the double entry basis. From January 1897, George Llewellyn Dennis was employed to provide bookkeeping services to Richard Vinicombe Dennis. George Llewellyn Dennis was the eldest child of Alexander Dennis the younger of Eeyeuk and gained commercial experience at woolbrokers John Sanderson and Co., Melbourne after an education at Toorak College (Henderson 1936, p.56). The structure of this ledger did not change during 1893 to 1900 and there is no evidence of the involvement of a professional accountant. A surviving cash book dating from 6 October 1898 served an integral role in updating the ledger.

Surviving audited financial statements for Barenya Station, Queensland show that Thomas Brentnall of Melbourne accounting firm Yeo, Brentnall & Co., acted as accountant/auditor for William Dennis & Co. in the 1890s.[37] While it is possible that Thomas Brentnall was connected in a professional capacity with the Western District station operations of the Dennis family, no evidence was found to support any association.

Summary

The pre-Federation accounting records of the Dennis family were structured primarily on a personified basis but indicate an interest in monitoring aspects of financial performance by means of the maintenance of separate ledger accounts for sheep and station (Tarndwarncoort) and a Robertson's station account. The surviving books of account were not maintained on a double entry basis and there is no evidence of their use in the preparation of separate profit and loss accounts or balance sheets for the family's Western District operations. The appointment of George Llewellyn Dennis in 1897 as bookkeeper for Richard Vinicombe Dennis did not lead to any structural changes in the accounts and no evidence was found of the use of a professional accountant in connection with the Western District pastoral operations.

French[38]

A small multi-purpose note book of Archeson Jeremiah French contains a diverse range of information related to station life during 1841-57 (Box 1298/2). Apart from the maintenance of ledger accounts, records were kept at varying times throughout this period for stores, shearing tallies, wool production, sheep issued as rations, items borrowed/returned, horses, kitchenware, mail sent and the associated cost and family birthdays/deaths among other things. The financial records related to the period January 1841 to October 1845 and consisted of a personalized ledger. The personal accounts were not prepared on the double entry basis but provide evidence of bookkeeping barter. They were not ruled off on a periodic basis. The amounts involved in settling obligations were often not entered as debit entries; rather the word "settled" was written in the debit column thus leaving many accounts unbalanced. There is no evidence of the preparation of profit and loss accounts or balance sheets.

A store account was recorded in 1849 only and although details of receipts of stores were recorded along with details of where those stores were allocated (for example, kitchen, hut and house), there was no evidence of a periodic stocktake and thus no details of particular inventory items at any point in time. From 1849, shearing tally particulars were recorded perhaps in response to the use of itinerate shearers rather than station hands for shearing. The information commonly reported to 1857 consisted of totals of sheep shorn per shearer, rates of pay for shearing, and the extended consideration due for each shearer adjusted by amounts due for wool washing. Normally, the shearers' wages were totalled in a separate entry as a record of the direct annual cost of shearing. Various wool performance measures were recorded from 1851. The annual wool clip information recorded to 1857 varied but normally consisted of particulars of the total weight of wool, average weight per bale and the average weight of wool per head. The items borrowed/returned particulars concerned implements such as axes, nails and ploughs together with other items such as tea, soap and tobacco.

Summary

The multi-purpose note book of Archeson Jeremiah French shows a regard for maintaining a record of various facets of pastoral station life in the early pioneering days. While records of various transactions to around 1850 related to specific dealings with individuals, the wool performance measures and cost of shearing particulars recorded from this time depicted facets of station performance.

Hood

The surviving nineteenth century accounting records of the Hood family consist primarily of financial records. The earliest ledger pertained to Bolac Plains for the period April 1854 to January 1859. This ledger was partially prepared on a double entry basis and provides evidence of bookkeeping barter. The ledger featured personal and non-personal accounts and shows a regard for the determination of aspects of station financial performance under the cash basis of accounting. The non-personal accounts used included stores, wages, petty charges, petty sales, sheep, cattle and horses. The balances of these accounts were periodically transferred to the station account.[39] Initially, the acquisition cost of the station was charged to the sheep account but was later reflected in the station account. Therefore, the accumulated balance in the station account was a measure of overall station performance since acquisition providing an adjustment was made for the initial cost of the station. On the sale of the station to Robert Jamieson in January 1859, a "nett profit" on sale was recorded in the station account based on the difference between the sale price and the accumulated balance of that account.

The earliest ledger for Merrang dates from 22 December 1856 to 1867 and was structured on the same basis as the above-described Bolac Plains ledger until February 1859 when the person who kept the books for Robert Hood from April 1854 evidently became disassociated with the station. This ledger was ruled off on both 22 December 1857 and 1858. A "proof" of balance of the "Merrang station" ledger account as at these two dates was effectively a trial balance. This proof showed the contributions by Robert Hood and his liabilities. A note to the station account balance as at 22 December 1858 stated "this is the actual cost of the station to Mr Hood at this date" thus signifying that cost at a time subsequent to acquisition should be based on original cost as adjusted for the results of trading to balance date. After February 1859, the updating of this ledger became less purposeful and no attempt was made to systematically rule off the accounts in this ledger. A station expenses account was established from 1 January 1862 but was not totalled on a periodic basis. In effect, the bookkeeping emphasis was to record transactions as an end rather than as any means to an end. The ledger also contained inventory records from 22 December 1856 of the "number of cattle should be on station by books" and, from 1859 to 1862, a separate record of stock counts based on periodic general musters of cattle where the stock "short" numbers were identified.

A station day book complemented this Merrang ledger and contained various originating entries and also recorded journal entries to close particular accounts to the station account to February 1859. This day book also recorded among other things shearing tally records indicating the overall performance of each shearer employed in the 1857 and 1858 seasons and details of workers recruited such as commencement dates and pay rates. Another surviving ledger for Merrang spans the period 1863-80. This ledger was structured on the personified basis and was described as the "working ledger" of Robert Hood. Double entry bookkeeping was not adopted in this ledger. It appears that Robert Hood's Merrang financial records became less focused with the passage of time on depicting aspects of station performance. This trend is evidently due, at least in part, to the loss of the skills of the person who established both the Bolac Plains and Merrang recording systems.

A surviving cash book of Robert Alexander David Hood dates from 1 January 1881 when he commenced to lease Merrang from his father. This cash book shows evidence of the adoption of a double entry bookkeeping system which is confirmed by reference to a surviving ledger pertaining to the period 1883-85. This ledger contains both personal and non-personal accounts. The non-personal accounts were ruled off on a calendar year basis but the personal accounts were ruled off on an ad-hoc basis. There is no evidence of the determination of any trading results for the periods involved and no financial statements were found. The cash book was maintained until 30 April 1897. Peter Wares Tait of Camperdown evidently began to provide accounting services to the Hood family around this time.[40] The accountant, until his death on 29 March 1901, continued to act for Robert Alexander David Hood.[41] However, not any accounting records prepared or balanced by Peter Wares Tait for the Hood family were located and no financial statements were found for this period.

Summary

The surviving pre-Federation financial records of the Hood family provide an illustration of accounting systems in earlier years having a stronger focus on the determination of facets of station performance than those pertaining to later years. It seems that the person who maintained Robert Hood's books to 1859 possessed bookkeeping skills which were lost on that person's apparent departure from Merrang. The surviving records of Robert Alexander David Hood show a more systematic approach to recording than had prevailed in the working ledger of Robert Hood. However, the records do not show any evidence of the determination of station financial results on a periodic basis. The involvement of Peter Wares Tait from at least 1 January 1897 most probably led to an overhaul of the Merrang accounting systems which cannot be elucidated on account of the unavailability of any surviving records for the period 1897 to 1900. There were few surviving pre-Federation volume records found but those examined show a regard for control over livestock resources by means of the adoption of a perpetual inventory system, and the importance of records of shearing tallies.

Hope

The surviving pre-Federation accounting records of the Hope family with respect to Darriwill and Gnotuk stations are comprised primarily of financial records. The earliest surviving record of George Hope is a day book for the period 1852-84. This day book recorded various transactions including payments in money and in goods, sales, particulars of engagements of workers and purchases. As transactions were finalized, the term "settled" was written in a column to record completion. Although no ledger folio members were recorded, the recording of either "Dr." or "Cr." next to the name of each person entered in the day book provides evidence of the establishment and use of ledger records but none were found. A cash book maintained during 1865-70 evidently recorded George Hope's banking transactions. Receipts and payments were recorded on separate pages but no periodic totals were recorded. The only evidence of a regard for an accounting period was the use of fresh pages for transactions in each January. Another surviving book recorded various miscellaneous financial and non-financial operating information around 1879 such as account sales of sheep and cattle, stock account by paddock, sheep numbers shorn by paddock summaries and sales of sheep skins. The stock account by paddock recorded sheep numbers as at 17 October 1878 and movements of stock throughout the period to September 1879. Although another count evidently took place on 1 March 1879, there was no evidence of any reconciliations (by paddock or overall) to the later stocktake figures and no particulars of any subsequent counts were recorded.

The available evidence indicates that William Henry Tuckett of Melbourne began providing accounting services to the Hope family after the death of George Hope on 25 April 1884. William Henry Tuckett prepared the accounts of the Estate of George Hope during the pre-Federation period as evidenced in the surviving half-yearly financial statements for this period. The financial statements of the estate were prepared as at 25 October and 25 April and commonly comprised an abstract of receipts and disbursements, balance sheet, schedule of income, and schedule of income accounts of beneficiaries. Although not any journals or ledgers of the estate appear to have survived, the comprehensive and detailed nature of the surviving financial statements suggests strongly they were the output of a double entry bookkeeping system. Accrual accounting was applied involving the recognition of debtors and creditors. The financial statements did not contain any audit certification which suggests that they were unaudited.

According to the balance sheet of the Estate of George Hope as at 25 October 1884 (the earliest available balance sheet), the values for assets and liabilities as at 25 April 1884 were those as reported in the statement of assets and liabilities dated 30 June 1884 and lodged with the Master-in-Equity. Many of these stated asset valuations remained unchanged to 1900. The stated value of Darriwill real estate which had been determined on the per acre basis only altered due to the addition of specific incidental costs (survey fees and fees to bring the estate under the Transfer of Land Act) to the valuation as at 25 April 1884. The Darriwill sheep (as leased together with the Darriwill station to various family members from 25 April 1884) were recorded at an unchanged value from 25 October 1885 to 1900, thus not reflecting changes in sheep numbers which must have occurred during this period or changing market values (per head). Other stock were also accounted for on the same basis. The values attributed to the estate's household furniture, farming and garden implements and also carriages as at 25 April 1884 remained unaltered to 1900. The executors' expenditure on improvements was recorded as an asset during 1884 to 1900. No depreciation was charged on any class of asset during the pre-Federation period.

The earliest surviving ledger of the Hope family pertained to the operations of George Rowland and James Hassall Hope at Gnotuk during the period January 1884 to January 1891. This ledger consisted of various non-personal accounts such as bank, station, plant, livestock and various expense accounts along with personal accounts for station workers. The ledger was prepared on a double entry basis but the commitment to this system promptly ceased on 20 December 1884. From that date, the bank account together with two partners' drawings accounts were the only accounts maintained. In substance, the ledger became a cash book. The bank accounts was first balanced on 31 March 1885 and subsequently on each 1 January. The ledger accounts maintained to 20 December 1884 were not ruled off and no financial statements were found for the period spanned by this ledger if indeed any had been prepared.

Based on surviving financial statements, "W.H. Tuckett & Son" also acted as accountant with respect to the operations on Gnotuk. The surviving financial statements comprise a summary of receipts and disbursements, balance sheet, and a schedule of profit and loss account and related to the period 17 March 1893 to 31 March 1894 and the years ended 31 March 1895, 1896 and 1897. The involvement of the accounting firm might have been influenced by the magnitude of the borrowings of George Rowland and James Hassall Hope from the Estate of George Hope. The balance sheet as at 31 March 1894 recognized Gnotuk lands and also furniture as at 17 March, 1893 as assets while the costs of plant and improvements incurred since that date were also recorded as assets. Although evidence contained in a letter of 22 July 1896 from W.H. Tuckett & Son to a T. Colles, the legal representative of the executors, indicated that the Gnotuk lands were over-valued by approximately 14 per cent, the valuation of these lands remained unchanged in the balance sheet throughout the period to 31 March 1897. No depreciation was charged on any class of asset during this period. Livestock was stated throughout the period at fixed valuations per head for each class of livestock but unlike the financial statements prepared for the Estate of George Hope the valuations were based on stock numbers which were ascertained at each balance date. The profit and loss accounts disclosed classified station income and expenses and hence provide evidence of a focus on station profitability during this period. As observed in connection with the financial statements prepared for the Estate of George Hope, these financial statements also did not contain any audit certification.

Although not any journals or ledgers associated with these financial statements for Gnotuk have been traced, it is likely they were also the product of a double entry bookkeeping system. However, a personalized ledger along with livestock inventory records are available for Gnotuk from 31 December 1898 to Federation. These records do not provide any evidence of the involvement of a professional accountant. The livestock inventory records were regularly balanced and included information on lamb productivity but there is no evidence of any reconciliations with any stock count particulars in the pre-Federation period. Lambing productivity rates were provided by paddock and for the overall flock in both 1899 and 1900. Another surviving pre-Federation ledger dates from March 1895 and was of the partnership of brothers George Rowland and Dr William Waugh Hope in the operation of the Darriwill leasehold. This non-personalized ledger involved a double entry bookkeeping system and the adoption of the cash basis of accounting. Ledger accounts were systematically ruled off on 31 December 1896 and on a calendar year basis thereafter. The periodic profit or loss was not transferred to the partners' capital accounts and thus the accumulated balance remained in the profit and loss account. No evidence was found of the involvement of a professional accountant in the preparation of this ledger.

Summary

The structure of the surviving pre-Federation ledgers of the Hope family dating from 1884 possibly reflects the influence of William Henry Tuckett who seems to have become the accountant of the Hope family on the death of George Hope. Although the journals and ledgers maintained by the accounting firm have not been found, the surviving financial statements of the Estate of George Hope and those of George Rowland and James Hassall Hope were most probably prepared on the double entry bookkeeping approach. These financial statements indicate that many of the recorded asset valuations remained unchanged for extended periods of time even when recorded valuations were evidently overstated. The available pre-Federation volume records are sparse. The surviving livestock records show an interest in perpetual inventory systems but are not an example of the best use of such systems for control purposes. There is evidence of the use of lambing performance measures in 1899 and 1900 but no evidence was found of the determination of performance measures for wool production. The day book of George Hope for the period 1852-84 provides evidence of the existence of a ledger which would have almost certainly been maintained on a personified basis.

Jamieson[42]

The Jamieson financial and volume records date from 16 August 1842 and May 1841 respectively. The earliest surviving accounting record is of cattle numbers which indicated "original stock" numbers and additions to the herd while the earliest surviving financial record showed details of expenses on supplies and relates to the partnership of "Aplin, Carmichael and William Jamieson" in the Union station.[43] It seems that these expenses were those settled by William Jamieson himself rather than the partnership. This practice is explained by reference to the partnership agreement which stated "we [the partners] do hereby agree to pay each one third of the expenses of the station and also to pay the third party of the expenses necessary for carrying on a darrey *(sic)*". During 1844-48 when the Jamieson brothers were at Castlemaddie the financial dealings with certain individuals (presumably station hands) were detailed on a personified basis. This record involved the entering of monetary amounts in a single column ruled down the page and shows evidence of bookkeeping barter. From 1 January 1847 to August 1848 details of "station expenses" and "sold off the station" were maintained under the cash basis of accounting. For the year ended 31 December 1847, a surplus result was shown but no result was determined for the period to August 1848. A surviving statement of net worth (described as "Money on hand and stock present . . . station valued at") showed the station and cattle valued in combination while sheep were valued separately on a per head basis. Volume records maintained to 1848 comprised details of stock numbers and of cattle killed (for rations) and cattle sold.

While building and operating a flour mill in Geelong (1849-51), the Jamieson brothers implemented a day book and personalized ledger system of recording and subsequently adopted the same bookkeeping system on returning to station life at Eumeralla West in 1851. The day book was a multi-purpose record of transactions such as purchases, labour contractual arrangements, cheque and cash payments, settlements made and received in goods rather than money, and receipts from sales of stock and produce. These transactions were subsequently entered in the ledger which was not prepared on the double entry basis but provides evidence of bookkeeping barter. There is evidence of the determination of a cash surplus/deficit result for 1855 and 1856. The same bookkeeping system continued in use from 17 January 1859 when Robert Jamieson ventured into sheep on the acquisition of the Bolac Plains station. The day books came to be used to record various types of non-financial operating information such as: cattle killed for station / flour stores (1860), lambs marked / cattle branded / sugar stores (1863), sheep numbers (1864), potato stores (1865), and cattle numbers (1866). The lambing records indicated an overall lambing productivity rate for all ewes. The earliest bale records examined were prepared in 1859 and showed for each consecutively numbered bale the wool type and weight. Also shown was the total weight of the clip. The personalized ledgers also came to be used on occasions to record certain important qualitative information relating to particular individuals.[44] Further evidence of an infrequent attention to determining a cash surplus/deficit result was found for 1860, 1862 and 1871.[45] As station manager of Bolac Plains during 1873-75 when the Jamieson family resided in Scotland, Andrew Geddes maintained the day book and personalized ledger system already in use. Controls were implemented which involved the examination of the station books by a Bank of Victoria manager (Mortlake Branch), a H.G. Soilleux, and the regular reporting by the station manager to Robert Jamieson. In a letter to Robert Jamieson of 10 August 1873, H.G. Soilleux reported:

> Geddes has left his books for me to check, he puts everything down in the day book, but the ledger of course is not so complete as merchants books and a fresh set entirely would be necessary to show a fair statement, but he follows your working system and no doubt you will understand them. I do not think it advisable to suggest anything different as he would scarcely be able to keep a more complicated set.

This statement implies that the structure of the books would not enable a "fair" presentation of financial information. Andrew Geddes regularly corresponded with Robert Jamieson to report on station conditions and prospects and to provide periodic statements of "receipts and disbursements &c &c".

A second day book and personalized ledger recording system was implemented at Stony Point station upon its acquisition in November 1881.[46] Following the assumption of the bookkeeping function by Robert Jamieson the younger, who had won bookkeeping prizes at the Geelong Church of England Grammar School in 1879 and 1880 (Geelong Church of England Grammar School Archives, Corio), changes took place in the recording of non-financial operating information. Robert Jamieson the younger undoubtedly applied skills acquired at school in performing calculations with operating statistics from 1883 to arrive at measures of performance which evidently had not previously been derived. The wool production records for 1884 indicated by station the wool bale output for different types of wool and the totals of bales sold in different markets (that is, London and Geelong). From 1885, additional wool clip statistics were recorded along with the average weight of wool per head for each station. Lambing records available for Stony Point (1883) and Bolac Plains (1884; 1891 to 1900) indicated the lambing productivity rates of ewes in each paddock. Stock records show the adoption of a perpetual inventory system for control of livestock on Stony Point in 1883 and on Bolac Plains from 1891. Sheep count figures obtained on shearing feature in such records. The records of shearing tallies dating from 1883 indicated, by station, the daily performance of each shearer, the total sheep shorn per shearer over the shearing period and the overall total of sheep shorn. The overall total of sheep shorn was reconciled with the total of the tallies of each shearer. The payments due to each shearer based on shearing performance were also shown. For 1893 and 1894 "remarks" were recorded for each shearer which indicated the standard of their work during the season.

Following the death of Robert Jamieson on 8 November 1894, Peter Wares Tait of Camperdown was appointed to act as accountant on behalf of the executors of the deceased estate.[47] A double entry bookkeeping system involving a general journal and ledger was established and maintained by the accountant from 8 November 1894 (6/16/7 & 8). The assets and liabilities of the Estate of Robert Jamieson as at 8 November 1894 were recorded at values which were those accepted by the Master-in-Equity for death duty assessment purposes (6/16/1). Accrual accounting was adopted involving the recording of debtors and creditors. The recognition of a depreciation expense in connection with plant commenced in the year ended 31 December 1896 but no other assets were depreciated earlier or in the next four years. Unsold wool was only shown as an asset on one occasion (as at 31 December 1898) and stores was not recorded as an asset in any accounting period to 1900. The values attributed to Bolac Plains and Stony Point lands (with improvements) held as at 8 November 1894 remained unchanged during the pre-Federation period. The costs of improvements incurred from 8 November 1894 were charged to expense as incurred. Livestock was valued on the per head basis at varying amounts for each class of livestock based on the stock numbers held at each balance date. These per head valuations also remained unchanged to Federation. Balance sheets were written in the journal (6/16/7 & 8) and were prepared as at 1 January during 1896 to 1900 (the books become those of Robert Jamieson the younger from 1 January 1899). Although separate profit and loss statements were evidently not produced, the accounting system introduced enabled the determination of periodic profit results. The initial profit and loss result was for the period 8 November 1894 to 31 December 1895. The books were structured by the accountant to enable a periodic profit or loss to be determined for each station. Overall net profit or loss was determined after deducting from the combined station result the items: interest, annuities and personal account items. Peter Wares Tait also brought about the advent of a cash book and petty cash book from 8 November 1894 which were maintained by Robert Jamieson the younger throughout the period to 1900.

Peter Wares Tait also acted for the deceased estate and Robert Jamieson in Colony of Victoria income tax matters following his appointment as the first income tax year ended on 31 December 1894. However, despite the accountant's involvement as described, the personalized ledger structure maintained to 8 November 1894 continued to be adopted in the station ledger throughout the period to 31 December 1900. The station ledger was updated by Robert Jamieson from the cash and petty cash books as the day book had been discarded presumably in response to instructions from the accountant. It seems that Robert Jamieson perceived the accountant's function to be that as auditor according to a letter to AML&F of 4 January 1899 wherein he stated "I have arranged with Mr Tait to audit the books again this year and expect him round shortly". No separate financial statements for the Estate of Robert Jamieson have been sighted if indeed any were prepared. Hence, no definite conclusions can be drawn about whether the accounts were subject to audit. The volume records maintained during the period 8 November 1894 to 1900 were found to be similar to those maintained from 1883.

Summary

The surviving pre-Federation financial records of the Jamieson family show a commitment to the personification of station ledgers even when H.G. Soilleux and Peter Wares Tait became involved with the family's financial affairs. On the death of Robert Jamieson, a dual system of accounting emerged as Robert Jamieson the younger continued to maintain a personalized station ledger. Perhaps Robert Jamieson the younger considered that the ledger structure in place adequately met his information needs in running the stations while the accountant's system of accounting was perfunctory, to satisfy the information needs of parties outside the family including the other executors of the Estate of Robert Jamieson. The necessity of lodging an annual income tax return from 1894 seems to have contributed to the on-going involvement of the accountant in Jamieson family financial matters. The Jamieson records also show an increased interest in the use of volume records. Robert Jamieson the younger was able to apply skills acquired at school to enable various determinations of performance measures to be made, thus representing a constructive transfer of knowledge attained to pastoral industry operations. The maintenance of financial control over personal dealings and the increased use of non-financial operating information to determine key station performance measures appear to have comprised a workable system within the station community for running pastoral affairs on a day to day basis.

Kininmonth

There is a range of financial and volume records prepared for nineteenth century pastoral operations on Mt. Hesse. Three surviving "wages" books were written in the ledger format and date from November 1882 when Mt. Hesse was acquired by James Leonard Kininmonth to the time of Federation (and beyond). These ledger records were structured on the personified basis and provide evidence of bookkeeping barter. These ledgers were not prepared on the double entry basis and do not contain any evidence of specific cost control or attempts to determine station financial performance. The advent of periodic financial statements in connection with Mt. Hesse evidently occurred after the death of James Leonard Kininmonth on 14 December 1896. Surviving pre-Federation financial statements of the "Mt. Hesse Estate" (that is, Estate of James Leonard Kininmonth) consist of statements of income and expenditure for the years ended 31 December 1898 to 1900 and balance sheets as at 31 December 1899 and 1900. The financial statements for 1899 and 1900 were typewritten and recorded that they were prepared by James Gardener, accountant, of Geelong.[48] These financial statements did not contain any audit certification which suggests that they were unaudited.

The books from which these financial statements were extracted do not appear to have survived but it is likely they were prepared under a double entry bookkeeping system. It appears as if the cash basis of accounting was adopted by the accountant in preparing the accounts.

The per acre valuation of land accepted by the Master-in-Equity was also recorded as the valuation of Mt. Hesse lands (with improvements) in the balance sheets as at 31 December 1899 and 1900. Sheep and cattle were also stated in these statements at the same per head values accepted by the Master-in-Equity while the valuation of horses in 1899 and 1900 had declined from the valuation adopted as at 14 December 1896. Livestock valuations were based on stock numbers at each respective balance date. No depreciation was charged on plant based on the observation of a common balance sheet valuation shown for this item in 1899 and 1900. The costs of improvements incurred in 1898 were immediately charged to expense. While stores was shown as an asset at different values, wool (unsold) was not recorded as such in either balance sheet. The statements of income and expenditure showed classified station income and expenditure and hence provide evidence of a focus on station profitability. For the years ended 31 December 1899 and 1900, the statements also disclosed special receipts and special payments of the estate. Other surviving financial records consist of a petty cash book dating from 29 December 1896 and a sales book which recorded the sales of stock and produce from 1897. The folio numbers recorded in the petty cash book indicate the existence of a ledger of the estate at the time of recording.[49]

The surviving volume records comprise stock books, bale books and a book which recorded the weights of ram fleeces. Stock books date from December 1882. Sheep numbers were recorded on a per paddock basis and indicate the adoption of a perpetual inventory system. Cattle numbers were much smaller and related to the overall herd only. A perpetual inventory system was also maintained for cattle but stock counts appear to have occurred on a less regular basis than for sheep. Bale books were maintained from 1883 which recorded a consecutive number for each bale in the annual clip along with details of wool type and the weight of each bale. For each annual clip, the total weight of all bales was recorded. The ram fleece records maintained from 1883 showed the weights of individual ram fleeces as categorized on an aged ram basis. The average annual fleece weights for rams in different age groupings (1-5 years) were also recorded. The structure of these various volume records did not alter on the death of James Leonard Kininmonth.

Summary

James Leonard Kininmonth seems to have been content to rely at least on personalized ledgers, detailed stock and bale records and particulars of ram fleece weights for operating Mt. Hesse. The evidence shows the involvement of a professional accountant in the affairs of Mt. Hesse following the death of James Leonard Kininmonth and the advent of periodic financial statements which were evidently unaudited. The evidence also shows that James Leonard Kininmonth's death did not have any impact on the structure of the Mt. Hesse volume records.

Mackinnon[50]

The Mackinnon ledgers date from 1853 when Marida Yallock was acquired by Daniel Mackinnon and Hugh Scott. A complete set of personalized ledgers spans the period to 1900 (Box 2051, 2052 & 2054); the last 46 years of which involved the full ownership of the station by the Mackinnon family. Another surviving set of accounting records date from 1 January 1885 which comprises general journals and ledgers that were established and maintained by accountant Peter Wares Tait of Camperdown on the double entry basis (Box 2054 & 2058). The evidence shows that Peter Wares Tait became involved with the Mackinnon family on a professional basis from around 1 October 1884. The accountant's appointment coincided with the engagement of William Kinross Mackinnon as station manager in 1884 and the retirement of his father, Daniel Mackinnon, from active pastoral engagement. Peter Wares Tait continued to maintain a separate set of books and prepared annual accounts on the accrual basis of accounting until his death on 29 March 1901. He was paid on a quarterly basis for professional services provided to the Mackinnon family in the period to 19 February 1889 and subsequently for services in connection with the Estate of Daniel Mackinnon which appears to have operated Marida Yallock until at least 31 July 1897 when the deceased's spouse died.

The surviving personalized ledgers of the Mackinnon family were not prepared on the double entry basis but show the application of bookkeeping barter. The only surviving pre-Federation cash book for Marida Yallock was maintained during 1853-60 (Box 2047). This book recorded receipts and disbursements that were posted to the personalized ledger. After 1 January 1885, the personalized ledgers occasionally featured entries in the handwriting of Peter Wares Tait, indicating that the accountant assisted in the balancing of certain accounts on an ad hoc basis. From 1885, the personalized station ledgers were ruled off on an annual basis as at 31 December consistent with the accounting period adopted in the other set of accounting records. The personalized ledger approach to recording was evidently an effective system for managing the day to day station affairs in the period to 1900.

A journal entry dated 1 January 1885 recorded the assets and liabilities of Daniel Mackinnon as at that date. The Marida Yallock lands were valued on a per acre basis and livestock was valued on a per head basis. Plant, furniture, and wool (unsold) were also recognized as assets. In the period to 31 December 1888, the per acre valuation of land and the per head valuations of livestock remained unaltered. Plant and also furniture were not depreciated and the costs of improvements were charged to expense as incurred. Changes to the recorded asset values occurred on the death of Daniel Mackinnon. The per acre valuation of land and the per head valuations of each class of livestock were all stated at increased amounts as at 19 February 1889. The values of these assets and others were those as contained in the statement of assets and liabilities prepared as at that date and lodged with the Master-in-Equity. As was the practice in the pre-19 February 1889 period, livestock was valued at balance date (19 February from 1889) on the basis of stock numbers held as at each balance date. The recognition of a depreciation expense in connection with plant commenced in the year ended 19 February 1895. To Federation, no other assets were subject to depreciation and the costs of improvements continued to be charged to expense as incurred. The per acre valuation of land remained unchanged during 1889 to 1900 while the per head values of sheep and cattle changed for the first time since 1889 in 1899.[51] The asset unsold wool was recorded at estimated values during 1885 to 1900 while stores was not recognized as an asset on any occasion. Throughout the 1885 to 1900 period, periodic station profitability was determined and a listing of ledger balances (effectively a balance sheet) as at each balance date was recorded in the general journal (Box 2058). However, not any separate financial statements were found if indeed any were prepared at the time. Hence, no definite conclusion can be drawn as to whether the accounts, and particularly those of the estate, were subject to audit.

Various measures of performance were ascertained and recorded in the general journals and ledgers maintained by Peter Wares Tait. From 1892, a return on investment (assets) was determined. This measure of station profitability was based on the book values of land and livestock after deduction of an amount which related to a portion of Marida Yallock that was leased to another party. This deduction was not based on the per acre valuation as recorded in the accounts but on a higher valuation. From 1895, the wool ledger account ordinarily detailed the total sales weight of the annual clip; the total number of sheep and lambs shorn; the average weight of wool per head and the gross and net returns per pound. The evidence of the determination of such measures shows a regard for the periodic comparison of performance in both financial and non-financial operating terms.

The pre-Federation volume records comprise stock records from 1872 and bale records from 1896 (Box 2047). The stock records maintained during 1872-76 were generally untidy and detailed stock numbers on a per paddock basis. There is evidence of the recognition of discrepancies in paddocks at the time of stock counts but such entries appear to have been made on a spasmodic basis. From 1881, a perpetual inventory system was used involving the recording of overall livestock numbers for each class of livestock. Discrepancies were recorded on a periodic basis which, in the case of sheep, arose when the sheep were counted on being shorn in late November/early December. The bale records detailed a number for each bale in the annual clip and the weight of each bale. In 1900, the total weight of all bales was also recorded.

Summary
The surviving financial records examined indicate the adoption of a personalized ledger system throughout the pre-Federation period from 1853 and the adoption of dual systems of accounting from 1 January 1885. Peter Wares Tait's professional involvement with the Mackinnon family coincided with the appointment of William Kinross Mackinnon as station manager and continued after the death of Daniel Mackinnon. Despite the advent of an accountability relationship in 1884, the personalized ledger system continued to be maintained thus signifying its suitability for running station affairs on a daily basis. The evidence shows the determination of a profitability ratio from at least 1892 and performance measures for wool production from at least 1895. The surviving volume records indicate the existence of a perpetual inventory system for livestock from 1881 and a regard for control of livestock on a paddock basis from at least 1872.

Macknight and Irvine
The earliest surviving pre-Federation financial records relating to Dunmore date from December 1847 being around the time when William Campbell sold his interest in the station to Macknight and Irvine. This cash book spans the period to 1867 and recorded receipts and disbursements which were totalled on the calendar year basis. The cash book entry of 25 July 1865 shows that Horace Flower of Port Fairy (at the time known as Belfast) became what seems to have been a silent partner holding a one-third interest in the Macknight and Irvine partnership.[52] The only surviving volume record of the Macknight and Irvine partnership is a stock book maintained during 1856-64. The entries in this book related to cattle movements such as those bought,

sold, killed and branded but did not record total cattle numbers on the station.

A surviving account book recorded statements of assets and liabilities as at various dates during 1865-73. The earliest statement of assets and liabilities was prepared as at 24 July 1865, the day preceding the investment of monies in the Dunmore operation by Horace Flower. The major asset recorded, "Dunmore station", was stated at "estimated value" which evidently incorporated the livestock on the station. Other assets recorded included land certificates (which presumably related to the small portion of Dunmore lands held as freehold), stores, cash at bank and various debtors as detailed. The liabilities included loans, and accrued interest thereupon, and various creditors as listed. Hence, accrual accounting was applied. No further financial statements were recorded therein until 1869. Balance sheets were prepared under the accrual basis of accounting as at 31 December 1869, 1870, 1871 and as at 14 November 1872. The only indication of station profitability was the overall movement in the partners' capital accounts between balance dates. The balance sheet as at 14 November 1872 indicated that the station including livestock had been sold on 31 October 1872 and showed the "proceeds" of land, livestock, plant and stores as separate assets. The purchasers of the station were in fact Macknight and Irvine in partnership.[53]

From 31 December 1869, the assets of the partnership included land (most of which had then been purchased), livestock, wool, stores, and hay. Land was valued on the per acre basis and livestock was valued on the per head basis based on the stock numbers at each balance date. Wool (unsold) was recorded at "estimated value". Stores and hay were also shown at valuation. The valuation of purchased land remained constant during 1869-71. Although the per head valuations attributed to cattle and horses remained constant during 1869-71, the per head valuation of sheep increased in 1870. No assets were depreciated in preparing the accounts. The account book shows that James Greig, an accountant of Camperdown, was involved in a professional capacity with the partnership from at least 1872.[54] The balance sheet as at 14 November 1872 stated the following opinion of James Greig as at 26 November 1872:

> I hereby certify that I have audited & closed Messrs Macknight & Irvines books for the past year (from 1 January to 14 Nov 1872) and have found them to be correct and the net estate to amount to Eleven thousand eight hundred and fifty pounds fourteen shillings and nine pence sterling subject to a few items contingent specified above and in suspense.

It seems that the production of a balance sheet as at 14 November 1872 and the conduct of the audit by James Greig were linked to the reported sale of the station on 31 October 1872. The books which were "audited & closed" by James Greig were not traced.

Summary

Despite the apparent non-survival of pre-Federation journals and ledgers with respect to the Macknight and Irvine partnership, the surviving financial records show a concern for reporting the state of affairs with respect to the Dunmore operation at certain dates. This interest in balance sheet preparation evidently occurred in the period bounded by the admission and retirement of Horace Flower as a partner in Dunmore. The involvement of a professional accountant on the recorded sale of Dunmore (and possibly earlier) appears to have been motivated by a need to ensure the affairs of the then partnership were settled on the basis of the financial position as attested to by an external party with accounting skills. The surviving volume records show a regard for recording movements of cattle but do not portray the full application of a perpetual inventory system.

McIntyre

A small note pad of Duncan McIntyre containing personal ledger accounts and particulars of flocks of sheep has survived. This information related to operations on Ardachy during 1843-44.[55] The personal accounts were not prepared on the double entry basis but provide evidence of bookkeeping barter. These accounts were not always balanced even where final settlement appeared to have occurred. However, these accounts demonstrate a regard for maintaining evidence of the financial outcomes of dealings with certain parties. The particulars of flocks showed the numbers of sheep included in each of three flocks and the name of the shepherd who was responsible for each flock. It is evident that the sheep in flocks were occasionally counted although a discrepancy observed was not recorded even though the sheep counted figure became the new total of sheep in the flock. The evidence suggests that a form of perpetual inventory system was of benefit in maintaining control of livestock resources in an era before the advent of station fences.

Summary

Of saddle-bag portions, the note pad examined contained financial and non-financial operating information which was evidently helpful in the conduct of pastoral activity in the early days of European settlement in the Western District.

Millear, Maidment and Austin/Millear[56]

Surviving financial and volume records relating to the Millear family's interest in the Western District date from 1870 and 1862 respectively. The earliest financial record was located in a wool book and consisted of personal accounts in the names of shearers. These accounts were not prepared on the double entry basis but provide evidence of bookkeeping barter. The surviving ledger records (1886-92) prepared in the period following the dissolution of the Millear, Maidment and Austin partnership in 1877 show the use of personal and non-personal accounts and the adoption of a cash basis of accounting. Personal accounts contained both debit and credit entries while non-personal accounts primarily contained entries in a single column. The ledgers were not prepared on the double entry basis. Periodic accounting occurred on the calendar year basis and the statements of receipts and disbursements prepared during this period showed categorized receipts and disbursements. Separate totals were shown for receipts such as sales of stock, wool sales and for loans and dividends. Disbursements included station wages, shearing expenses, station stores, improvements, land tax and family (housekeeping) expenses. Separate schedules of annual station wages and shearing expenses detailed the total disbursements to each station hand and shearer respectively as drawn from the respective personal ledger accounts. The amounts for other categories of disbursements were extracted from the non-personal ledger accounts. No evidence was found of the involvement of a professional accountant in the maintenance of these ledgers and no other financial statements were found for the period to 1900. A surviving cash book (1889-1900) recorded receipts ("cheques received") and disbursements ("cheques drawn").

The surviving volume records examined primarily featured information on stock, stores, lambing, shearing, bale and wool production. Many of these were prepared for the partnership of Millear, Maidment and Austin. Stock records dating from 1863 show the adoption of a perpetual inventory system for control of livestock resources. Annual inventory summaries showing opening and closing livestock based on sheep shorn were commonly prepared in the period to 1900. Sheep were accounted for on a per paddock basis (at least during 1885 to 1900) and were subject to regular counts. Stores records (1867) showed details of incoming and outgoing stores and provide evidence of the adoption of a perpetual inventory system. Lambing records (1862-66) showed the lambing productivity rate of all breeding ewes (1862-63) and the productivity rates of "ordinary" and "selected" ewes (1864-66). The percentage of deceased lambs to total ewes turned out was also recorded during 1862-64. Later lamb marking records were prepared on a similar basis. Surviving shearing tally records dating from 1882 showed the daily and season performance of each shearer employed and the daily and season performance in the shed. The overall total of each shearer's tally was reconciled with the total number of sheep shorn in the season. Bale records (1867-77) showed the weight of each consecutively numbered bale in the annual clip as categorized into wool type classifications (combing, clothing, pieces and locks). The total number of bales and the total wool weight in each classification were also recorded. Wool production records (1870-77) showed a range of quantitative information for each annual clip. The annual wool production performance was expressed on an average weight per head basis for different categories of sheep (for example, rams, selected ewes, breeding ewes, wethers) and for the overall flock . These records also showed the gross return, expenses ("as per home invoices") and net return per head for both sheep and lambs during 1871-77.

Summary
The surviving pre-Federation accounting records related to the Millear family's Western District pastoral interests indicate a time-specific concern for control over livestock resources and stores. They also demonstrate an interest in shearing performance and bale weights and a reliance on station performance measures for monitoring wool and lambing production. The surviving financial records examined provide evidence of the preparation of a statement of receipts and disbursements for Edgarley during 1886-92. No evidence was found of the preparation of profit and loss statements and balance sheets or of the involvement of a professional accountant during the period to 1900. The surviving ledgers and the personal accounts found in the wool book were not prepared on the double entry basis.

Miller and Tulloh[57]
A personalized ledger maintained for operations on Pieracle station during 1848-52 has survived (4/1/1). This ledger shows evidence of bookkeeping barter and the practice of station workers approving their final settlement amount by signing their name or placing their mark on the appropriate ledger page. In many cases the signature or mark of a witness was also recorded. This practice allowed the workers to check the balance due to them based on the agreed rates for the employment period and the consideration previously given including the valuations attributed to goods received in lieu of cash. Double entry bookkeeping was not adopted in this ledger.

    Other surviving financial records indicate a regard for determining a station result and the apparent use of an imprest system (4/2/1). For the period February 1848 to 31 March 1849, a station result was calculated as the difference between the advance on wool and station expenditure. The amount of the difference was described as the "balance" and one-half of it was also recorded beneath this balance suggesting that Henry Miller and William France Tulloh were equal partners in terms of the distribution of surpluses. The items of station expenditure detailed included stores, wages, cartage, travelling expenses and license fees. An expense for stores evidently arose when the goods were purchased rather than when they were used. The personalized ledger did not contain any accounts for particular expense types hence the details of these expenses were obtained independently of the ledger. Consequently, it is difficult to confirm whether a cash basis of accounting was adopted although later dated evidence suggests that the cash basis was most probably adopted. A "cash account" (effectively cash book entries) maintained from 23 April 1849 to 1 December 1850 provides evidence of the amounts deposited by Henry Miller into the station bank account and a list of station disbursements over this period totalling the same amount.[58] Station revenue was not shown for this period. Hence, the station bank account was evidently operated on the imprest system which implies the adoption of the cash basis of accounting. No volume records were found for the Pieracle station when it was operated by Henry Miller and William France Tulloh.

Summary

The surviving pre-Federation financial records for Pieracle station with respect to the partnership of Henry Miller and William France Tulloh show the maintenance of personalized ledgers and provide evidence of a regard for deriving a station result. There is no evidence of the involvement of a professional accountant with Pieracle during its operation by the partnership (1848-64) and no volume records appear to have survived.

Officer

There is a range of surviving financial and volume records pertaining to the operation of Mt. Talbot by the Officer family in the nineteenth century. Ledger records are available for the periods 1852-80 and 1889-95. The ledger records were prepared on a personified basis and provide evidence of bookkeeping barter. They were not prepared on the double entry basis. Although no specific expense accounts were maintained in the ledgers, monthly, year to date and calendar year totals of station expenses were prepared and recorded therein during 1853-56 and monthly totals are also detailed for the period January 1858 to March 1858. The monthly expense records show a regard for accrual accounting notion as the costs of labour was recorded at one-twelfth of the respective annual contracted rates. Despite the interest in ascertaining station expenses, there is no evidence of the determination of a periodic profit or loss result. Other financial records comprise day books which related to the periods 1852-65 and 1871-76 and a shearing record book dating from 1885. The day books primarily recorded details of issues of rations and other goods and payments made to hawkers on behalf of station hands that were subsequently recorded in the personal ledger accounts. The shearing record book contained a personalized ledger that was maintained to record details of transactions with shearers only. The earliest surviving ledger book (1852-55) contained lists of orders and cheques drawn but no further records of this kind appear to have survived. No evidence was found of the involvement of a professional accountant in station accounting.

The surviving pre-Federation volume records related to ration issues, shearing tallies, bale weights and included particulars of performance measures for wool production. The rations issued records available for 1863-64 provide evidence of control over the issue of flour, sugar, tea, tobacco and soap rations. The entries in these records were made on a weekly basis to show the total quantity issued for each ration type and also details of rations of different types issued to individual station hands and to the men's hut. Shearing tally records are available for the periods 1857-60, 1863-64, 1868-78, 1885-88, 1890-94 and 1896 to 1900. These records commonly showed the daily and season totals of stock shorn and the daily and season performance of each shearer. The season total of stock shorn was reconciled with the total of the season tallies of each shearer. For 1863-64, another more detailed shearing record showed the daily tallies in each of six shearing runs for each shearer and the overall daily total of stock shorn. This record appears to have been prepared in the shearing shed as each run was completed and was subsequently used to prepare the other tally records as described. Bale records are available for 1863 or 1864, 1873-75, 1885-88, 1890-94 and 1896 to 1900. These records commonly showed a bale number for each bale, details of wool type and the weight of each consecutively numbered bale. For each annual clip the total weight of all bales was recorded. From 1885, there is evidence of the determination of performance measures with respect to the annual wool production. Measures commonly recorded for both sheep and lambs were the average weight of wool per head and the net proceeds (price) per pound.

Summary

The pre-Federation pastoral financial records of the Officer family show
the maintenance of personalized ledgers in the periods as specified from
1852-95. There is evidence of a regard for control of expenditure in the
1850s but no evidence of the determination of station profitability. Not
any pre-Federation financial statements were found if indeed any were
prepared and there is no indication of the involvement of a professional
accountant based on the records examined. Perhaps a professional
accountant became involved with Mt. Talbot in 1895 to assist the
Officer family on the advent of income tax in the Colony. However, the
unavailability of any general journals and ledgers for the period 1895 to
1900 hampers considerably the elucidation of this possibility. The
surviving volume records show an interest in the control of issues of
rations and in shearing performance and the depiction of bale weights.
The later available evidence of the determination of performance
measures for wool production shows a desire to assess key aspects of
station performance.

Ritchie[59]

The surviving nineteenth century accounting records of the Ritchie
family with respect to the Blackwood station consist of both financial
and volume records. The earliest surviving ledger dates from 1855-60
and was prepared on a personified basis (6/1/1). This ledger was not
prepared on the double entry basis but provides evidence of bookkeeping
barter. A later surviving ledger spanned the period 1893 to 1900 and
was prepared on the double entry basis (6/1/3).[60] This ledger featured
non-personal accounts including a profit and loss account in a section of
the ledger described as "general ledger". The ledger also contained
personal accounts in a separate section titled "customers' ledger". Wages
were recorded as expenses (debit entries) in the general ledger on the
accrual basis of accounting. The credit entries were posted to personal
accounts in the customers' ledger. Payments of wages were debited to
the respective personal accounts. Profit results were determined for the
years ended 30 September 1895 to 1900.[61] Only three accounts in the
general ledger (bank, bills receivable and bills payable) that were not
closed annually to the profit and loss account and there is no evidence of
the preparation of any balance sheets in this period. Costs of plant and
improvements were charged to expense as incurred. There is no evidence
of any involvement of a professional accountant in the maintenance of
either of these ledgers.

　　　Cash and day books are available for the periods 1852-56, 1866-79,
1886-93 and 1899 to 1900.[62] The earliest surviving record of cash
transactions (1852-56) only recorded details of transactions with

William Rutledge & Co., a general merchant, wool broker and stock and station agent at the time. The first surviving day book was maintained from 31 March 1866 to 31 March 1879 and recorded a range of transactions. This day book provides evidence of the use of a personalized ledger during this period as folio numbers were recorded to assist in updating the station ledger which does not appear to have survived. The day book and surviving correspondence records indicate that the station books were audited from at least 1868 (three years after the death of Daniel Ritchie) to 31 March 1886 and possibly later. The audit was conducted by Stanislaus James Bayly, a solicitor of Warrnambool, in the period to his death on 2 December 1874 and subsequently by William Powling, solicitor of Belfast, the deceased's former partner in the firm of Bayly and Powling.[63] Presumably, the executors of the Estate of Daniel Ritchie were seeking comfort in the form of an examination of the books maintained by John Ritchie, the station manager at Blackwood. No audit certificates were found if indeed any were prepared. However, the signature of the auditor involved was commonly written in the day book on the last page of entries for each 31 March financial year. The cash books prepared during 1886-93 and 1899 to 1900 recorded receipts and disbursements on a more systematic basis than had occurred under the earlier day book method of recording.

Surviving correspondence records show that William Simpson, an accountant of Melbourne, was providing professional services to John Ritchie in 1873 in his capacity as manager of Blackwood for the executors of the Estate of Daniel Ritchie (2/1/491/1-2). On 1 January, 1874, William Simpson and Benjamin Goldsmith formed a partnership (2/1/491/3) and a professional association between Simpson and Goldsmith and the Ritchie family existed during 1874 and early 1875 (2/1/491/4-5; 2/1/8/40; 2/1/44/89). The appointment of William Simpson was related to the administration of the Estate of Daniel Ritchie. In a letter to John Ritchie of 14 July 1873 with respect to the "Blackwood Estate A/ct", Stanislaus James Bayly wrote "the writer . . . has placed these accounts in the hands of a professional accountant for the purpose of having them prepared in the forms required by the Courts" (2/1/44/72). The reference to the Courts seemingly relates to the Master-in-Equity of the Supreme Court of Victoria as indicated in Stanislaus James Bayly's letter to John Ritchie of 12 November 1873. This letter stated "He [William Simpson] says you and I will be obligated to go before the Master . . ." (2/1/44/76). According to John Ritchie's letter to William Simpson of 27 August 1873, the information supplied to the accountant included a valuation of stock as at 31 March 1873 and the executors' records of "the inventory of the stock, plant, when the Executors took possession on 31 March 1866"

(2/2/2). Delays in the preparation of "the accounts" (2/1/491/4-5; 2/1/44/80) were experienced, much to the annoyance of Stanislaus James Bayly (2/1/44/77). The accounts were evidently finalized by Simpson and Goldsmith in January 1875 (2/1/44/89). No further involvement of William Simpson or Simpson and Goldsmith in the affairs of the Ritchie family is evident from the surviving records. None of the accounts (or any books of account) prepared by these accountants appear to have survived.[64]

Other surviving financial records included statements of valuations dated 25 March 1886 as prepared by a A.A. White. There also survives separate sheep valuation statements prepared at this time by a N. Gow and a L. Kaufmann.[65] As Robert Blackwood Ritchie took ownership of Blackwood in 1886, it is likely that these valuations were conducted at the time of the change in ownership. The statements prepared by A.A. White contained valuations of livestock, implements, goods, chattels and fencing posts. However, no valuation was recorded for the Blackwood lands. Also available are abstracts of expenditure for the years ended 31 March 1878-82.[66] These abstracts detailed the date of each expenditure together with the name of the other contracting party as appropriate and classified the costs into categories such as fencing, materials, shire rates, buildings and special expenditure. Each category was totalled and a total of all categories of expenditure was also recorded. Such evidence of cost aggregation shows a regard for cost control from at least 1878. As no ledger records are available for this period, no valid conclusion can be drawn as to whether these abstracts were drawn from the ledger or prepared independently as a separate task.

Surviving volume records for Blackwood to 1900 consist of stock books (1870-82 and 1893 to 1900), shearing tallies (1869-70 and 1885), bale records (1866-78 and 1886-90) and lambing productivity records (1871-82). The stock records indicate the adoption of a perpetual inventory system for the control of livestock resources (5/2/6-8). Sheep were accounted for on a per paddock basis (1871-82 and 1893-94) and discrepancies at stock counts were recorded as appropriate. Stock counts commonly took place every three months. A separate stock record relating to the period 1894 to 1900 showed the overall flock numbers including opening and closing inventory and movements throughout the year to shearing time. The closing sheep numbers represented "total sheep shorn" at shearing and overall discrepancies were recorded as appropriate. Stock records for cattle (from 1896) and horses (from 1893) were accounted for in overall number terms. Shearing tally records detailed the daily and season performance of each shearer and the total numbers of sheep shorn each day and during the season.[67] The season total of stock shorn was reconciled with the total of the season tallies of each shearer.

The bale records contained particulars of each bale in the annual clip and commonly featured measures of performance for wool production (Group 4).[68] These records showed a bale number for each bale, details of wool type and the weights of each bale as measured at the station and also in London. The total weight of the annual clip was also shown. The measures of performance recorded were the average weight of wool per head (1868 and 1872-74); the average wool income (presumably net) per head (1872 and 1874) and the average weights of wool per head for washed sheep, washed lambs and washed sheep and lambs (1886).[69] Also recorded in 1886 were the average bale weight for four different categories of wool: greasy wool, washed lambs wool, washed sheep's wool and washed wool. The lambing records indicated the lambing productivity rates of ewes of different ages and the overall lambing productivity rate for the season (5/2/6).

Summary

The surviving financial records of the Ritchie family to Federation indicate the adoption of a personalized ledger approach and the subsequent adoption of a double entry system of accounting which focused on the determination of periodic profit but continued to involve the maintenance of personal ledger accounts. The evidence shows that solicitors Stanislaus James Bayly and William Powling were, at different times, auditors of the books of the Estate of Daniel Ritchie and that accountants William Simpson, and Simpson and Goldsmith were involved on a professional basis with the Ritchie family in 1873 and 1874-75 respectively. The accountants were appointed to prepare financial information in a form suitable for dealing with the Master-in-Equity. No further evidence of the involvement of professional accountants in the period to 1900 was observed. The surviving abstracts of expenditure show a regard for cost control during 1872-82 and the surviving shearing records indicate a concern for accuracy in recording shearers' productivity on which they were paid. The pre-Federation volume records examined demonstrate a regard for control over livestock and wool resources and provide evidence of the use of various performance measures for wool and the determination of rates of production for lambing. Overall, the surviving accounting records show a progressive focus on the use of a range of key station performance measures including periodic profit.

Robertson/Patterson

The surviving financial records relate to both Warrock and Capaul stations. Two incomplete sets of ledger records were examined. The first set (1876-89) evidently pertained to Capaul and the other related to Warrock (1887-99). These surviving ledger records were structured on the personified basis and were not prepared on the double entry basis. They show evidence of bookkeeping barter. There also survives for Warrock wages books (1888-95), and a cash book (1888 to 1900) which recorded disbursements only. The wages books contained accounts which were duplicates of those relating to station workers including shearers as recorded in the relevant ledgers. However, these personalized wages ledgers were different in the regard that station workers were required to sign their names on the relevant ledger pages as evidence of their receipt of wages. As amounts due to permanent station hands were settled in cash on a quarterly basis, they recorded their signature on four occasions in each year. This practice enabled the worker to check the accuracy of the details recorded and presented an opportunity for the station owner to have discussions with his workers about station and other affairs. There is no evidence of any involvement of a professional accountant at either Warrock or Capaul stations in the period to Federation. A surviving letter book of George Robertson Patterson (1894 to 1900) shows particulars of revenue and expense items with respect to the 1894 and 1895 calendar years which were evidently prepared independently of the surviving ledger records and forwarded to the Commissioner of Taxes.

The surviving volume records pertained to Warrock only and related to shearing and bale weights from 1887. The shearing records indicated the daily numbers of sheep shorn and the total numbers shorn in the shearing season. From 1900, additional details of shearing were recorded including particulars of sheep shorn (merino lambs, grown merino lambs, cross bred sheep and cross bred lambs) and the performance of each shearer in the season. Bale records showed a bale number for each bale, details of wool type and the weight of each bale in the annual clip.

Summary

The examination of the surviving pre-Federation financial records of Warrock and Capaul stations shows the use of personalized ledgers and the use at Warrock of separate wages books which contained certain personal accounts as duplicated in the station ledgers. Despite the advent of income tax in the Colony in 1894, the structure of the surviving ledger records examined did not change around that time. The preparation of shearing and bale records at Warrock show an interest from at least 1887 in recording certain facets of wool production.

Russell, P.[70]

The relevant surviving nineteenth century accounting records of the Philip Russell family pertain to both the Carngham and Langi Willi stations. For Carngham, the earliest surviving financial record book dates from 1843 and features different approaches over time in the maintenance of ledger accounts (584/2). In the period 1843-1853 when Carngham was operated by Philip Russell and Robert Simson, the ledger featured a broad range of non-personal accounts and also personal accounts. There is evidence of bookkeeping barter and a mixture of single and double entry bookkeeping. From 1853, when Philip Russell became the sole proprietor of Carngham, the ledger accounts were maintained on a personified basis until January 1861. During 1843-60, there is no evidence of the use of the ledger to prepare periodic financial statements. During 1861-63, the ledger was transformed to feature a range of non-personal accounts. It was maintained on the double entry basis and half-yearly statements of receipts and disbursements and balance sheets were recorded therein.[71] Receipts were classified into categories which comprised sheep, cattle, horses, mines and rents while labour, improvements and miscellaneous categories were adopted for disbursements. Land and livestock were valued in the balance sheet on a per acre and per head basis respectively. Livestock valuations were determined on the basis of stock numbers at each balance date. The per acre valuation of land changed in 1862 when the value increased while the per head valuation of sheep, cattle and horses were subject to much variation during this short period. Mining rights were also shown as an asset at values which fluctuated. The costs of fencing, improvements and stores were recorded as disbursements, although stores on hand were recorded in the balance sheets as at 1 August 1862 and 1 February 1863.

Philip Russell departed Australia for Britain at the beginning of 1861 and seems to have returned to Australia between April 1863 and January 1864 (Brown, 1935, p.371; 1971, pp.195 and 220). Thus, the changes in the structure of accounting records in 1861 were linked to his absentee ownership and the associated obligation for the station manager, James Aitken, to be accountable for the resources placed under his control. For the period after 1863, the ledger does not provide evidence of the continuation of periodic accounting and shows a renewed focus on personal accounts. From around 1868, it seems that the ledger became more of a private ledger of Philip Russell rather than a station ledger. A surviving cash book (1868-75) recorded receipts and disbursements (584/3). Other separate surviving ledger records for Carngham (1868-75) were also prepared on a personified basis (584/4). For Langi Willi, a surviving ledger maintained during 1875-81 also shows the adoption of a personalized recording system. This ledger does not provide evidence of periodic accounting as ledger accounts were ruled off as contractual arrangements and transactions were completed.

The Ballarat Trustees Executors and Agency Co. Ltd acted for the executors of the Estate of Philip Russell and almost certainly maintained the books of the estate for the period from its advent on 14 July 1892 to 1900.[72] Although not any journals and ledgers of the estate appear to have survived, there survives audited financial statements of the Estate of Philip Russell for the years ended 30 June 1894, 1896, 1897 and 1901. These annual statements comprised a statement of receipts and expenditure and also a balance sheet. The comprehensive and detailed nature of these surviving statements suggests they were produced under a double entry bookkeeping system. The 1894 financial statements were audited by stockbroker Augustus Shepherd while the 1896, 1897 and 1901 statements were audited by Frederick Downes, a stockbroker and accountant of Ballarat. Both attested that the financial statements were "examined and found correct".[73] Throughout the period 1894 to 1901, many of the recorded valuations of the assets of the estate evidently remained unaltered including valuations of sheep, cattle, horses, crops, stores, carriages, and tools and implements. The stable valuations observed were those recorded in the statement of assets and liabilities as at 14 July 1892 and lodged with the Master-in-Equity. For livestock, the stated valuations observed for each class of livestock were based on both the stock numbers and the per head valuations determined as at 14 July 1892. Nonetheless, stock numbers undoubtedly altered during the period to 1900. Based on the valuations of land which were observed, recorded land valuations evidently remained unchanged during 1894 to 1901. The valuations as at 30 June 1894 for Langi Willi and Carngham real estate were marginally higher than those contained in the statement of assets and liabilities lodged with the Master-in-Equity.[74] Station expenditure items were shown separately for each station while station receipts were those for the combined station operations. Costs of improvements were immediately charged to expense. Unsold wool was shown as an asset indicating a regard for the notion of accrual accounting.

Wool books for Carngham (1872-86; 1891 to 1900) and Langi Willi (1870 to 1900) were examined.[75] For each station, there was shown for each consecutively numbered bale both the wool type and bale weight. The total weight of the annual clip was also shown for each station. From 1871 and 1873 performance measures were recorded for wool production at Langi Willi and Carngham respectively. These normally consisted of the average weight of wool per head; the average net proceeds (price) per head and the average net proceeds per pound. In the surviving Carngham bale records, comparative wool performance measures were recorded for other Western District stations comprising Mawallock and Stoneleigh stations in 1873 and Ercildoun in 1877 (Box 446).[76] In 1873, the measure compared was the average net proceeds per pound while the 1877 performance comparison with Ercildoun involved the average weight of wool per head, the average (presumably net) proceeds (price) per head and the average (presumably net) proceeds per pound. From 1896, comparative wool production reports detailed key operational statistics and performance measures for Langi Willi and Carngham along with three other nearby stations comprising Trawalla, Mawallock and Caranballac. The key performance measures commonly reported for these stations were the average weight of wool per head (and per lamb and per sheep); the average gross and net proceeds per head and the average net proceeds per pound. Further, a surviving statement of net return on wool showed for both Carngham and Langi Willi the annual net wool receipts during 1882-98 and the average net receipts for each station during this 17 year period.

Summary
The surviving ledger records relating to Philip Russell's interest in Carngham and Langi Willi show diversity in their structure. The first major change was to a personalized ledger approach when the partnership with Robert Simpson in Carngham was dissolved in 1853. The involvement of James Aitken, as manager of Carngham when Philip Russell was in Britain during 1861-63, brought periodic accounting and the preparation of financial statements by means of a non-personalized system of recording. Notwithstanding, a personalized ledger system was evidently reintroduced in 1864 on Philip Russell's return to Australia. The surviving financial records indicate the involvement of professional accountants in the operations of Carngham and Langi Willi after the death of Philip Russell. The surviving ledger records of Philip Russell do not provide evidence of any motivation to determine station profitability on a regular periodic basis. Alternatively, there was found to be an interest in the determination of performance measures for wool production and a regard for performance comparisons with other wool growing stations in the Western District.

Russell T. *et al.*[77]
The surviving accounting records related to the nineteenth century operation of Barunah Plains by the Russell family consist of stock books and also financial records that were evidently prepared by the Geelong Branch of AML&F on behalf of James Russell.[78] A story by Civelli (1991) in the *Geelong Advertiser* with respect to Barunah Plains indicated that all accounting records were destroyed in 1978 when the

Russell family sold the station. The press story stated that "orders were given for all the record books to be placed in a heap, chain sawed and then burned" (Civelli, 1991, p.1). In a letter to the editor of the *Geelong Advertiser*, Geordie Russell replied:

> To say that all records were ordered to be burnt is not quite true - many records and letters dating back to our early ownership, together with journals, are in the La Trobe Library. Other letters and records are in the hands of the family (Russell, 1991, p.6).[79]

The stock books examined in the study were made available by Geordie Russell.

These stock books related to the periods 1880-82 and 1887-89 and pertained to sheep only. Sheep were accounted for on a per paddock basis under a perpetual inventory system.[80] Sheep were counted on a regular basis, commonly in March, June and November. Discrepancies on stock counts were recorded as appropriate.

A surviving cash book (6/14/6) and ledger (6/14/1) dating from 23 September 1897 were prepared by AML&F for James Russell. These records were evidently maintained by James Gardener, the Geelong manager of AML&F. The ledger was prepared on the double entry basis and features both personal and non-personal accounts. It includes statements of income and capital account for the period 23 September to 31 December 1897 and the year ended 31 December 1898 and also statements of income account for the years ended 31 December 1899 and 1900.[81] Balance sheets as at 31 December 1897, 1898, 1899 and 1900 were also recorded in the ledger. The cash basis of accounting was adopted in 1897 but a regard for accrual accounting was evident from 1898 in the recognition of the expected net proceeds of the sale of wool in London as an asset. The Barunah Plains land (with improvements) were valued in combination on a per acre basis. The stated real estate valuation did not alter in the period to 1900. The stated valuations of plant, furniture and stores as at 31 December 1897 also remained unaltered during the period to Federation. Throughout this period, livestock was valued on a per head basis using different amounts for each class of livestock based on stock numbers at each balance date. The per head valuation of sheep changed on one occasion (in 1899) in the pre-Federation period. In contrast, the per head valuations of cattle, horses and pigs remained constant during this period. The costs incurred on plant, improvements and stores after 23 September 1897 were immediately charged to expense and no depreciation expense was recognized in the accounts during 1897 to 1900. It appears that the pre-Federation accounts of James Russell were unaudited.

Summary

The surviving nineteenth century volume records examined show the adoption of a perpetual inventory system at Barunah Plains from at least 1880. These records indicate a regard for control over stock resources. The surviving financial records available were prepared for James Russell from 23 September 1897 on the double entry basis and show the preparation of periodic reports in the form of profit and loss statements and balance sheets. These financial records were prepared by AML&F, a major lender to James Russell during 1897 to 1900.

Chapter 7 examines the structure and usage of pre-Federation accounting information based on the case by case findings reported in this chapter. It provides a generalized perspective of accounting practice in Western District pastoralism from 1836 to 1900.

NOTES

1. Table 6.1 is based on Table I in Carnegie (1995, p.8).
2. In the case of the Dennis family, a bushfire destroyed the shearing shed in 1944 but not the Tarndwarncoort homestead where the surviving pre-Federation financial records were stored. In an oral history interview held on 3 December 1990, Norman Dennis (a descendant of the pioneering Alexander Dennis) remarked "any records in the old woolshed would have been burnt when the shed was burnt" (Carnegie, 1990).
3. According to Napier (1989, p. 240), "financial accounting records (in the widest sense) tend to survive where managerial records are destroyed".
4. The location numbers presented in this discussion of surviving Armytage records relate to those records held at the La Trobe Library (manuscript number MS 7829).
5. The dissolution of the partnership between Charles Henry Armytage and George Fairbairn in January 1869 did not result in any changes to the structure of the Mt. Sturgeon accounting records (Blake & Riggall/Fairbairn, George, and Fairbairn Pastoral Company/No.4, University of Melbourne Archives).
6. The carriage account was evidently used to record costs related to the station horse teams. Miscellaneous expenses were included in the station expenses accounting including fruit trees, fowls, seed, mail, potatoes and expenses for "self".
7. The evidence shows that William Henry Tuckett's appointment as accountant for the Estate of Charles Henry Armytage began on 1 September 1876. The minutes of a meeting of executors of the Estate held on 7 June 1877 indicate that William Henry Tuckett's remuneration, set on a annual basis, commenced from that date. In the same meeting, the executors signed a cheque payable to William Henry

Tuckett which was the first cheque approved in the minutes for payment to the accountant for an amount consistent with the level of remuneration due from 1 September (including any minor outpockets subsequently described in the minutes as "petties"). William Henry Tuckett's name was not listed as a liability in the statement of assets and liabilities of the deceased as at 26 April 1876 and there is no available evidence to suggest that he was Charles Henry Armytage's accountant prior to that date.

8. William Henry Tuckett's firm was named W.H. Tuckett & Son in 1889 on the admission of Charles Helton Tuckett as a partner. The firm name changed again in 1897 to W.H. Tuckett & Sons on the admission to the partnership of another son, Philip Sydney Tuckett. William Henry Tuckett died in Melbourne on 19 September 1904 at the age of 87 years (Sutherland Smith, 1992, p.58).

9. The Master-in-Equity performed functions in connection with the enforcement and collection of death duties in Victoria (*Duties on the Estates of Deceased Persons Statute* 1870; Griffith, 1965, pp.249-251; Jacobs, 1969, pp.1-10).

10. As mentioned previously, improvement costs were capitalized as an asset rather than treated as an expense in the records of the Estate of Charles Henry Armytage.

11. On examination, the surviving Beggs' records held at the Gold Museum, Ballarat, were not catalogued.

12. For example, an allowance for creditors included as expenditure in a prior period would lead to the inclusion of the same amount in 1 January receipts to contra the payment of the creditors in that period.

13. This discussion of the surviving Black Bros., and Black Bros. & Smith records provides location numbers of the La Trobe Library where the records are located. These manuscripts are numbered MS 8996 (named "Niel Black & Co.") and MS 10761 respectively.

14. The balance of Mrs Black's account with "the executors of the late N. Black" was transferred to an account in the name of the Black Bros. on 13 June 1887. The stock book (1874-98) also indicates that a stock count took place on 13 June 1887 and shows brought forward stock numbers as at that date. (The entries in this stock book from 1874 to 15 May 1880 related to the operations of Niel Black while those from his date of death to 13 June 1887 were evidently in connection with the Estate of Niel Black).

15. See *Terang Express*, 22 November 1927.

16. Surviving financial statements to 1896 are held in Box 2718/4 while Box 2718/5 contains those subsequently prepared.

17. W.H. Foley had earlier acted as accountant for a Mr R. Buchanan and John Smith when they operated Tallangatta station in North-East Victoria. W.H. Foley appears to have first prepared the accounts for the Tallangatta partnership for the year ended 31 December 1884 (Box 2718/1).

18. The balance sheet of Black Bros. & Smith as at 14 January 1894 shows that Niel Walter Black had become a partner in Grassdale Estate. During

the subsequent period to Federation, the partnership of Black Bros. & Smith comprised four partners.

19. This discussion of the surviving Clyde Company/Russell, G. records provides location numbers of the La Trobe Library where the records are held (manuscript number MS 9248).

20. These periodic returns are published in Brown (1952, 1958, 1959, 1963 and 1968).

21. In a letter to George Russell of 22 December 1840, William Cross wrote "these [printed forms] will save you much labour & at the same time be satisfactory to the partners here" (Brown, 1952, p.403).

22. Brown (1968, p.xxiii) reported that one of George Russell's letterbooks was missing. As a consequence, there is no record of outwards correspondence with the Glasgow agent after June 1854.

23. William Cross had become a partner of the Clyde Company by the early 1840s (Brown, 1958, p.148).

24. The wages book (described as a ledger by Brown, 1952, p.182) for the period 1839-42 has still not been found.

25. Leslie Manor was purchased by George Russell at auction on 26 February 1867 (Brown, 1935, p.376). The other stations were Barunah Plains, Mawallok and Stoneleigh.

26. The series numbers detailed in this discussion of the surviving Cumming records relate to those records held at the University of Melbourne Archives under the name "Mount Fyans".

27. The ledger (LS3/6/11) only is held at the University of Melbourne Archives.

28. A profit result had also been determined for the period 1 January 1898 to 7 May 1898.

29. Stonehenge Estate was acquired by Claude Percival Fyans Cumming, a younger brother of William Burrow Cumming (Henderson, 1936, p.495).

30. The location numbers detailed in this discussion of the surviving Currie records relate to those records held at the La Trobe Library (manuscript number MS 8074).

31. The listing in the journal of ledger balances as at 1 January 1876 details the folio numbers of the former ledger (that is, "O.L.") and the newly established ledger (that is, "N.L.").

32. A memorandum from the Commissioner of Taxes of 28 May 1896 concerning the income tax affairs of John Lang Currie was addressed to H.M. Strachan (Box 847). In 1898, Strachan, Bostock & Co. amalgamated with Shannon, Murray & Co. as Strachan, Murray and Shannon Pty Ltd (University of Melbourne Archives).

33. In a letter to Peter Wares Tait of 13 February 1900, Patrick Sellar Lang stated "I may say that Mr. Strachan does not now keep the Books of the Trust. Mr Gillespie keeps them posted himself". Patrick Sellar Lang was also an executor of the Estate of John Lang Currie.

34. From October 1851, wool sales were recorded in the station account and the accumulated credit balance of the sheep account as at July 1852 appeared in the station account.

35. In some years, the debit entries were totalled in September while the credit entries were totalled in July.
36. This report included a valuation of wool but not for sheep.
37. These financial statements comprise profit and loss accounts for the years ended 30 June 1892 and 1895 and balance sheets as at those dates.
38. This discussion of the French note book provides a location number of the La Trobe Library where the book is held (manuscript number MS 10053).
39. The duration of the first accounting period was two years as the ledger was not ruled off on a systematic basis until 17 April 1856. Thereafter, the ledger was ruled off on 17 April of each year.
40. The first mention of Peter Wares Tait in the cash book of Robert Alexander David Hood was made on 5 April 1897 when a cheque was drawn in the accountant's favour. Underneath the last entry in the cash book was a note in the accountant's handwriting which stated "see Bank Book now from 1 January 1897". This evidence suggests that Peter Wares Tait maintained the books of Robert Alexander David Hood from 1 January 1897.
41. In the statement of assets and liabilities of Peter Wares Tait prepared as at his date of death and lodged with the Master-in-Equity, Robert Alexander David Hood was a debtor on account of professional services rendered by the accountant.
42. The deposit numbers listed in this discussion of the surviving Jamieson records relate to those records held in the AML&F collection at the Noel Butlin Archives Centre, Australian National University, Canberra.
43. The Union partnership agreement was dated 20 July 1842, although the partnership may have commenced prior to this date. However, this first volume record shows that the partnership terminated on 20 January 1843 when C.D. Aplin removed his share of the stock from the run.
44. Details of the death of two of Robert and Johanna Douglas Jamieson's children (William and Alice) are shown in the "A. Morrison Exps. Scotch College" ledger account while details of the death by drowning of two station hands are shown in the respective personal ledger accounts.
45. A partly completed statement found for 1872 suggests a limited interest in the preparation of an annual surplus/deficit result.
46. Although non-personal ledger accounts were prepared in the Stony Point ledger to record the acquisition of the "estate" (land and buildings), stock and furniture, the credit entries shown were matched with debit entries which showed the settlement by cheque of the contract amounts and the accounts were closed off.
47. The executors of the estate were pastoralists Albert Austin, William Cumming and Robert Jamieson the younger. Both Albert Austin and William Cumming were neighbours of the Jamieson family.
48. The financial statements for 1899 were dated 16 February 1900 at Geelong.
49. These folio numbers were in different handwriting from that of the person who originally entered the transactions.

50. This discussion of the surviving Mackinnon records provides location number details of the La Trobe Library where the records are located (manuscript number MS 9470).

51. The settlement of the Estate of Daniel Mackinnon and the inheritance of Marida Yallock by Donald Mackinnon may have occurred in 1899 and, if so, these changes in values may have been in response to instructions given by the new owner.

52. Henderson (1941, pp.247-251 and 372-379) and Hone (1974a) do not contain any mention of an investment by Horace Flower in Dunmore.

53. The entry in Charles Hamilton Macknight's diary for 31 October 1872 stated "station sold by Auction in Melbourne, Macknight and Irvine bought it".

54. James Greig might have provided accounting services to the partners in 1872 as entries in the diary of Charles Hamilton Macknight refer to a "Mr Grieg" who was reported to have arrived at Dunmore on 6 March 1871 and to have left the station two days later. Mr Grieg and James Greig may have been the same person.

55. The note pad had been used to record stock numbers in 1839 when Duncan McIntyre was working in Van Diemen's Land.

56. On examination, the surviving Millear, Maidment and Austin/Millear records held at the La Trobe Library had not been accessioned and catalogued. The pre-accession number of the collection is PA 791.

57. This discussion of the surviving Miller and Tulloh records presents series numbers of the University of Melbourne Archives where the records are held under the name "William France Tulloh".

58. The disbursements were posted to the personal accounts in the ledger.

59. This discussion of the surviving Ritchie records presents series numbers of the University of Melbourne Archives where the records are located under the name "R.B. Ritchie & Son Pty Ltd".

60. Another ledger prepared during 1879-86 has been catalogued at the University of Melbourne Archives (6/1/2) but had subsequently been misplaced and was therefore not available for examination.

61. From 1896, the profit results were no longer accumulated in the profit and loss account but were transferred (including the accumulated balance at the time) to Robert Blackwood Ritchie's private account.

62. No specific series numbers are attributed to these surviving cash and day books.

63. William Powling was taken into partnership by Stanislaus James Bayly around July 1869 (*Port Fairy Gazette*, 6 November 1903).

64. The surviving probate records with respect to the Estate of Daniel Ritchie do not contain any statement of assets and liabilities of the deceased as at his date of death.

65. These statements are available in Second Accession, Management File No.1.

66. These abstracts are available in Second Accession, Management File No.2.

67. These tally records are available in Second Accession, Management File No.2.

68. No specific series numbers are attributed to these surviving bale records.
69. Some of these wool details are found in the day book for 1866-79 (at rear).
70. Except where otherwise indicated, the location numbers detailed in this discussion of the surviving Philip Russell records relate to those records held at the Geelong Historical Records Centre.
71. These financial statements spanned the period 1 February 1861 to 31 January 1863.
72. The surviving records of the Ballarat Trustees Executors and Agency Co. Ltd pertaining to the Philip Russell family included accounting working papers, draft financial statements, audited financial statements of the Estate of Philip Russell for the year ended 30 June 1901 and income tax returns of the estate during 1894 to 1900 (Union Fidelity Trust Papers, Gold Museum, Ballarat).
73. This certification was used in each of the four financial years as specified.
74. There are three possible reasons for these differences. Firstly, the valuations reviewed by the Master-in-Equity were subsequently adjusted upwards. Secondly, additional land was acquired in the period 14 July 1892 to 30 June 1894 and, thirdly, certain costs incurred during this period (for example, land subdivision or survey fees) were capitalized as assets.
75. The 1872-86 wool book for Carngham is held at the La Trobe Library (manuscript number MS 8924).
76. As seen earlier, evidence of performance comparisons with Stoneleigh was also found in the surviving pre-Federation records of the Beggs family and the Clyde Company/Russell, G. Evidence of performance comparisons with Mawallock was also observed in the case of the Clyde Company/Russell, G.
77. The deposit numbers detailed in this discussion of surviving records in connection with Barunah Plains relate to those records held in the AML&F collection at the Noel Butlin Archives Centre, Australian National University, Canberra.
78. These financial records indicate that the partnership of Andrew and James Russell in Barunah Plains was dissolved on 23 September 1897 and that James Russell operated the station as sole proprietor from that date.
79. The surviving records lodged at the La Trobe Library did not include any pre-Federation financial or volume records.
80. There was a total of 59 flocks (segmented by specific paddock location) in 1880.
81. The capital items recorded in 1897 related to the acquisition of the station by James Russell and the financing support provided by Andrew Russell while the capital items shown in 1898 related to a special account.

CHAPTER 7

STRUCTURE AND USAGE OF NINETEENTH CENTURY PASTORAL ACCOUNTING INFORMATION

Based on the findings reported in the previous chapter for the 23 pastoral entities comprising the research sample, this chapter examines the structure and usage of accounting information prepared for pre-Federation pastoral industry engagement in the Western District. In so doing, this chapter identifies generally adopted accounting practices and certain minority practices and also delineates changes in accounting practice throughout the period 1836 to 1900. The chapter comprises three main sections. The first section presents an analysis of the accounting information observed in surviving financial records. The second section analyses accounting information of a non-financial operating nature as contained in surviving volume records. A discussion of the combined use of financial and volume records in pre-Federation pastoralism follows in the third section.

Accounting Information of a Financial Nature

This section analyses the structure and usage of pre-Federation pastoral accounting information of a financial nature. In the first instance, a discussion is presented of the nature of ledgers and originating entry records maintained in periods before professional accountants became involved with station accounting in the Western District. Then follows a discussion of the evidence of a regard for expenditure control during these periods and an examination of the progressive involvement of professional accountants in the establishment and maintenance of financial recording systems and the preparation of accounts from 1872. The major accounting practices adopted in preparing pre-Federation accounts are examined along with certain minority practices which are regarded as important in this study by virtue of the scant evidence unearthed of their application. An examination of financial records lags from Western District pastoral occupation to the earliest dated surviving ledger, day/cash book and financial statement records follows to assist in assessing the urgency for preparation of particular kinds of records.

Ledgers

Surviving pre-Federation ledger records were found for 21 of the 23 pastoral entities in the research sample. As evident in Chapter 6, the station ledgers and originating entry records examined were prepared to the early 1870s by Western District pastoralists or their station managers without the assistance of professional accountants. The earliest surviving station ledgers examined were found to be commonly prepared on a personified basis or primarily on that basis and they generally provide evidence of the adoption of bookkeeping barter. They were not usually prepared on the double entry basis. Table 7.1 summarizes the findings reported in Chapter 6 with respect to the nature of the earliest surviving ledger records found for these 21 entities.

TABLE 7.1: Nature of Earliest Surviving Ledger Records

Entity (21)	Dates of Earliest Ledgers	Personalized Basis (fully or primarily)	Evidence of Bookkeeping Barter	Double Entry Bookkeeping Systems (fully)	Ledger Signing by Station Workers
Clyde Company/					
Russell, G.	1836	•(a)	•		
Dennis	1840	•	•		
French	1841	•	•		
Corney	1842	•	•		
McIntyre	1843	•	•		
Russell, P	1843		•		
Jamieson	1844	•	•		
Miller and Tulloh	1848	•	•		•
Officer	1852	•	•		
Mackinnon	1853	•	•		
Hood	1854		•		
Beggs	1855	•	•		
Ritchie	1855	•	•		
Cumming	1856	•	•		
Armytage	1863	•	•		
Millear, Maidment and Austin/Millear	1870	•	•		
Currie	1876			•	
Robertson/					
Patterson	1876	•	•		•
Kininmonth	1882	•	•		
Hope	1884			•	
Russell, T *et al.*	1897			•	

Note:
(a) The earliest ledger featured the use of both personal and non-personal accounts from 1 January 1838.

The table shows the earliest surviving ledger record found was prepared by George Russell for the Clyde Company (1836-39). Unlike most of the early ledger records, this ledger featured a mix of single and double entry bookkeeping and the use of personal and non-personal accounts from 1 January 1838. The earliest surviving Currie ledgers (1876-81) were prepared on the double entry basis by William M. Fergusson who provided professional accounting services to John Lang Currie from at least 1876. Of all the entities in the research sample, the Currie ledgers were the earliest surviving ledgers that were prepared by a professional accountant even though accountants were found to have been involved with Macknight and Irvine and also Ritchie from 1872 (and possibly earlier) and 1873 respectively.

Ledgers prepared on a personified basis or primarily on that basis are concerned with reflecting the financial positions of dealings with particular parties. The recording focus evident in the ledgers examined involved the accurate and detailed statement of transactions with station workers and other parties involved with the station community. In the case of station workers, these ledgers normally recorded particulars of a personnel nature. For non-itinerate station workers, personal ledger accounts typically showed the length of employment, agreed rates of pay and a description of the role performed (for instance, shepherd, boundary rider, cook and domestic servant). Itinerate workers comprised shearers and other casual labourers. For shearers, the entries in personal ledger accounts commonly indicated the dates of employment, the numbers of sheep shorn during the period and the agreed rate of payment based on 100 head shorn. For workers engaged on other short-term projects such as fencing, the ledgers normally stated the nature of the work undertaken and showed, where relevant, the piece rates involved (for example, rates based on the number of fencing post holes dug). Amounts due to station workers were normally recorded as credit entries in ledger accounts.

Personal ledger accounts also recorded details of settlements made either in money or in goods. Goods rendered in settlement of obligations were recorded at their current cash equivalents and included livestock, tobacco, boots, clothing and blankets. This use of money as a unit of account in instances where money was not available or unnecessary relied upon the accurate recording of issues of goods from station stores and also livestock at their current cash equivalents. The evidence shows that endeavours were made to accurately reflect the details of such transactions in personal ledger accounts. Details of settlements made were commonly recorded as debit entries in ledger accounts. In the cases of Miller and Tulloh, and Robertson/Patterson, evidence was found of station workers approving their settlement amount by signing their name (or placing their mark) on the appropriate personalized ledger page.

Some early ledgers (Armytage; Beggs; Cumming; Dennis) were prepared primarily on a personified basis. Non-personal accounts were found to be used for items such as carriage, incidentals and sundries. These accounts often appeared to have been used to record transactions involving relatively minor sums of money. However, the extent of the usage of such accounts represented a very small proportion of the total number of accounts entered in the respective station ledgers.

Ledgers prepared on a personified basis or primarily on that basis were, in effect, a combined debtors' and creditors' record. The bookkeeping emphasis was to accurately portray the amounts due from and owed to parties as an end in itself. These ledgers were generally not structured to provide detailed representations of aspects of performance and financial position and were thus not used to measure underlying attributes of economic activity. However, the records maintained would enable the pastoralist or station manager to monitor strictly the states of affairs of all personal dealings and to produce evidence, where necessary, to settle any disputes with, or satisfy queries from, particular parties. As such, these detailed ledgers constituted a lifetime record of station operations, showing station settlement and development from an individualized financial perspective.

As identified in Chapter 6, some early ledgers maintained in the period to the late 1850s (Clyde Company/Russell, G., 1838-39; Russell, P., 1843-53; Hood, 1854-59) were found to feature the combined use of personal and non-personal ledger accounts. All of these ledgers show the adoption of both single and double entry bookkeeping in their preparation. Chapter 6 also presented evidence of a regard in a few cases for the elucidation of aspects of performance and financial position in early ledger records. In particular, the Dennis ledgers indicate an interest in monitoring certain aspects of financial performance from the 1840s while the Hood ledgers to 1859 depict a regard for ascertaining station financial performance on the cash basis of accounting. The Clyde Company ledgers are an exemplifier in terms of their use to prepare periodic financial reports for the British-based partners. The Clyde Company ledgers show considerable sophistication in their preparation from 1839 and, by 1845, the partners were provided with half-yearly information on both station profitability and financial position as prepared on the accrual basis of accounting. The financial statements prepared by James Aitken during 1861-63 when Philip Russell of Carngham and Langi Willi was residing in Britain represent another early illustration of a desire to keep absentee owners informed about periodic financial performance and financial position. As evident in Chapter 6 and as discussed later in this chapter, the involvement of professional accountants in station accounting in the Western District from the early 1870s brought about changes in the structure of ledgers associated with an emerging focus on the maintenance of ledgers as a means to an end.

As indicated above, combinations of both single and double entry bookkeeping were found to exist in some early ledger records as described. The first instance of the adoption of a double entry basis of accounting occurred in the ledger records of the Clyde Company in 1839. Another early application of the double entry basis was made by James Aitken during 1861-63 while he was station manager for Philip Russell. Both cases involved an accountability relationship. As stated earlier, William M. Fergusson was found to have maintained ledgers on the double entry basis for John Lang Currie during 1876-81. On the basis of the available records examined, all other financial recording systems maintained to 1875 were not prepared on the double entry basis.

Originating Entry Records

Surviving day and/or cash books were found for 18 entities in the research sample. These books served as originating entry records for the preparation of ledgers in those cases where ledgers were available for examination. For these 18 entities, Table 7.2 shows the dates of the earliest surviving day/cash books examined. Day books were found to be more prevalent in the early decades of pastoral settlement from 1836. Early day books were used to record a wide range of transactions as they occurred such as labour contractual arrangements, purchases, cash and cheque payments, settlements made and received in goods at their current cash equivalents, issues of rations, and receipts from sales. The surviving day books were, in effect, a multi-purpose record of day by day financial dealings with various parties including station workers. Transactions were commonly recorded on a detailed basis and much of this detail was usually transcribed into the ledgers.

On occasions, day books were also used to record certain operating particulars. The Jamieson volume records found for the period 1860 to the early 1880s were prepared in day books. Shearing tally records along with particulars of payments to shearers (1857-58) were recorded in the surviving Hood day book. A certain Beggs Brothers day book (1886-89) stated sheep count figures and particulars of transfers of sheep. However, the prime focus of day books was on the detailed representation in financial terms of dealings of various kinds.

**TABLE 7.2: Nature of Earliest Surviving Originating Entry
Records**

Entity (18)	Dates of Earliest Surviving Day Book	Dates of Earliest Surviving Cash Book	Cash book lags (years) from Dates of Earliest Surviving Day Book
Clyde Company/			
Russell, G	1840	1857	17
Macknight and Irvine		1847	
Miller and Tulloh		1849	
Jamieson	1851	1855(a)	4
Hope	1852	1865	13
Officer	1852		
Mackinnon		1853	
Hood	1856	1881	25
Dennis	1861	1898	37
Ritchie	1866	1886	20
Russell, P		1868	
Armytage	1869	1870	1
Currie		1876	
Beggs		1886	
Robertson/Patterson		1888	
Millear, Maidment			
and Austin/Millear		1889	
Corney		1895(b)	
Russell, T *et al.*		1897	

Mean and Median Lags (years)

Mean Lag			16.7
Median Lag			17.0

Notes:
(a) Details of "cash received" and "paid out" for the six months ended 30 June 1855
     were recorded in a ledger.
(b) A cash account recorded in a ledger recorded receipts and disbursements from 1
     December 1871 to 31 December 1891.

As mentioned earlier, entries recorded in day/cash books to the mid
1870s were found to be commonly entered as a separate process into the
ledger. Only two instances were identified which involved the use of
journal records during this period. A separate journal book was prepared
by George Russell for the Clyde Company from at least 1843 while
journal entries were found to be recorded in the Hood day books during
1856-59 to close particular accounts to the station account. The Clyde
Company records were maintained on the double entry basis while the
Hood records were partially prepared on this basis. Consistent with the
general adoption of recording systems which were not prepared on the
double entry basis, general journals were also uncommon in the period

before the involvement of professional accountants in station accounting.

Cash books commonly detailed receipts and disbursements and were less of an operational record than day books which portrayed transactions involving money and/or goods and, in some cases, certain operating particulars. As such, cash books, particularly in the later decades of the nineteenth century, were often orientated toward the representation of transactions which involved the pastoralist's bank and/or woolbroker as a clearing house. Of the two types of originating records, the earliest day books were found to have been maintained in periods prior to the advent of cash books for those entities whose surviving records included both day and cash books. Table 7.2 shows that cash books followed day books in all seven cases. The mean and median cash book lags as the period between the dates of the earliest surviving day and earliest surviving cash books were determined to be 16.7 years and 17 years respectively. The table also indicates that cash books were the sole originating records from the early 1870s in cases where no earlier originating records were found. The Armytage day book dating from 1869 was the last instance revealed of the later use of cash books.

Control of Expenditure

Some evidence was found of a regard for the control of station expenditure in surviving records to the early 1870s. As discussed earlier in this chapter, the surviving Clyde Company/Russell, G., Dennis, Hood and Russell, P. records provide evidence of an interest in station financial performance. With the exception of the Dennis records, these early records also provide evidence of a concern for the classification of costs into categories of expenditure. The basis for this classification was evidently linked to a desire to maintain control over the costs of the major inputs to pastoral production such as labour, stores, improvements, tools and implements, travelling and sheep dressing. Other evidence to the mid 1870s was found of a concern for the control of expenditure in the absence of evidence of a regard for ascertaining station financial position (Miller and Tulloh, 1848-49; Officer, 1853-56 and 1858). The surviving Miller and Tulloh records show a concern for the classification of costs into categories of expenditure while the surviving Officer records detailed monthly, year to date and calendar year totals of all expenditure (1853-56), and monthly totals only in 1858. Based on all the surviving evidence, the determination and recording of station expenditure on a monthly basis was most uncommon.

Of the five cases identified above as portraying a concern for the control of expenditure (as classified), three of them involved accountability relationships. As station managers, George Russell and James Aitken were dealing with equity interest holders who were based in Britain. In the other case, William France Tulloh, as managing partner (as the evidence suggests), was accountable to his Melbourne-based partner, Henry Miller. Across the entire research sample, it is evident that this focus on the control of expenditure to the early 1870s was not widespread. In the absence of accountability relationships, the evidence suggests a much stronger focus on monitoring the financial status of dealings with particular parties and a later emphasis on making plain the pastoralist's overall cash position through the preparation of cash books.

Involvement of Professional Accountants

Of the surviving evidence which spans various periods during 1836 to 1900, 15 entities were found to have used professional accounting services from 1872. Table 7.3 provides summary details, in ascending date order, of the earliest use of professional accounting services by these 15 entities together with details of later observed involvements of professional accountants in the pre-Federation period. As noted in this table, the earliest observed professional involvement in station accounting was that of solicitor, Stanislaus James Bayly, who performed an audit function in connection with the Estate of Daniel Ritchie from at least 1868. Of the 15 entities detailed in the table, four were identified as having first used professional accounting services in each of the 1870s and 1880s, while seven were found to have first appointed professional accountants in the 1890s. Three accountants provided professional services for 10 of these 15 entities. Peter Wares Tait provided services to five entities while James Gardener and William Henry Tuckett acted for three and two entities respectively. William Henry Tuckett was the only professional accountant named in Table 7.3 found to have been a pastoralist himself. He operated Spring Bank station in the Western District during 1862-69 (Billis and Kenyon, 1974, p.278).

As supported by the findings reported in Chapter 6, the initial appointment of a professional accountant in eight of these 15 cases occurred either immediately on or subsequent to the death of the pioneering pastoralist. The eight cases are as follows (the figures in brackets indicate the lag, if any, in years from date of death to the date of the earliest evidence of the involvement of a professional accountant): Ritchie (8); Armytage; Hope; Beggs (6); Jamieson; Russell, P. (2); Hood (6) and Kininmonth (2). The absence of any lag in the cases of Armytage, Hope and Jamieson conveys the immediate involvement of professional accountants upon the deaths of the pastoral

TABLE 7.3: Use of Professional Accounting Services to Federation

Entity (15)	Year of Earliest Observed Involvement of a Professional Accountant	Name of Earliest Involvement of Professional Accountant	Later Involvements Observed	
			Year	Name
Macknight and Irvine	1872	James Greig(a)		
Ritchie(b)	1873	William Simpson	1874	Simpson & Goldsmith
Currie	1876	William M. Fergusson	1896	Hugh M. Strachan
			1898	Peter Wares Tait(a)
Armytage	1876	William Henry Tuckett J. Wemyss Syme(a)	1882	James K. Bickerton(a)
Hope	1884	William Henry Tuckett		
Mackinnon	1884	Peter Wares Tait		
Beggs	1887	Thomas Edward White		
Black Bros. (& Smith)	1887	W.H. Foley and Joshua Edward Vines(c)	1889	Joshua Edward Vines
Jamieson	1894	Peter Wares Tait		
Russell, P	1894	Ballarat Trustees Executors and Agency Co. Ltd/ Augustus Shepherd(a)	1896	Frederick Downes(a)
Cumming	1895	Peter Wares Tait		
Clyde Company/ Russell, G	1896	James Gardener		
Hood	1897	Peter Wares Tait		
Russell, T *et al.*	1897	AML&F/James Gardener		
Kininmonth	1898	James Gardener		

Notes:
(a)   These involvements were as auditor.
(b)   Stanislaus James Bayly, solicitor, acted in an audit capacity in connection with the Estate of Daniel Ritchie from at least 1868.
(c)   In 1887 and 1888, W.H. Foley acted for the partnership of Black Bros. & Smith while Joshua Edward Vines acted for the Black Bros. partnership.

pioneers involved and the advent of deceased estates. For Ritchie, Beggs, Russell, P., and Kininmonth, the appointment in each case was found to be linked to the death of the pastoral pioneer and the administration of the deceased estate. In the case of Hood, the observed involvement of Peter Wares Tait in 1897 may have been prompted by other considerations such as the advent of Colony of Victoria income tax in 1894. In two of these eight cases (Armytage and Russell, P.), professional accountants were also identified as being involved with the administration of deceased estates in an audit role. Further, Peter Wares Tait was found to have audited the accounts of the Estate of John Lang

Currie. Another case of the involvement of a professional accountant seems to have been influenced by the death of a neighbouring pioneering pastoralist. As explained in Chapter 6, William Cumming was an executor of the Estate of Robert Jamieson who died on 8 November 1894. The executors of this estate appointed Peter Wares Tait to act as accountant on their behalf. The accountant appears to have been appointed to act for the Cumming family in late 1894/early 1895. Thus, the involvement of Peter Wares Tait with the Cumming family seems to have been linked to the death of Robert Jamieson. In total, nine of the 15 cases (or 60 per cent) involving the observed use of professional accounting services in the pre-Federation period were identified as being linked, either directly or indirectly, to the passing of pioneering pastoralists and the consequent advent of deceased estates.

In two of the other six cases, the use of a professional accountant pertained to the operation of pastoral partnerships which involved partners who were not related. The involvement of a professional accountant, as auditor, was found to be linked to the sale of Dunmore station in 1872 and the dissolution of the three-person Macknight and Irvine partnership. There was an apparent need to ensure the partners' settlement was subject to external reference in order to bring the matter to a satisfactory conclusion. The later-constituted entity, Black Bros. (& Smith), comprised different partnerships including that of the Black brothers and John Smith in Grassdale Estate. The appointment of a professional accountant may have been motivated by a desire for the Black brothers to periodically confirm the maintenance of continued trust in their managing partner who was responsible for the day to day financial and operating dealings of the partnership.

Differing factors appear to explain the use of professional accounting services for the remaining four cases of Currie, Mackinnon, Clyde Company/Russell, G., and Russell, T. *et al.* By 1876, John Lang Currie had built Eildon, a substantial St. Kilda residence, and as shown in Chapter 5 had developed a broad range of business interests. From about this time, Currie seems to have devoted less time to the personal supervision of his pastoral interests than was previously the case (*Australasian*, 19 March 1898). The appointment of a professional accountant may have been linked to a desire to maintain control over affairs which had become more subject to the influence of others. As discussed in Chapter 6, the involvement of a professional accountant with the Mackinnon family began in 1884 on the engagement of William Kinross Mackinnon as station manager of Marida Yallock on the retirement of his father, Daniel Mackinnon, from pastoral industry engagement. The 1896 involvement of a professional accountant in the affairs of Clyde Company/Russell, G. followed the death of George

Russell eight years earlier and related to the transfer of control of Golf Hill station from Philip Russell to his sister, Janet. Finally, the involvement of AML&F (effectively James Gardener as the evidence suggests) in accounting for the operations at Barunah Plains was connected with the dissolution of an unhappy partnership between Andrew and James Russell and the sale of Andrew's interest to James in 1897.

Table 7.3 notes the instances where professional accountants were found to be engaged as auditors. In total, six different auditors were identified as being associated with the entities involved. The audit certification statements examined focused on the perceived accuracy of the accounts. Of the six auditors, four used the certification "examined and found correct" while "audited and found correct" was used by another. The statement "found them [the books] to be correct" was written by James Greig in the earliest audit report sighted. James Greig's report contained the only qualified audit opinion as evidenced in his statement, "subject to a few items contingent specified above and in suspense".

As indicated in Chapter 6, the involvement of professional accountants typically heralded periodic accounting and a focus on determining station financial performance and financial position. The annual cycle was adopted in the cases identified except for the Estate of George Hope (1884 to 1900) where the half-yearly cycle was implemented. The professional accountants typically prepared the accounting books on the double entry basis or, where such records were not available, were likely to have adopted double entry accounting based on the comprehensive and detailed nature of the surviving financial statements examined. The emerging focus on measuring underlying attributes of economic activity involved the application of accrual accounting. Accrual accounting normally involved the recognition of debtors and creditors in the accounts. Except in the case of Armytage, the use of day books ceased on the appointment of professional accountants or before. However, in certain cases ledgers structured on a personified basis, or primarily on that basis, continued to be maintained on that basis despite the advent of new financial recording systems introduced by the accountant. As the findings in Chapter 6 show, such personalized ledgers were found to be maintained in the cases of Armytage, Mackinnon, Jamieson and Cumming in respective periods following the engagement of professional accountants on a continuing basis. Of these four cases, only one (Armytage) did not involve the use of the services of Peter Wares Tait. This on-going reliance on personalized ledger structures was evidently central to the operation of a workable system in these station communities for conducting pastoral affairs on a day to day basis.

Where deceased estates were involved, the valuations of assets and liabilities recorded initially in accounting records were commonly those appearing in statements of assets and liabilities lodged with the Master-in-Equity to enable the determination and collection of death duties. Of the eight cases discussed earlier where the first-time appointment of a professional accountant occurred either immediately on or following the death of a pastoral pioneer, five (Armytage; Hope; Jamieson; Kininmonth; Russell, P) involved the use of such valuations in recognising the initial assets and liabilities of the deceased estate in the accounts. In the case of Beggs, such valuations were only listed in the ledger maintained for the Estate of Francis Beggs. In the other two cases (Hood; Ritchie), no conclusions could be made about the use of these valuations for accounting purposes based on the surviving evidence. For Cumming and also Mackinnon, Peter Wares Tait had already provided professional accounting services to these families prior to the death of the pioneering pastoralists but reflected the valuations prepared for the Master-in-Equity in the books of the respective deceased estates where they were different from those already recorded at death. Hence, in a total of seven cases the valuations prepared for the Master-in-Equity were commonly recorded as the initial values of assets and liabilities in the accounts of the deceased estates involved. The mandating of the valuation of assets and liabilities for government revenue collection purposes provided a convenient and reliable means for professional accountants to implement double entry, accrual based accounting systems with a consequent emphasis on the preparation of periodic financial statements.

As mentioned earlier, there were a few cases identified up to the 1870s where statements of financial performance and balance sheets were prepared but only in the case of the Clyde Company/Russell, G. were these found to be a regular feature of station accounting. It was not until the era of the involvement of professional accountants with the pastoral entities identified that such statements with their focus on financial outputs became commonplace in station accounting.

Major Accounting Practices Adopted in Preparing Accounts

The major assets of a pastoral entity are grazing land and livestock. Until the 1860s, most grazing land in the Western District was held under license. Notwithstanding, throughout the pre-Federation period freehold land was found to be valued in accounts on the per acre basis. Alternatively, livestock was found to be valued in accounts on the per head basis at varying amounts for each class of livestock depastured. As the evidence revealed, these assets along with others such as plant, wool, stores, furniture and carriages were often initially brought to account at valuation on the death of a pastoral pioneer. Liabilities such as bank loans, bills payable and creditors including accrued wages were stated at the respective amounts owing as at a particular date. No other liabilities were stated in connection with labour consistent with the absence of a range of employee entitlements in pre-Federation industrial relations.

The accounting practices observed for the major classes of assets in the surviving pre-Federation accounts are summarized in Table 7.4. The table shows there was a propensity for land valuations to be stated in the accounts at per acre values which remained unaltered. This propensity was very strong in cases where professional accountants were engaged. In the cases of Cumming and Mackinnon where professional accountants were involved, the stated per acre values only altered once on the occasion of the death of the respective pastoral pioneer. In the other three instances indentified where stated per acre values varied, no evidence was found of the involvement of professional accountants. Of these, the Clyde Company/Russell, G. (1845-53) and Russell, P. (1861-63) entailed accountability relationships by virtue of foreign ownership and absentee ownership respectively. The third instance of the Clyde Company/Russell, G. (1859-77) did not involve an accountability relationship as was previously in place but involved the use of stable values in the accounts during 1867-77.

Table 7.4 also depicts an almost equal preparedness to record stable and varied per head valuations in the accounts for livestock. Commonly, livestock valuations were determined on the basis of stock numbers at each balance date. However, in the cases of Armytage (1876 to 1900), Hope (1884 to 1900) and Russell, P. (1894; 1896-97; 1901), all of which involved the use of the services of professional accountants, the stated livestock valuations during the respective accounting periods were based on per head values and stock numbers at the commencement of the *initial* accounting period. This practice was at least questionable as stock numbers and per head values undoubtedly altered during these respective periods to 1900. In all three cases, the livestock valuations reported throughout were those recorded in the statements of assets and liabilities lodged with the Master-in-Equity. All three cases also involved the use of stable per acre land valuations as shown in the table. Both Armytage and Hope were clients of William Henry Tuckett.

TABLE 7.4: Accounting Practices for Major Classes of Assets

Entity (12)	Period	Land (per acre valuation)	Livestock (per head valuations)	Improvements	Plant (including tools and implements)	Wool	Stores	Depreciation Advent	Depreciation Class of Assets
Armytage	1876 to 1900	Stable	Stable(a)	Asset	Asset	Asset	Asset (to 1877)		
Black Bros. (& Smith)	1886 to 1900	Stable	Varied	Asset	Asset	Asset	Asset	1887	Improvements / Plant
Clyde Company/ Russell, G	1845-53	Varied	Varied		Asset	Asset	Asset	1859	Improvements
	1859-77	Varied	Varied	Asset					
	1896	Asset	Asset						
Cumming	1895 to 1900	Varied(b)	Varied(b)		Asset / Asset (from 1898)		Asset	1898	Plant
Currie	1876-81	Stable	Stable		Asset				
	1894; 1897	Stable	Stable(c)	Asset	Asset			1894(d)	Various
Hope	1884 to 1900	Stable	Stable(a)	Asset	Asset				
	1893-97	Stable	Stable	Asset	Asset				
Jamieson	1894 to 1900	Stable	Stable		Asset	Asset (only 1898)		1896	Plant
Kininmonth	1899 to 1900	Stable	Stable		Asset	Asset	Asset	1895	Plant
Mackinnon	1885 to 1900	Varied(b)	Varied(b)		Asset	Asset	Asset		
Macknight and Irvine	1869-72	Stable	Varied						
Russell, P	1861-63	Varied	Varied				Asset (1862-63)		
	1894; 1896-97; 1901	Stable	Stable(a)			Asset	Asset		
Russell, T et al.	1897 to 1900	Stable	Varied		Asset	Asset (from 1898)	Asset		

Notes:

(a) Throughout these years, livestock valuations were based on both stock numbers and per head valuations as at the commencement of the *initial* accounting period.

(b) Stated valuations of land (with improvements) and livestock were restated as at the date of death of the pastoral pioneer. No further restatement of land valuations occurred in the respective periods to Federation.

(c) The valuations of Larra sheep and cattle were constant in 1894 and 1897 while the valuations of livestock on other stations varied. It is unclear whether the different valuations in 1897 were due to changes in stock numbers or changes in per head values adopted or both.

(d) Depreciation was incorporated in these balance sheets as a valuation adjustment rather than a process of allocation.

It was found to be accepted valuation practice to include improvements in valuations of station real estate. Statements of assets and liabilities lodged with the Master-in-Equity recorded station land and improvements at a combined valuation. As Table 7.4 shows in the instances of Armytage, Black Bros. (& Smith), Clyde Company/Russell, G. (1859-77), Currie (1894; 1897) and Hope, improvements were recorded in the accounts as a separate class of asset. With the exception of Currie, where no conclusion can be drawn based on the unavailability of the associated ledgers, improvements were stated in the balance sheets of these other four entities at cost. For Armytage and Hope, the improvement costs incurred from the date of death of the respective pastoral pioneer were those capitalized as assets. In the cases of Currie (1876-81), Jamieson, Kininmonth, Macknight and Irvine, Russell, P. (1894, 1896-97, 1901), and Russell, T. *et al.*, the stated land valuations were based on stable per acre land values while the costs of improvements were immediately written off in the accounts. Hence, in these cases improvements undertaken since the initial valuation of station real estate were not regarded as an identifiable financial resource for accounting purposes. The other cases (excluding Clyde Company/Russell, G, 1896) involved the use of varied per acre land values and an implicit recognition of improvements as an asset to the date of the last valuation of station real estate for incorporation in the accounts. Therefore, it is evident there was diversity rather than uniformity in accounting for improvements.

Accounting for the costs of plant including tools and farming implements as assets was found to be a common practice as shown in Table 7.4. In comparison with improvements, the greater tendency to record plant as an asset may have been related to the ability to more readily identify the specific costs involved, whereas the costs of improvements would often include the labour costs of those who also performed regular station duties. Table 7.4 also shows a propensity to record unsold wool and stores as assets in the accounts. However, there was a greater propensity to recognize plant as an asset. The earliest instance of the recognition of depreciation as a process of allocation was observed in 1859. Table 7.4 shows a regard for recognising a depreciation expense on this allocation basis in only four other cases; all of which eventuated in accounting periods following the involvement of professional accountants. The recognition of depreciation expense in three of these four cases followed the advent of Colony of Victoria income tax in 1894 and pertained to plant on each occasion. In all three cases the professional accounting services were rendered by Peter Wares Tait and involved accounting for the affairs of deceased estates.

Although specific classes of assets and liabilities were shown in surviving pre-Federation balance sheets, no evidence was found of the classification of assets or liabilities into current and non-current/fixed categories or any other dichotomy. Hence, items in surviving balance sheets were not grouped to elucidate notions of liquidity.

Minority Accounting Practices

Evidence of the use of accounts to derive return on investment (assets) was found in only two cases (Armytage; Mackinnon). In both cases the services of professional accounting services had been used in periods prior to the time of the return on investment determinations. For Armytage, return on investment was based on average annual profits over a seven-year period (1888-94) while return on investment was determined annually from 1892 in the case of Mackinnon. Only in the case of Armytage was there any evidence found of a concern for budgeting. The budget statement examined was of estimated expenditure (as categorized) for 1882-83. The practice of documenting financial projections for planning and control purposes was evidently uncommon in the period to Federation. While there was scant evidence of written budgets, this does not suggest there was a lack of planning in nineteenth century pastoralism.

Financial Records Lags by Type

An examination of particular financial record lags is necessary to elucidate any varying degrees of urgency in the preparation of different types of financial records. For the purpose of this analysis, the surviving financial records have been classified into three categories as follows: ledgers, day/cash books and financial statements. Table 7.5 shows the lags (in years) from occupation to the earliest surviving financial records categorized by type for all of the 23 entities comprising the research sample.[1] The 17 entities whose surviving financial statements were available for examination include the 12 entities detailed in Table 7.4 along with Beggs, Hood, Millear, Maidment and Austin/Millear, Miller and Tulloh, and Ritchie. As explained in Chapter 6, statements of receipts and disbursements with respect to the income and capital accounts of the Estate of Francis Beggs were prepared in July 1887 for the accounting periods spanning the six and a half years from 29 December 1880. In the cases of Hood, and Millear, Maidment and Austin/Millear the financial records incorporated periodic receipts and disbursements while the only financial statement found for Miller and Tulloh was most probably of this kind. The surviving Ritchie financial records showed periodic profitability during 1895 to 1900 but did not feature any statements of financial position.

TABLE 7.5: Lags from Occupation to the Earliest Surviving Financial Records

Entity (23)	Date of Pastoral Occupation	Ledgers (21)	Day/Cash Books(a) (18)	Financial Statements (17)
Armytage	1857	6	12	19
Beggs	1855	-	31	32
Black Bros. (& Smith)	1885			-
Clyde Company/ Russell, G	1836	-	4	2
Corney	1840	2	55	
Cumming	1856	-		39
Currie	1844	32	32	32
Dennis	1840	-	21	
French	1841	-		
Hood	1854	-	2	-
Hope	1840	44	12	44
Jamieson(b)	1841	3	10	53
Kininmonth	1882	-		17
Mackinnon	1840	13	13	45
Macknight and Irvine	1842		5	27
McIntyre	1843	-		
Millear, Maidment and Austin/Millear	1858	12	31	28
Miller and Tulloh	1845	3	4	3
Officer	1847	5	5	
Ritchie	1842	13	24	53
Robertson/Patterson	1844	32	44	
Russell, P	1843	-	25	18
Russell, T *et al.*	1851	46	46	46

Mean and Median Lags (years)

Mean (c)		10.0	20.9	26.9
Median (c)		3.0	17.0	28.0

Notes:
(a) The financial records lags shown relate to the earliest day book or earliest cash book from occupation or whichever is the shorter period.
(b) The earliest Jamieson financial records (1842) showed details of expenses on supplies which has not been classified for the purposes of this table.
(c) These lags have been calculated on the basis of the numbers of entities in the table heading for each record type.

Table 7.5 also presents the mean and median lags determined for each of these three types of records. Assuming a tendency did not exist for particular types of financial records to be destroyed or discarded while other types were retained, the cross-record differences in the mean and median lags show the urgency was greatest for the preparation of ledger records. In turn, the table shows a greater urgency for the preparation of day/cash books than financial statements, many of which were prepared from the early 1870s by professional accountants. It is possible that ledger records might have been regarded by the descendants of pioneering pastoralists to be of greater interest for heritage purposes than day/cash books. It is also possible that pre-Federation financial statements might have been considered to contain sensitive information and were withheld from lodgement in public collections or were possibly removed from private collections prior to examination. Notwithstanding these possibilities, on the basis of the records available for examination it is generally evident that different degrees of urgency prevailed in the preparation of pre-Federation financial records.

Using the information in tables 7.3 and 7.5, Table 7.6 shows the lags (in years) from occupation to the earliest surviving financial record

TABLE 7.6: Lags from Occupation to the Earliest Surviving Financial Records and the Earliest Involvement of a Professional Accountant

Entity (15)	Date of Pastoral Occupation	Earliest Financial Record Lag	Earliest Professional Accountant Involvement Lag
Armytage	1857	6	19
Beggs	1855	-	32
Black Bros. (& Smith)	1885	-	2
Clyde Company/Russell, G.	1836	-	60
Cumming	1856	-	39
Currie	1844	32	32
Hood	1854	-	43
Hope	1840	12	44
Jamieson	1841	3	53
Kininmonth	1882	-	16
Mackinnon	1840	13	44
Macknight and Irvine	1842	5	30
Ritchie	1842	13	31
Russell, P	1843	-	51
Russell, T *et al.*	1851	46	46
Mean and Median Lags (years)			
Mean		8.7	36.1
Median		3.0	39.0

and the earliest involvement of a professional accountant in station accounting for the 15 entities found to have used professional accounting services to Federation. Of these 15 entities, the earliest surviving financial records pre-dated the earliest observed involvement of a professional accountant in 13 cases. In the other two cases (Currie; Russell, T *et al.*), the respective lags were common. The mean and median lags also recorded in Table 7.6 highlight the magnitude of the variance between the initial focus on financial record keeping and the involvement of professional accountants in station accounting. The discussion now turns to the contents of surviving volume records examined.

Accounting Information of a Non-Financial Operating Nature

The structure and usage of pre-Federation accounting information of a non-financial operating nature is analysed in this section. The surviving volume records have been classified for analysis hereunder into six categories as follows: stores, stock, shearing, bale, wool production and lambing production. There follows an examination of the lags from occupation to the earliest volume records by type and a discussion of the influence professional accountants may have had on the establishment and maintenance of volume record systems.

Stores

As discussed earlier in this chapter, issues of stores to station workers and related costings of issued items were commonly recorded in personal ledger accounts. However, evidence of the preparation of specific records for stores was found in seven cases. The entities involved and the dates of the earliest surviving stores records found are as follows: Clyde Company/Russell, G. (1838); French (1849); Jamieson (1860); Officer (1863); Armytage (1865); Millear, Maidment and Austin/Millear (1867) and Begg (1886). Of these earliest stores records, those of Officer and Armytage comprised particulars of issues of stores while the French records showed details of receipts and issues of stores. The earliest Jamieson stores records showed details of quantities purchased and the related costs of certain store items. The earliest stores records of the Clyde Company/Russell, G., Millear, Maidment and Austin/Millear, and Beggs provide evidence of the adoption of a perpetual inventory system for the control of stores resources. A perpetual inventory system was also evidently adopted in the case of Armytage in 1876. The surviving evidence of the adoption of a perpetual inventory system by Armytage and Beggs relates to the periods following the passing of Charles Henry Armytage and George and Francis Beggs respectively.

The adoption of a perpetual inventory system for stores would have enabled an assessment of the correlation between the physical quantities of store items identified on periodic counting and those which should have been held on the basis of records of receipts and issues from the store. The identification of discrepancies would provide the pastoralist or station manager with an opportunity to mount corrective actions, where necessary, to ensure future losses of stores were minimized.

In the cases of French, Officer, and Millear, Maidment and Austin/Millear, the only specific volume records for stores which appear to have survived relate to 1849, 1864-5, and 1867 respectively. Hence, the only evidence of the maintenance of specific stores records for other than short time spans pertains to the other four pastoral entities mentioned.

Stock

In total, specific records for livestock were found for 15 of the entities in the research sample. The existence of stock records indicates a regard for the control of livestock resources. Table 7.7 shows the date of the earliest surviving stock records examined for each of these 15 cases and provides details of the nature of these records. The earliest surviving stock records found were those of the Clyde Company/Russell, G. dating from 1837. These records show the adoption of a perpetual inventory system for monitoring sheep which were depastured in flocks in a period before the advent of fences. The earliest surviving record of the adoption of a perpetual inventory system for monitoring sheep depastured in paddocks was evidently prepared by the Beggs Brothers in 1860. Table 7.7 and the discussion of the evidence of stock records in Chapter 6 depict the widespread adoption of perpetual inventory systems for livestock. The use of perpetual inventory systems for livestock would have enabled the pastoralist or station manager to assess the magnitude of any stock losses or gains and the degree of any unplanned mixing of stock segmented by flock or paddock. The regular identification of discrepancies would provide evidence of the effectiveness of station workers such as shepherds and boundary riders in supervising livestock and also those workers engaged in the construction and upkeep of fences and gates. The maintenance of stock records would have enabled the verification of the livestock carrying capacity of land for land tax assessment purposes from the time of its introduction in 1877.

TABLE 7.7: Nature of Earliest Surviving Stock Records

Entity (15)	Date of Earliest Stock Records	By Paddock	Description
Clyde Company/			
Russell, G	1837(a)		Perpetual inventory system
Jamieson	1841(b)		Maintained records of livestock numbers/ killed/sold
McIntyre	1843(a)		Regard for perpetual inventory ideas
Hood	1856(b)		Perpetual inventory system
Macknight and Irvine	1856		Emphasis on recording stock movements
Beggs	1860	•(c)	Perpetual inventory system
Millear, Maidment and Austin/Millear	1863	•(d)	Perpetual inventory system
Ritchie	1870	•	Perpetual inventory system
Mackinnon	1872	•	Perpetual inventory system from 1881
Armytage	1876	•	Perpetual inventory system
Hope	1878	•	No reconciliations observed with sheep count figures
Russell, T *et al.*	1880	•	Perpetual inventory system
Kininmonth	1882	•	Perpetual inventory system
Currie	1886	•	Perpetual inventory system
Black Bros. (& Smith)	1887	•	Perpetual inventory system

Notes:
(a) Records maintained for flocks.
(b) Records related to cattle herd.
(c) Records were seemingly prepared on a paddock basis from 1860.
(d) Records are available on a by paddock basis from 1885.

The surviving volume records show that perpetual inventory systems were adopted for both livestock and stores by the following four entities (dates specified in each case are of the earliest livestock and stores records respectively): Clyde Company/Russell, G. (1837/1838); Beggs (1860/1886); Millear, Maidment and Austin/Millear (1863/1867) and Armytage (1876/1876). Except in the case of Beggs, the dates of the earliest surviving records of each type are either identical or only vary slightly. Further, the surviving stock records provide evidence of the practice of recording the numbers of sheep shorn as closing/opening inventory figures. The shearing season provided an opportunity to count sheep (and lambs) and to identify and record any discrepancies based on the details maintained of stock movements since the previous count. Hence, records of shearing tallies and stock records prepared under a perpetual inventory system were interdependent.

Shearing

Surviving records of shearing were found for 11 entities in the research sample. As the discussion in Chapter 6 indicated, such records consisted predominantly of shearing tallies. Table 7.8 shows the date of the earliest surviving shearing records examined for each of the 11 cases and depicts the emphasis on the recording of shearers' tallies. In cases where shearers' tallies were found to be recorded daily or in the single case where they were observed for each flock, the aggregate of each shearer's tally for the season was reconciled with the respective total of sheep shorn in the season. These reconciliations demonstrate a strong regard for the elimination of error in recording.

Shearing tally records were important for at least three reasons. Firstly, because shearers were piece-work contractors paid on the basis of their actual performance in the shed. Hence, the maintenance of accurate records of the quantities of sheep shorn by each shearer was needed to settle contractual arrangements on an amicable basis. Secondly, inefficient and superior shearers could be identified on the basis of their performance during the season, thus enabling future selections of shearers to be informed. Finally, the determination at shearing of sheep numbers for the purpose of determining the effectiveness of controls over livestock resources enabled corrective

TABLE 7.8: Nature of Earliest Surviving Shearing Records Examined

Entity (11)	Date of Earliest Shearing Records	Shearers' Tallies			Shearing Performance Measures	Record of Total Sheep Shorn (By Paddock)	Daily Record of Total Sheep Shorn
		Daily	By Flock	Season Tallies only			
Currie	1846(a)				•(b)		
Clyde Company/ Russell, G	1847	•					
French	1849			•			
Officer	1857	•					
Hood	1857			•			
Ritchie	1869	•					
Armytage	1873			•			
Hope	1879					•	
Millear, Maidment and Austin/Millear	1882	•					
Jamieson	1883	•					
Robertson/Patterson	1887						•

Notes:
(a) The surviving shearing tally records examined date from 1898.
(b) The performance measures recorded were the average shearing per day and the average shearing per man per day.

actions, if any, to be implemented. As mentioned earlier, stock count figures derived at the time of shearing were found to be used as inputs in stock records.

The evidence reported in Chapter 6 of surviving shearing records indicates there was much similarity in the structure of shearing tally records kept at those stations where the daily performance of each shearer was recorded. Further, the evidence shows the structure of the earliest records of shearers' daily performance tended to remain substantially unchanged in later years to 1900. The only evidence found of the determination of shearing performance measures were contained in a comparative report of shearing for Larra (1846-79). This report showed the average numbers of sheep shorn per day and the average shearing per shearer per day over a period of 34 years. However, this comparative report of John Lang Currie is unique in the context of the shearing records examined in this study.

Bale

Surviving bale records were found for a total of 11 entities in the research sample. The nature of the earliest surviving bale record in each of these cases is summarized in Table 7.9. The earliest surviving bale record was of the Clyde Company/Russell, G. for 1846. It recorded for each consecutively numbered bale in the annual clip details of both wool type and bale weight. Subsequent Clyde Company/Russell, G. bale records (1848-56) did not state individual bale weights. The Cumming bale records for 1860 showed the number of bales of

TABLE 7.9: Nature of Earliest Surviving Bale Records

Entity (11)	Dates of Earliest Bale Records	Bale Numbering		Bales per Flock (No Weights)
		Wool Type	Weights	
Clyde Company/ Russell, G	1846	•	•	
Jamieson	1859	•	•	
Cumming	1860	•		•
Officer	1863	•	•	
Ritchie	1866	•	•	
Millear, Maidment and Austin/Millear	1867	•	•	
Russell, P	1870	•	•	
Armytage	1876	•	•	
Kininmonth	1883	•	•	
Robertson/Patterson	1887	•	•	
Mackinnon	1896	•	•	

particular wool types for each of the flocks depastured (12 in all) but did not feature details of individual bale weights. As the discussion in Chapter 6 indicated, the other bale records examined consistently stated individual bale weights along with details of wool types and commonly recorded the total weight of each annual clip.

The recording of individual bale weights on production allowed the pastoralist or station manager to ascertain the overall weight of wool in the annual clip. It also provided a check upon the accuracy of the particular bale weights recorded on dockets provided by woolbrokers. In the absence of specific bale weights any errors in weighing bales at locations distant from the pastoral station may not have been recognized. The bale records which stated individual bale weights show much commonality in their structure. The only variation of note was in connection with the Millear, Maidment and Austin/Millear records which were segmented to show for each wool type the total number of bales and the total weight of the bales involved.

Wool Production

Records of wool production excluding specific bale records were found for 13 entities in the research sample. The surviving records of wool production commonly reflected a range of annual operating statistics and performance measures. Bale records which made plain information about bale weights complemented the wool production records as knowledge of the total weight of production was necessary to determine certain performance measures. Records of shearing tallies also complemented the determination of certain performance measures. The evidence of the types of performance measures found to be used for wool production is summarized in Table 7.10. This table shows the dates of the earliest observed determination of each of the various performance measures based on wool production. Some measures involved the use of non-monetary amounts to portray a key aspect of station productivity. Other measures involved the use of monetary amounts to depict a station financial return.

The average weight of wool per head measure was found to be used in 12 of the 13 cases. The calculation of this most commonly identified measure was dependent upon knowledge of the total weight of production and the total numbers of sheep shorn. Its determination enabled an assessment of station productivity based on wool production. Other key measures in use included the average net proceeds per head (nine cases) and the average proceeds per pound (four cases). These two

TABLE 7.10: Types of Performance Measures Determined for Wool Production(a)

Entity (13)	Average weight per head (12)	Average Return per head			Average Return per pound			Per Bale Ratios		Ram Fleece weights (individual) (2)	Receipts per acre (1)
		Gross (3)	Expenses (2)	Net (9)	Gross (2)	Expenses (1)	Net (4)	Average weight (4)	Net return (1)		
Clyde Company/											
Russell, G	1847			1864			1847	1846			1864
French	1851							1851			
Beggs	1866			1866			1866				
Ritchie	1868			1872				1886			
Millear, Maidment and Austin/Millear	1870	1871	1871	1871			1871				
Russell, P	1871			1871							
Currie	1883			1898	1883				1883	1896	
Kininmonth										1883	
Jamieson	1885										
Officer	1885			1885							
Mackinnon	1895	1895		1895							
Cumming	1895	1898	1898	1898							
Armytage	1899				1886	1886	1886	1876			

Note:
(a)   The dates given are those of the earliest use of each measure identified.

measures involved the use of sales proceeds (gross and/or net) and total sheep numbers or total weight of production respectively. The determination of either of these measures allowed an assessment of station financial return based on wool production. Where either or both of these measures were determined, the average weight of wool per head measure was also found to have been ascertained. Table 7.10 indicates a regard by 10 of the 13 entities involved for the determination of both station productivity and station financial return based on wool production. The average weight per bale ratio (four instances) as a further indicator of station productivity required a knowledge of the total weight of production and the total number of bales, details that were found to be commonly recorded in surviving bale records. Two instances were observed of the determination of individual ram fleece weights, a practice which aided the selection of rams of superior productivity for station stud purposes. The evidence reported in Chapter 6 of the periodic determination of performance measures for wool production would have enabled a longitudinal comparison of station performance. Such periodic determinations would have assisted the pastoralist or station manager in identifying the factors which gave rise to variations in station productivity and station financial return.

As reported in Chapter 6, evidence was also found in four cases (Beggs, Clyde Company/Russell, G; Currie; Russell, P) of the longitudinal comparison of key performance measures for wool production with those ascertained for other stations in the Western District. Only in the case of Currie did the performance comparison solely involve stations under family ownership. The evidence of the types of performance measures used in the inter-station comparative reports examined is summarized in Table 7.11. This table shows the adoption in all four cases of the average weight of wool per head and the average net return per head indicators while the average return per pound (gross and/or net) was used in three of these four cases. The table also demonstrates a reliance for inter-station performance assessment on a range of measures to depict aspects of station productivity and station financial return based on wool production. Only in the case of Beggs did the comparative reports involve less than four different performance measures. Such evidence shows a concern for a prime value-creating process in pastoralism and an apparent need for a better understanding of the determinants of wool production.

TABLE 7.11: **Inter-Station Performance Comparisons for Wool Production**

Entity (4)	Comparison periods (in ascending date order)	Comparison sample size (in total)	Average weight per head	Average return per head		Average return per pound		Net return per bale	Receipts per acre
				Gross	Net	Gross	Net		
Clyde Company/									
Russell, G	1864-73	5	•		•(a)		•(a)		•
Beggs	1877-79	3	•		•				
Russell, P	1873	3						•	
	1877	2	•		•(a)		•(a)		
	1896-1900	5	•	•	•		•		
Currie	1898-1900	2	•		•	•	•		•

Note:
(a)   Presumably the net return per head and per pound measures were determined.

Lambing Production

Stock records which showed numbers of lambs produced in the absence of lambing productivity rates were not regarded as lambing production records in this study because they did not focus on input/output relationships. In total, records which depicted lambing productivity rates based on breeding ewes were found for eight entities in the research sample. The entities involved and the dates of the earliest surviving lambing production records examined are as follows: Clyde Company/Russell, G. (1840); Millear, Maidment and Austin/Millear (1862); Jamieson (1863); Beggs (1868); Ritchie (1871); Armytage (1881); Currie (1887) and Hope (1898). The Clyde Company/Russell, G. records of 1840 showed the overall productivity rate for all flocks and an upper range of productivity for some flocks. The earliest surviving Jamieson lambing records showed an overall lambing rate for all ewes. Except in the case of Millear, Maidment and Austin/Millear, the other surviving lambing records (including the Jamieson records from 1883) showed the lambing productivity rates of ewes in each paddock (or effectively by the ages of ewes) or by age and commonly the overall productivity rate for the season. In the case of Millear, Maidment and Austin/Millear, the surviving lambing productivity records showed the performance of ewes classified as ordinary, selected, and of all breeding ewes on the station.

The determination of lambing productivity rates shows a keenness to make plain another aspect of station productivity. Further, the evidence presented in Chapter 6 of the periodic determination of lambing productivity rates would have permitted a longitudinal comparison of station breeding performance. Such periodic determinations would have enabled the identification of factors which contributed to variations in lambing performance and, of course, to elucidate wool production performance in subsequent periods. Although the evidence shows a concern for inter-station comparative performance for wool production, no such evidence was found for lambing production.

Seven of the eight entities which were found to have prepared records on lambing production also prepared wool production records. The lags (in years) between the dates of the earliest observed preparation of wool production and lambing production records in each of these seven cases are shown below (a minus sign depicts the evidence of the earlier availability of lambing production records). The order of presentation is based on the ascending dates of the availability of lambing production records: Clyde Company/Russell, G. (-6); Millear, Maidment and Austin/Millear (-8); Jamieson (-22); Beggs (2); Ritchie (3); Armytage (5) and Currie (4). The mean variation (in years) is 3.1 years if the impact of the sign is taken into account. Wool production records lagged the lambing production records only in the three earliest cases of surviving lambing production records.

Volume Records Lags by Type

Table 7.12 shows the lags (in years) from occupation to the earliest surviving volume records for each of the 20 entities involved by record type: stores, stock, shearing, bale, wool production, and lambing production. As the table indicates, only stores records and lambing production records were available in the minority of cases. However, these outcomes do not suggest that such records were of lesser importance than others. As indicated earlier, details of issues of stores and any related costings were often included in personal ledger accounts. Although a focus on the recording of stores issues may not have constituted a complete control system over stores resources, it demonstrates a desire for information on the allotment of items and the financial consequences of settlements involving goods rather than money. Further, in some cases where the surviving evidence does not indicate the determination of lambing productivity rates, rough estimates of such may have been gleaned from stock books which recorded quantities of lambs only on a per flock/paddock basis and/or for the overall sheep population. In these cases, reliance may have been placed on such rough estimates even if they were not accurately determined and recorded at the time.

Table 7.12 also shows the mean and median lags for each of these six record types. Assuming all types of pre-Federation volume records were considered to be of equal interest for heritage purposes, the differences in the mean and median lags for certain types of records suggests a greater urgency for the preparation of some forms of records

TABLE 7.12: Lags from Occupation to the Earliest Surviving Volume Records

Entity (20)	Date of Pastoral Occupation	Stores (7)	Stock (15)	Shearing (11)	Bale (11)	Wool Production (13)	Lambing Production (8)
Armytage	1857	6	19	16	19	19	24
Beggs	1855	31	5			11	13
Black Bros. (& Smith)	1885		2(a)				
Clyde Company/ Russell, G	1836	2	1	11	10	10	4
Cumming	1856				-(b)	39	
Currie	1844		42	2		39	43
French	1841	8		8		10	
Hood	1854		2	3			
Hope	1840		38	38			58
Jamieson	1841(c)	19	-	24	-	26	4
Kininmonth	1882		-		1	1	
Mackinnon	1840		32		56	55	
Macknight and Irvine	1842		14				
McIntyre	1843		-				
Millear/Maidment and Austin/Millear	1858	9	5	24	9	12	4
Officer	1847	16		10	16	38	
Ritchie	1842		28	27	24	26	29
Robertson/ Patterson	1844			43	43		
Russell, P	1843				27	28	
Russell, T *et al.*	1851		29				
Mean and Median Lags (years)							
Mean		13.0	14.5	18.7	18.7	24.2	22.4
Median		9.0	5.0	16.0	16.0	26.0	18.5

Notes:
(a) As explained in Chapter 6, these stock records were a continuation of those prepared for the Estate of Niel Black and, before that, for Niel Black himself.
(b) The Mt. Fyans merino stud was established in 1860; the year of construction of the Mt. Fyans woolshed (Cumming, 1992, p.40).
(c) Robert Jamieson acquired the Bolac Plains sheep operation in 1859. Thus, the lags for sheep records have been determined using this date rather than 1841 when the Jamieson brothers depastured cattle.

over others. For instance, the evidence suggests records of stock and stores were generally prepared in advance of other types of volume records while shearing and bale records were generally prepared in advance of records of wool and lambing production. Of course, the determination of performance measures for wool and lambing production required more complex arithmetic calculations than mere addition and subtraction. Table 7.12 also shows that stores, stock, shearing, bale, wool production, and also lambing production records were found for a total of four (Armytage; Clyde Company/Russell, G; Jamieson; Millear, Maidment and Austin/Millear) of these 20 entities, thus signifying the importance of all six types of volume records for pastoral industry engagement at least in these cases.

Influence of Professional Accountants

The influence, if any, of professional accountants on the structure and usage of pre-Federation accounting information of a non-financial operating nature is partly examined in Table 7.13. Table 7.13 details the lags (in years) from the time of initial involvement of professional accountants to the dates of the earliest surviving volume records by type. Of the 20 entities detailed in Table 7.12, there is evidence in five cases only of the earliest surviving volume records of any type dating from the time of initial involvement of professional accountants. With the possible exception of Armytage, where the earliest surviving stock, bale, and wool production records found date from the engagement of William Henry Tuckett in 1876, it is evident that professional accountants generally had virtually no initial influence on the structure

TABLE 7.13: **Lags from Earliest Involvement of Professional Accountants to the Earliest Surviving Volume Records**

Entity (5)	Date of Engagement of Professional Accountant	Stores (-)	Stock (2)	Shearing (-)	Wool Bale (2)	Wool Production (4)	Lambing Production (3)
Armytage	1876		-		-	-	5
Cumming	1895					-	
Currie	1876		10			7	11
Hope	1884						14
Mackinnon	1885				11	10	
Mean Lags (years) (a)						4.3	10

Note:
(a)   Determined for wool and lambing production only.

and usage of surviving accounting information of a non-financial operating nature.

The most discernible possible influence of professional accountants relates to wool production performance records. As shown in Table 7.13, there are four cases including Armytage where the earliest determination of performance measures for wool were found in the respective periods from the initial appointment of professional accountants to 1900. Table 7.13 also provides evidence of three cases including Armytage where the earliest lambing production records were dated in periods following the involvement of professional accountants. However, on taking into account the lengths of the respective lags shown in Table 7.13 for Currie, Hope, and Mackinnon, it is evident in at least these cases that the possible influence of professional accountants on the structure and usage of non-financial operating information is problematic.

The involvement of professional accountants in station accounting may have resulted in a decreased reliance on non-financial operating information for pastoral industry engagement in cases where the accountant concentrated on the implementation of double entry accounting systems and the determination of financial outputs. However, the findings reported on a case by case basis in Chapter 6 do not elucidate any dismantling of volume record systems that were in place on the initial involvement of professional accountants or any enhancement of the pre-existing systems of this genre.

Combined Use of Financial and Volume Records

With a focus on the earliest surviving accounting records, this section addresses the combined use of financial and volume records in pre-Federation pastoral industry engagement. In particular, the degrees of urgency for the preparation of major types of financial and volume records (as previously identified) are analysed. Also included in this section is an analysis of the nature of the earliest performance records identified in cases where performance was observed to be measured in both financial and non-financial operating terms in the period to Federation.

The foregoing discussion highlights the preparation of financial and volume records in pre-Federation pastoral industry engagement. Based on the earliest surviving financial and volume records, it is evident that varying degrees of urgency prevailed in the preparation of certain types of records. The combined evidence of mean and median lags from occupation for both financial and volume records shown in tables 7.5

and 7.12 respectively, and summarized in Table 7.14, provides some
pertinent insights.

TABLE 7.14:   Ranking of Mean and Median Lags from
               Occupation   to   the   Earliest   Surviving
               Financial and Volume Records

Record Types	Mean Lags	Ranking	Median Lags	Ranking
Ledgers	10.0	1	3.0	1
Stores	13.0	2	9.0	3
Stock	14.5	3	5.0	2
Shearing	18.7	4	16.0	4
Bale	18.7		16.0	
Day/Cash books	20.9	5	17.0	5
Lambing production	22.4	6	18.5	6
Wool production	24.2	7	26.0	7
Financial statements	26.9	8	28.0	8

This table depicts the rankings of the mean and median lags (in years)
for nine different record types. The rankings specified of the mean and
median lags are generally consistent and show that ledgers were
generally relied upon for pastoral industry engagement by the entities
involved at an earlier time than any other types of records. In ascending
median lag order, the table shows the early use of stock records followed
by stores records in time. The lags ascertained for shearing and bale
records and day/cash books follow and are similar. There follows
evidence of the later preparation of records of lambing and wool
production performance. The mean and median financial statements
preparation lags were both ranked last and were 16.9 (mean) years and
25.0 (median) years subsequent to the lags determined for ledgers. In
general, a lesser urgency was found to exist for the preparation of
records which focused on performance measurement in financial and
non-financial operating terms.

Table 7.14 indicates a general focus on measuring lambing and
wool production performance subsequent to when certain key statistics
were first made plain in volume records. Records such as stock books,
shearing tallies and bale books reflected the operating statistics
necessary for the determination of the performance measures found to be
determined. Personalized ledgers or those prepared primarily on a
personified basis were not intended to facilitate the preparation of
periodic profit and loss statements and balance sheets. Although some
early pre-Federation ledgers were structured to facilitate the periodic
preparation of financial statements, it is evident that the involvement of

professional accountants from the early 1870s resulted in the wider preparation of periodic statements of financial performance and financial position.

In total, there were 17 entities whose surviving records included one or more of the following four types of performance records: lambing production, wool production, shearing performance and financial statements. As the findings in Table 7.14 relates to the entire research sample, it is necessary to analyse the nature of the earliest surviving performance records prepared in cases where performance was found to be measured in both periodic profit and also other terms. Table 7.15 shows the lags (in years) from occupation to the earliest performance records for the 12 entities whose surviving records included financial statements and one or more of the following types of records: lambing production; wool production and shearing performance. Of these 12 entities, five (Armytage; Clyde Company/Russell, G; Hope; Mackinnon; Russell, P.) involved accountability relationships at the time the earliest surviving performance records were prepared. In four of these cases, the earliest surviving performance records depicted periodic profit while the earliest surviving financial statements and other performance records were prepared in the same year in the other case. Of the remaining seven cases, six were found to have involved the earlier preparation of performance measures of a non-profit nature while in the other case the earliest surviving financial statements and other performance records were prepared in the same year. These findings indicate that financial statements were generally not prepared with the

TABLE 7.15: Lags from Occupation to the Earliest Surviving Performance Records

Entity (12)	Date of Pastoral Occupation	Lambing Production (8)	Wool Production (11)	Shearing Production (1)	Financial Statements (12)
Armytage	1857	24	19		19
Beggs	1855	13	11		32
Clyde Company/ Russell, G	1836	4	10		2
Cumming	1856		39		39
Currie	1844	43	39	2	32
Hope	1840	58			44
Jamieson	1841	4	26		53
Kininmonth	1882		1		17
Mackinnon	1840		55		45
Millear, Maidment and Austin/Millear	1858	4	12		28
Ritchie	1842	29	26		53
Russell, P	1843		28		18

same degree of urgency as other station performance measures in those cases where accountability relationships did not exist.

Conclusion

In the absence of accountability relationships, the evidence suggests that the nature of accounting information required for pre-Federation pastoral industry engagement was a blend of various types of non-financial operating statistics and also financial particulars of the state of dealings with those parties who were connected with the station community. Following the establishment of records of non-financial operating statistics, there emerged a general focus on the use of such statistics to measure lambing production and wool production performance. This focus on input/output relationships in physical unit terms was evidently regarded as appropriate, if not essential, for assessing major aspects of station productivity. Some wool production measures also involved the use of monetary amounts (sales) to depict an annual station financial return based on either inputs (sheep shorn) or outputs (per pound) or both. Personalized ledgers provided information relating to the status of financial dealings with others and represented a combined debtors' and creditors' record and effectively provided a lifetime record of station activity from an individualized perspective. There was little evidence of a regard for expenditure control in the absence of accountability relationships. Instead, there appeared to be a stronger focus on the maintenance of records of cash position.

The type of information required for accountability purposes and for government levy collection purposes had a stronger financial focus with a much greater emphasis on statements of financial performance and position. There was also an emphasis on expenditure control where accountability relationships existed in periods preceding the involvement of professional accountants. The initial involvement of professional accountants in station accounting was often connected with the death of the pastoral pioneers. The introduction of death duties in 1870 and the need to prepare and lodge a statement of assets and liabilities with the Master-in-Equity to enable the determination and collection of death duty acted as a spur on many occasions for the appointment of professional accountants. The advent of deceased estates also brought an obligation for executors, as stewards, to account for the resources under their effective control. The further requirement to report financial information to the Colonial government from 1894 for income tax purposes also generally sharpened the focus in the period to Federation on the measurement of financial outputs and sharpened the propensity to recognize depreciation as an expense in the accounts.

The advent of double entry accounting and periodic financial statements were not necessarily seen to be a superior means of running the stations internally. This would explain why the pre-existing volume recording systems and, on occasions, the simpler financial recording systems were retained for day to day station operations. As indicated earlier, the external reporting systems introduced by professional accountants were added as an overlay in some cases. In accounting for assets there was a propensity for professional accountants to use values which were either constant or subject to infrequent change. This preference for stating steady values was particularly evident for land and, to a lesser degree, for livestock. In some cases, livestock values were repeatedly based on both the stock numbers and per head values as at the commencement of the *initial* accounting period. The adoption of such valuation practices, especially on entering the 1890s when land values and livestock prices were generally depressed, had the potential at least to delimit the relevance of the financial statements involved and suggests that they may not have been central to financial decision making. Despite the increased emphasis on the preparation of statements of financial performance and financial position during the last three decades of the pre-Federation period, periodic profit results were not commonly featured in the surviving inter-station comparative reports examined. Instead, there was an emphasis on inter-station performance comparisons for wool production. Such performance measures were possibly perceived to be more cogent indicators of station productivity and return than those based on the capital/income dichotomy.

The findings show that the influence of professional accountants on accounting change was primarily related to financial records. The impact of professional accountants on the structure and usage of accounting information of a non-financial operating nature, in general, was evidently negligible. In one or two cases, professional accountants possibly influenced the implementation of wool production and lambing production records. Whatever impact, if any, professional accountants had on the establishment of volume recording systems and the use of measures of non-financial operating performance, it did not result in a paradigm shift as found to occur on their involvement with financial recording systems. Notwithstanding this paradigm shift, there was evidence in only two cases of the use of accounts to ascertain return on investment (assets). Professional accountants also did not appear to focus on the preparation of financial or production budgets as there was only one case found of a concern for budgeting (which was of limited focus concerning estimated expenditure). What scope existed for documenting projections for planning and control purposes appears to have been overlooked by the professional accountants involved.

Having depicted the structure and usage of pre-Federation pastoral accounting information based on the findings reported in Chapter 6, the next chapter endeavours to provide explanations for the accounting practices observed.

NOTES

1. Tables 7.5, 7.12, 7.13 and 7.14 are based on Tables II, III, IV and V respectively in Carnegie (1995, pp.10, 14 & 17-18).

PART III

PROBABLE EXPLANATIONS AND
CONCLUSION

CHAPTER 8

EXPLANATIONS FOR ACCOUNTING PRACTICES

This chapter attempts to provide explanations for the pre-Federation pastoral accounting practices observed in this study. In particular, it endeavours to identify and discuss the key factors which appear to have impacted on the structure and usage of accounting information prepared for pre-Federation pastoral industry engagement in the Western District. The identification and discussion of key environmental factors of the genre addressed in Chapter 2 draws upon the examination of the nineteenth century pastoral industry environment and station environment presented in Chapter 3 and the backgrounds of those pastoralists whose surviving records comprise the research sample as provided in Chapter 4. This study recognizes that accounting is an element of the organizational and social context and is influenced by factors specific in location and time. Although generalized conclusions are drawn about the likely impact of cultural, legal and political, professional, educational, economic and other factors, there is no attempt to rank these factors in any order of importance.

Cultural
As evident in Chapter 2, there is a growing literature on the impact of culture in shaping the accounting environment of a country. It is a logical development of this literature for accounting historians to examine culture as one of a range of major environmental factors to assist in explaining bygone accounting practices in a local, time-specific context.

The accounting literature elucidates the structuring of ledgers on a personified basis prior to the development of records beyond mere personal accounts (Littleton, 1933, pp.49-61; Jackson, 1956, pp.295-302). As found in this study, pre-Federation ledger records were commonly prepared on a personified basis or primarily on that basis in the absence of accountability relationships. The advent of accountability relationships typically brought accounting change in the structure and usage of financial information, although in certain cases where double entry bookkeeping systems were introduced the personalized ledger systems already in place continued to be used for day to day station operations.

Pastoral accounting records emerged in early days of European pastoral settlement when conditions were harsh. An elucidation of the harshness of the conditions in the Western District was provided by Norman Dennis of "Tarndwarncoort" in an oral history interview held on 3 December 1990 as follows:

> It has to be remembered that these people [early settlers] had no idea of the type of season they were coming to, the productivity of the land, the severity of the droughts, the wetness of the winters and the coldness of the winds. They probably lived pretty much by a pick and an axe and a skinning knife. They had the anxiety of the Aboriginals and their spears, they had the anxiety of the Aboriginals hunting, fires getting out of hand and also had the anxiety of whether or not they'd be able to sell their wool, if they could get it to the market. With bookkeeping I daresay it was just the barest essentials (Carnegie, 1990).

The "barest essentials" in terms of financial records were commonly personalized ledger systems which met the information needs of the pastoralist or station manager in communities of settlers where there undoubtedly existed a sense of camaraderie in the difficult, isolated conditions.

The personification of pastoral ledger records can be explained as reflecting an organisational culture in an isolated environment where Western District stations were interdependent communities comprising station personnel including itinerant workers under the overall direction and care of a pastoralist. Such isolated communities had varying populations ranging to over one hundred people whose combined efforts resulted in the development of typically substantial pastoral holdings in periods before the advent of inland Western District towns. In an oral history interview held on 1 August 1991, Robert Jamieson III of "Stony Point" (son of Robert Jamieson the younger) at the age of 88 years stated that "the stations used to be the local community in several ways because they had a lot of people there" (Carnegie, 1990-91). Pastoralists would be conscious of their role as providers which would extend to the provision of facilities and rewards involving money and goods to attract and retain capable and trustworthy people to serve in the development of the station and the pastoral industry generally. Robert Jamieson III also stated in the same interview that his grandfather "realised that if you were going to have the place [station] well run, you want to get the right sort of people if you could".

Under the cultural perspective adopted in this study, personalized ledgers appeared to be symbolic of the station culture which shaped the world views of the pastoralist. Within isolated interdependent station communities, station accounting appeared to be dominated by world views that reflected an organisational culture of interpersonal communal exchanges and the pastoralist's paternalistic control of the station community. It follows that personalized ledgers came to define and were defined by the organizational culture as the context within which world views are determined. The personalized ledgers reflected a commitment to make plain the financial positions of dealings with station personnel and other parties involved with the station community. The propensity to personify ledger accounts indicates that accounting information was seen to be necessary to reflect and exercise financial control over a range of dealings with those connected with the pastoralist's community.

As discussed in Chapter 3, there developed from around the mid 1850s a culture referred to as colonial liberalism which embodied the rejection of world views implicit in settler capitalism. Settler capitalism was particularly rejected by a growing number of people in Melbourne and country towns. Within these urban communities, the prevailing world views represented a national culture which, as discussed in Chapter 3, brought Western District pastoralists generally into conflict with their colonial liberalism adversaries. From 1870 onwards, world views implicit in colonial liberalism brought economic consequences on the death of the pastoral pioneer. These broader community views appear to have affected station accounting by means of the application of legislation which reflected the rejection of the notion of settler capitalism. (An examination of legal and political factors follows.)

National culture also seems to explain the practice of "rendering account" by persons who, as accountors, report on the nature and consequences of their activities to accountees. From an early time in England, the procedure of rendering account was a common law requirement for a variety of agents (Mills, 1990, p.62). As pointed out by Mills (1990, p.62) "although the requirement was non-statutory in origin, medieval legislation helped to institutionalize various aspects of the process and provided for severe remedies if an agent refused examination". As discussed in Chapter 2, the obligation to account in England was enforced by the courts by means of a system of writs. Thus, rendering account by accountors in accountability relationships is a long-standing tenet of English society and has been formulated at law as a function of national culture. As New South Wales and subsequently Victoria were British Colonies among others in Australia, this acceptance of rendering account was implicit in the colonial era and also formulated at law under the Australian legal system which was modelled on the English legal system.

Under the cultural perspective encompassed in this study, the preparation of financial statements in cases where accountability relationships existed seemed to be symbolic of the national culture which shaped the world views of the parties involved. Hence, the act of preparing periodic financial statements for accountees appeared to reflect a culture of rendering account in business dealings involving accountors and accountees. The form and content of the financial statements prepared in such circumstances was evidently affected by a range of factors including the requirements of accountees or their "home" agents, the educational background of accountors, the use or not of professional accounting services, and also government requirements. These factors will be addressed in more detail in the following sections of this chapter. The financial statements provided information on an accountor's stewardship of the resources under control and at least permitted accountees to periodically reassess their level of confidence and trust in accountors.

It seems that the personalized ledger systems prevalent in cases where accountability relationships did not exist may not have been regarded as ideal by those involved in banking and professional accounting. They held world views that reflected their particular training and/or experience. By way of illustration, in 1873 Soilleux (a Jamieson family banker) cast doubt as to whether the personalized ledger system would enable a "fair statement" to be prepared. In the case of professional accountants, double entry accounting systems were found to be introduced or were evidently adopted (in cases where ledgers were not available) at the time of their initial involvement in station accounting. In many cases, the involvement of professional accountants was motivated by the Victorian Government's interest in personal wealth and income by means of the imposition of death duties and income tax respectively, and by their capacity and preparedness to produce periodic financial statements for accountability purposes. (An examination of this professional factor is made later in this chapter.) Although professional accountants appointed to act for the Armytage, Cumming, Jamieson and Mackinnon families introduced systems of accounting to conveniently produce financial information to satisfy the expectations or needs of parties external to the respective families, personalized ledgers continued to be used within the station community for running pastoral affairs on a day to day basis. In effect, the evidence of the existence of two financial accounting systems in periods following the engagement of professional accountants portrays the station micro-community as an important cultural influence throughout the period to Federation.

Legal and Political

A possible early influence on the volume records maintained from 1839 was the legislation, as discussed in Chapter 3, which introduced a stock assessment. This legislation required the reporting on a six-monthly basis of livestock numbers to the colonial government. The legislation did not mandate the keeping of livestock records but sanctions were provided for under the Act for making false declarations or statements. (For illustrative purposes, the official form completed under the Act in the case of the Clyde Company/Russell, G. for the half year ended 31 December 1839 is reproduced in Appendix B.) The adoption of the practice of recording livestock numbers in stock records from 1839 would have been perceived as important for evidence purposes alone if not also for livestock monitoring purposes. As evident in Appendix B, the Act also imposed a type of regular census in the form of six-monthly reporting of the names of those persons who were "on the establishment". This requirement may have contributed to the propensity to personify ledger records as there was a need to monitor changes in station population in personalized terms.

The passage of legislation in the 1870s imposing death duties and also land tax on estates only in excess of 640 acres were products of colonial liberalism. These levies imposed economic burdens on pastoralists and other wealth holders to contribute in desired portions to the financing of public services and also facilities including the development of the colony's infrastructure. The later introduced, but more broadly applicable, colonial income tax also had economic consequences for large-scale pastoralists as they were not exempted from paying income tax even though they were also subject to land tax.

The advent of land tax in the Colony of Victoria did not have implications for the structure and usage of pastoral accounting information of a financial nature as grazing land was independently valued for assessment purposes based on the per acre carrying capacity of the land. Hence, the advent of land tax on certain estates did not necessitate the preparation of any financial information for the colonial government. However, as shown in this study, the legislation which introduced death duties in the colony impacted on the structure and usage of accounting information of a financial nature. However, this impact was staggered because the advent of accounting change was linked to the mortality of the pastoral wealth holders. In the case of income tax, taxpayers including pastoralists were affected from 1895 on the advent of this fund raising measure. In fact, the increased propensity to recognize depreciation as an expense in pastoral accounting records appears to have been linked to the deductibility of depreciation under the colonial income tax legislation.

It is clear that legislation was necessary to command the payment of levies assessed on pastoralists in the colonial period. However, the influence of national culture on the nature of legislation introduced and the consequences of legislative change on accounting should not be ignored. In effect, political factors masquerade for prevailing world views. As a chain of impacts, cultural change influences political change which in turn influences legislative change which in turn influences accounting. At the onset of new legislation, it follows that the advent of any accounting systems introduced to enable compliance with that legislation is symbolic of the national culture as the context within which prevailing world views are determined. The role of state agencies in accounting development has also been illustrated in the Australian Royal Charter attempts made in the early decades of the twentieth century (Chua and Poullaos, 1993; Poullaos, 1993, 1994).

Professional

Based on the research sample, the availability of professional accounting skills in the Colony had an impact on pastoral accounting in the Western District from the early 1870s. Until 1887, accounting services were provided in Victoria in the absence of any professional accounting bodies.[1] As indicated in Chapter 1, the advent of an organized accounting profession occurred in the Colony of Victoria on the formation of The Incorporated Institute of Accountants, Victoria (IIAV) which was incorporated under the *Companies Statute* 1864 on 1 March 1887 as a company limited by guarantee (Macdonald, 1936, p.11). Notwithstanding, pre-1 March 1887 practitioners who were perceived as competent comprised a group of people whose training and/or experience in accounting shaped their world views.[2] These world views of the preferred structure and usage of accounting information constituted a "professional culture". From the early 1870s, pastoral accounting became progressively influenced by a professional culture as circumstances came about which necessitated the involvement of professional accountants. Emerging from this culture came the IIAV and later constituted accounting bodies in Victoria. The objects of the IIAV were stated in clause 3 of the Memorandum of Association to be:

(A) To aim at the elevation of the profession of Accountants by the dissemination of professional knowledge and the inculcation of sound practice.

(B) To increase the confidence of the banking mercantile and general community in the employment of recognised

     Accountants and Auditors by admitting to the Institute such persons only as shall in future save as hereinafter provided pass satisfactory examinations in the theory and practice of the work, and by the prevention of illegal and dishonourable practices.
(C) To afford means of reference for the amicable settlement of professional differences and to decide upon questions of professional usage and etiquette.
(D) To promote good feeling and friendly intercourse amongst the members.
(E) To watch over and promote the interests of the profession generally (IIAV, 1887, pp.7-8).[3]

     The merits of local professional accounting bodies were expressed by Thomas Brentnall,[4] a pioneer accountant in Melbourne and foundation member of the IIAV, who stated:

    It was gradually borne in upon a few of us that if those who were holding themselves out as public practitioners were to gain the confidence and support of the public, there must be a standard fixed which would connote the possession of the necessary qualifications for this special work. To that end a meeting was held on April 12, 1886, at which thirty practising accountants met to consider the propriety of establishing an "Association of those having kindred interests in their common calling, and a desire to place their profession on a higher plane than it had previously occupied in public esteem." We knew the position attained by the Institute of Chartered Accountants in England and Wales, which had been incorporated by Royal Charter in 1880, by the Society of Accountants and Auditors in 1885, as well as the three Scottish Institutes which had come into existence some years previously. With these examples before us, we had no difficulty in arriving at the conclusion that our object could best be attained by following their footsteps (Brentnall, 1938, p.64).

     As pointed out in Chapter 2, this concept of how members of a social stratum establish and preserve their status, and how collective social mobility is attained is commonly known as "social closure" (Larson, 1977; Macdonald 1985, p.54).
     As hinted by Brentnall (1938, p.64), Australian accountants were active importers of the British model rather than the American model of the accounting profession which resulted in the inevitable proliferation of bodies (Parker, 1989, pp.12-19; Carnegie, 1993, pp.61-62; Parker & Carnegie, 1997). As indicated in Chapter 1, The Australian Institute of Incorporated Accountants (AIIA) was Victoria's second professional accounting body and was based in the Western District throughout its

life span of 46 years. (An inventory of surviving primary records of the AIIA held by the Victorian Public Records Office is shown in Appendix C). The AIIA was incorporated on 13 December 1892 under the *Companies Act* 1890 as a company limited by guarantee and was dissolved in 1938. Originally based at Port Fairy, a coastal town in the Western District, the headquarters of the AIIA were relocated to the inland city of Ballarat on 28 June 1893. Of its foundation membership of 55, 60 per cent resided in the Western District. The objects of the AIIA were similar to those of the IIAV and stated in clause 3 of the Memorandum of Association to be:

(A) To provide an Organisation to which all Accountants of first rate ability and standing may be admitted on a footing of equality and fairness.

(B) To make strong and permanent effort to advance the rank of the practice of Accountancy from its present general acceptance - that of a mere calling - to what the Institute conceives it should be received as - viz., one of the learned professions.

(C) To consequently prescribe and insist upon - by adequate examination and enquiry - a high standard of attainments and personal character, without which no accountant shall be entitled to the *imprimatur* of the Institute; thus affording a strong guarantee as to the ability of its members to efficiently discharge the important duties they are called upon to perform.[5]

(D) To exercise watchful care over the advancement and welfare of the profession - by taking pains to diffuse the latest progressive ideas on points of professional practice, as well as sound information generally; by acting when it may be so requested as a friendly arbiter of professional disputes; and generally by constituting itself a genial safe-guard of the interests of its members, as well as a promoter of good fellowship among them (AIIA, 1892).

Of the professional accountants identified in Table 7.3, four were foundation members of either the IIAV or the AIIA. William Henry Tuckett and James Knight Bickerton were foundation members of the IIAV (IIAV, 1887, p.5). Peter Wares Tait and Frederick Courthorpe Downes were founding members of the AIIA (AIIA, 1892).[6] William Henry Tuckett was appointed to act for both the Armytage and Hope families prior to the advent of the IIAV in 1887. James Knight Bickerton was engaged to act as auditor for the Estate of Charles Henry Armytage also before 1887. Peter Wares Tait was engaged by the Mackinnon family in 1884 while his other four pastoral engagements identified by reference to surviving business records examined in this study (Cumming; Currie; Jamieson; Hood) all began after the establishment of the AIIA in 1892. Frederick Courthorpe Downes was, among other auditing engagements, auditor of the Ballarat Trustees Executors and Agency Co. Ltd and acted as auditor for the Estate of Philip Russell in periods after 1892. In summary, this analysis shows professional accounting services were provided to Western District pastoralists by at least three of these four accountants in periods prior to the advent of the IIAV and AIIA. However, the development of their accounting practices, particularly in the case of Peter Wares Tait, may have been enhanced as a consequence of becoming a member of a local professional accounting body.

Chapter 7 identified the circumstances, as far as possible, leading to the appointment of professional accountants for the 15 entities involved in the research sample. The most common reason for their appointment was the advent of deceased estates. The introduction of death duties in 1870 and the requirement to prepare and lodge statements of assets and liabilities for duty assessment purposes brought economic consequences for the pastoral families involved. Of course, the advent of deceased estates also brought an obligation for accountors to report the consequences of their activities to accountees. Once involved in pastoral accounting by means of the preparation of statements of assets and liabilities, professional accountants were prepared to assist accountors in periodically discharging obligations under accountability relationships and, from 1895, were further willing to assist pastoralists in preparing annual income tax returns for the colonial government. Oehr (1899) provides evidence that executorship accounting roles were sought by professional accountants in pre-Federation Victoria.[7] As reported in Chapter 7, accountability relationships also existed in various other cases involving the use of professional accountants in pastoral accounting. Overall, legal and political factors and/or a culture of rendering account in business dealings appear to have been the main determinants for the engagement of professional accountants. However, once appointed, professional accountants focused on generating financial outputs under double entry accounting systems which were symbolic of a professional culture. Professional culture was intended to be captured and monopolized by those who sought social closure on the advent of an organized accounting profession.

As pointed out in Chapter 1, Musson (1893) and subsequently other authors stressed the importance for pastoralists to maintain a "proper" set of books. Most of these authors proposed double entry accounting systems for pastoralists. At a colonial government level, the Under Secretary of the New South Wales Department of Agriculture and Mines in 1894 stated:

> Without a proper system of bookkeeping many an agriculturalist
> may go heedlessly and ignorantly on to bankruptcy, as lacking a
> knowledge of how accurately to keep his accounts, he cannot
> ascertain his position, whereas by a properly maintained system
> of bookkeeping he would be able to ascertain his financial
> position at once, and so prevent so serious a catastrophe as
> bankruptcy (Hawkesbury Agricultural College Annual Report,
> 1894, p.6 as cited in Juchau, 1993, p.59).

Of course, this emphasis in the literature on "proper" accounting
systems was based on the view that many pastoral recording systems
then in place were "improper". Based on surviving business records,
this study has provided evidence of the combined preparation of
financial and non-financial operating information in pre-Federation
pastoral industry engagement with an emphasis on the use of this
information for day to day station operations. Although pre-existing
financial recording systems appear to have been fit for their intended
operational purpose, it is evident that documented and other calls for
pastoral accounting reform in Australia had a favourable impact on the
demand for accounting services and, hence, the fee earning potential of
professional accountants including those prepared to provide services to
Western District pastoralists.

As mentioned earlier, the influence of professional accountants on
pastoral accounting change was particularly evident in the case of
financial records. This emphasis on the preparation of financial
information is also very strongly evident in the nature of questions set
for "Book-keeping" examinations conducted by the IIAV during 1891-
1899.[8] An investigation of the content of these surviving examination
papers showed a total emphasis on the financial accounting function. (A
summary of the content of examination papers on "Book-keeping" held
by the IIAV during this period is presented in Appendix D). As is noted
in Appendix D, the first questions to include the item depreciation in
the surviving "Book-keeping" examination papers appeared in 1894, the
first year for which returns of income were required to be prepared under
the Colony's income tax legislation which permitted depreciation to be
treated as an allowable deduction.[9] Appendix E presents a reproduction
of the earliest question specifically on station accounting found in the
surviving "Book-keeping" examination papers which appeared in the
Associates' Examination conducted in June 1898. This question required
the preparation of station accounts for a pastoral partnership. It is
evident that the IIAV's members (and certainly all or the majority of
those on the body's Examining Committee) perceived a need for
prospective members to be proficient in using double entry
bookkeeping to prepare accounts and present financial statements. The

lack of focus in examinations on evaluating input/output relationships in physical terms may assist in explaining why the impact of professional accountants generally on the structure and usage of the pastoral accounting information of a non-financial operating nature was found to be seemingly negligible in this study.

Further elucidation of a lack of concern by pre-Federation professional accountants for the evaluation of performance in physical terms is found in the first and second editions of Vigars's *Station Book-keeping: A Treatise on Double Entry Book-keeping for Pastoralists and Farmers* published in 1900 and 1901 respectively. An associate member of the Corporation of Accountants of Australia (CAA) by 1902, Vigars (1901, p.4) intended this book to "aid towards a complete system of Book-keeping being more largely adopted upon Stations and Farms".[10] In addition to providing a descriptive list of books used in double entry bookkeeping in both these editions, Vigars presented a descriptive list of other books which "may be recommended" for the pastoralist (1900, pp.10-11; 1901, pp.10-11). These other books included a store day book, wool book, shearer's tally book, and also sheep, cattle, and horse paddock books. Apart from providing a specimen of a sheep paddock book in the first edition (1900, pp.70-71) and presenting an example of posting the entries in the store day book to the ledger in the second edition (1901, pp.82-83), there was no further discussion or illustration of these other books. No guidance of any kind was given on how the information recorded therein could be used for station performance measurement purposes. It is evident that Vigars was particularly concerned with the wider adoption of "a complete system of [double entry] Book-keeping" by pastoralists rather than with a balanced focus on financial and non-financial operating information.

Many professional accountants in pre-Federation Victoria and other Australian colonies may have possessed little or no knowledge of internal accounting techniques or what is now referred to as "management accounting". The early literature on accounting concentrated on "external accounting" with little or no coverage of internal accounting techniques (Boyns & Edwards, 1996, p.27). For example, the earliest known printed book on accounting published in Australia by Dimelow (1871-73) at Ballarat titled *Practical Book-keeping Made Easy* did not feature any examination of internal accounting techniques (Carnegie & Parker, 1994), nor did the first-known accounting book published in Melbourne by Wild (1874) titled *Book-keeping by Double Entry Made Easy* (Carnegie & Varker, 1995).[11] Even in the more highly industrialized Britain, there was no specific literature on internal accounting techniques until the late 1880s (Fleischman & Tyson, 1993, pp.505-506; Parker, 1969, p.20). Prior to this time, knowledge of internal accounting techniques was acquired through means such as parental influence, working under skilled supervision, and factory or other site visits.[12]

The accuracy of books maintained or audited by professional accountants in the nineteenth century was seen to be of paramount importance by the practitioners themselves (Oehr, 1899, p.298; Strangward, 1899, p.222).[13] As evidenced in this study, audit certification statements focused on the correctness of the accounts examined. Such a focus is borne out in a legal case involving Thomas Brentnall as a witness. As recollected by Brentnall (1938, p.81), the following dialogue between the judge and himself occurred:

> "Mr Brentnall, are you prepared to stake your reputation as an accountant upon the accuracy of your statements as set forth in the report?" "Yes, your honour." "Then I have no further comment to make. The case is dismissed."

Although Musson was a scientist (Juchau, 1993, p.59), he also argued the virtues for books to be "in themselves neat and precise" (Musson, 1893, p.186). A concern for objective information seems to explain the propensity for professional accountants involved in pre-Federation pastoral accounting to repeatedly use dated valuations for certain assets such as pastoral land in preference to current values which might have been regarded as unsuitable in an industry affected by changes in climate and prices set in international markets. According to Power (1996, p.21), "accounting exercises that are inherently subjective such as valuation, can acquire an institutionalized objectivity by virtue of being widely supposed to be valid". This study provides some evidence which suggests that certain key asset valuations were objective because of their stability rather than because of any correlation with objective commercial evidence (see Wolnizer, 1987).

In summary, professional accountants played an increasing role in pastoral accounting in the Western District from the early 1870s. As evidenced in this study, they typically brought changes in the structure and usage of financial information consistent with their world views. The focus on financial outputs was also discerned in surviving pre-Federation examination papers of the IIAV.

Educational

The educational backgrounds of Western District pastoral pioneers and their sons appears to have impacted generally on the structure and usage of pastoral accounting information prepared in the colonial era. It is difficult to assess the direct impact of this environmental factor in many cases. However, certain probable influences may be identified.

As discussed in Chapter 5, a 70 per cent majority of pastoral pioneers in the Western District came from Scotland and many of these were found to have obtained their formal education in their homeland. Mepham (1988a) wrote about the "Scottish Ascendancy" in accounting texts which occurred in the eighteenth century when a number of important accounting texts emanated from Scotland.[14] Mepham (1988a, p.151) attributed this ascendancy to the achievements of the "Scottish Enlightenment" which is a commonly used term to describe a period during which emerged what Stewart (1854, p.551) referred to as a "sudden burst of genius". The duration of the Enlightenment is commonly considered to span from the Act of Union (1707) to the death of Sir Walter Scott (1832) (Mepham, 1988a, p.151). According to Young (1967, p.11):

> . . . the Scots thinkers of the Enlightenment not merely refused to recognize any distinction between the pure and applied sciences, but were prepared to treat the practical applicability of their speculations as a yardstick of their merits.

It was during this era of emphasis on the criterion of "practical applicability" that many important Scottish books of accounting were written and studied in Scottish educational institutions and also by individuals in private. As commented upon by Mepham (1988a, p.166), such texts "must surely rank as achievements of the Enlightenment in that they were important contributions to the development of systematic business systems which were of considerable practical use and extremely influential". As the pioneering pastoralists emigrating from Scotland with a background of formal education were educated during the latter decades of the Enlightenment, it is evident that they brought with them the benefits of an education which was considered to have a more practical orientation than that generally obtainable in England (Edwards, 1989a, p.278). Given the farming backgrounds of many of the Scottish emigrants, the early emphasis on both financial and volume recording systems for Western District pastoral industry engagement appears to have been influenced by their education in Scotland.

Little evidence was found of the particular subjects studied at Scottish educational institutions by the pioneering Western District pastoralists who were identified as having been afforded a formal education. It seems that the educational background of George Russell of the Clyde Company aided his implementation and maintenance of a wide range of financial and volume recording systems for pastoral operations in the Colony. As pointed out in Chapter 5, George Russell attended classes in arithmetic, mathematics and bookkeeping conducted

at the University of Edinburgh in 1830. These classes were given by a
"Mr Wallace who taught students and other young men" (Brown, 1935,
p.39). It seems reasonable to suggest that Mr Wallace was Professor
William Wallace who held the Chair of Mathematics at the University
of Edinburgh from 1819 to 1838 (University of Edinburgh, 1957,
p.217).[15] However, as recorded by George Russell "I only attended these
classes five or six weeks, and did not derive any great benefit from
them" (Brown, 1935, p.39). As Professor Wallace "was regarded as an
able teacher" (University of Edinburgh, 1957, p.218), it appears as if a
knowledge of bookkeeping may have previously been acquired by
George Russell. During 1841-43, Charles Myles Officer studied writing
and bookkeeping in the arithmetic subject taken in Fourth and Fifth
Class at the Edinburgh Academy (The Edinburgh Academy Archives;
The Edinburgh Academy, 1843, p.3). The successful completion of
these studies may have been a factor contributing to the emphasis on
expenditure control at Mt. Talbot during at least 1853-56 and the first
three months of 1858.[16]

Students undertaking studies at certain universities until 1833, and
possibly later, were not exposed to bookkeeping in the form of a
separate subject. The *Edinburgh University Almanack* of 1833 does not
contain any mention of bookkeeping studies (University of Edinburgh,
1833). Hence, students in the Faculty of Arts such as Charles Hamilton
Macknight may not have studied bookkeeping at all (University of
Edinburgh Archives). In so far as the B.A. degree at Trinity College
was concerned, students such as Archeson Jeremiah French were
exposed to classics, mathematics, science and philosophy until 1833
(University of Dublin, 1993, p.C2).

As discussed in Chapter 5, the sons of pioneering Western District
pastoralists were commonly educated at private boarding schools in
Melbourne or Geelong, the most popular establishments being Geelong
Church of England Grammar School, Geelong College, Melbourne
Church of England Grammar School and Scotch College. As evidenced
in the Scholastic Report included in the *First Annual Report of the
Committee of Management of the Geelong Grammar School* (as cited
in Bate, 1990, p.17), the School taught bookkeeping from 1855 to all
students. The *Annual Report, Prize List and Prospectus of The Geelong
College* for 1863 indicated that bookkeeping was occasionally
substituted for writing, but only "where a pupil has made such progress
as not to require so much time for writing" (The Geelong College,
1863, p.8). According to Bate (1990, p.32), "commerce was not highly
regarded" at Geelong College around that time. It was not until 1875
that a bookkeeping prize was instigated at the school (The Geelong
College, 1875). It seems commercial subjects were taught at the

Melbourne Church of England Grammar School from 1858, the year in which Frederick John Halden was appointed the Commercial Master (Kiddle, 1937, pp.25 & 128).[17] It was not until 1867 that commercial subjects were introduced at Scotch College (Scotch College Archives, Melbourne). The School's 1870 *Annual Report, Honor List & Prospectus* referred to the prominence given to studies in bookkeeping as follows "Writing, Book-keeping, Spelling, Grammar, Geography, and Composition - all practical subjects - occupy a prominent place in our programme, and engage a large proportion of our time and attention" (Scotch College, 1870, p.5).

Although the sons of pioneering Western District pastoralists attended private schools and had opportunities to acquire bookkeeping and other skills, it may have taken many years in certain cases before the locally educated progeny became involved with Western District station accounting. In certain cases the sons either sought or were required to gain working experience elsewhere before returning to the Western District stations of their families. For instance, as pointed out in Chapter 5, Robert Alexander David Hood, James Hassall Hope and William Kinross Mackinnon all gained pastoral industry experience at stations in other Australian colonies while George Herbert Armytage and Hugh Norman Beggs held positions after their schooling in a pastoral company and a bank respectively. In other cases, it is possible that station accounting remained within the domain of the pastoral pioneer until he retired from active pastoral industry participation or died. As discussed in Chapter 6, the influence of education in the case of the Jamieson volume records represented a constructive transfer of knowledge acquired at school to pastoral industry engagement. Robert Jamieson the younger demonstrated a flair for bookkeeping by winning prizes at the Geelong Church of England Grammar School in two successive years.

Local private schools also educated a number of those who subsequently acted as professional accountants in the Colony of Victoria. For instance, Joshua Edward Vines attended the Geelong Church of England Grammar School during 1876-80 and was awarded a bookkeeping prize in 1878 (Geelong Church of England Grammar School Archives, Corio). Joshua Edward Vines subsequently became widely regarded for his expertise in financial matters and, in addition to his involvement with the Black family as discussed in Chapter 6, he undertook private work in and around Terang (*Terang Express*, 27 November 1922). Peter Wares Tait completed his schooling at Scotch College in 1870. His results in that year of third in his arithmetic class and equal fourth in his geometry class (Scotch College Archives, Melbourne) demonstrated a flair for detail which he carried into his career as one of the earliest public accountants based in the Western District and, perhaps, its most influential accountant in the colonial era. It is not known whether he also studied bookkeeping at Scotch College but it seems reasonable to suggest that his formal education incorporated studies in bookkeeping.

Perhaps the influence of local formal education on station accounting was more often felt on occasions when a pastoral pioneer died or when accountability relationships emerged for other reasons. In such circumstances the pastoral pioneers' sons who had studied commercial subjects including bookkeeping at school were likely to have been more prepared than their fathers might have been to use professional accounting services. Pastoral pioneers who had developed successful station operations from the early days of European pastoral settlement without the aid of professional accountants may have resisted any approaches or urge to engage them once their stations were well-established. Local formal education was also likely to have contributed to the wider use of arithmetic in station affairs. As indicated in Table 7.14, the surviving evidence of the determination of performance measures for wool and lambing production was generally prepared subsequent to the preparation of records of operating statistics. The necessity to use more complex arithmetic calculations than addition and subtraction may have contributed to these overall time variations. Notwithstanding, it is likely that the locally educated sons of pastoral pioneers would have been generally willing to apply their newly acquired knowledge to assist in station operations.

In the Western District at Ballarat, James Dimelow operated the Township Commercial Academy (subsequently renamed the Ballarat Commercial College) from 1860 to 1879 and wrote his book on accounting published in sets during 1871-73 (Carnegie & Parker, 1994). Although Dimelow provided opportunities to acquire a knowledge of bookkeeping, not any connection between Dimelow and the pastoralists whose records were examined in this study was found. In addition, no association between Dimelow and the pre-Federation professional accountants identified in this study was identified.

Economic

Certain economic factors appear to have impacted upon the structure and usage of pre-Federation pastoral accounting information. At a macroeconomic level, probable economic factors included currency problems, growing economic complexity and the economic depression of the early 1890s. As addressed in Chapter 3, currency problems presented difficulties to Port Phillip District settlers in periods before the advent of a system of branch banking and prior to the standardisation of the currency. These conditions necessitated the adoption of barter in isolated station communities and the practice of bookkeeping barter as identified in this study. As indicated in Chapter 2, Baxter (1956, p.272) and Parker (1986, p.85) pointed out that accounting's role in an economic climate where banks and money in circulation are scarce is to lubricate barter. Although the personalized ledger records observed may have made barter easier, barter transactions in themselves constituted only one form of interpersonal communal exchanges in station communities. Further, this study provides evidence of the preparation of a variety of other accounting records for purposes other than to facilitate barter.

The level of economic activity within a country is a determinant of the sophistication of accounting systems adopted generally. A country's economy becomes more complex and generally more regulated as the level of economic activity and the size of the public sector expand. In the Colony of Victoria, the taxation arrangements became more diverse as the economy developed. Income tax was introduced in 1895 following an economic depression which came after the 1870s-80s boomtime. The Victorian government was experiencing severe deficits on account of the early 1890s depression (Mills, 1925, p.89). The government had endeavoured to subsidize its declining revenues during the depression years by increasing the rates of existing taxes but these measures did not attract sufficient funds (Fayle, 1984, p.674). Despite opposition from pastoralists who were still required to pay land tax under what they generally perceived to be a double taxation regime, income tax "passed into the fiscal practice of the Colony" (vanden Driesen and Fayle, 1987, p.29). These economic influences were manifest throughout Victoria and affected Western District pastoralists.

The economic depression in Eastern Australia also exposed deficiencies in accounting and auditing practices throughout the Colony of Victoria (Anon, 1893, p.1014; Macdonald, 1936, p.22; Maskell, 1944, p.210; Davison, 1978, pp.111-112; Griffiths, 1982, p.43). Such deficiencies may have been linked to "a host of amateurs and sharp operators" which operated together with "a majority of respectable auditors" in the period prior to the incorporation of the IIAV in 1887 (Davison, 1978, p.111). Davison (1978, p.112) argued it was "a popular fear of bad bookkeeping" that contributed to the growth of the organized accounting profession in the 1890s. Hence, it seems that the economic depression served as a catalyst for the development of the organized accounting profession in Victoria.

At a microeconomic level, the lending policies and practices of pre-Federation pastoral companies and banks are also relevant to an explanation of accounting practices. Gleanings of these policies and practices were found in the surviving minute books of the Boards and Account Committees of these financiers and in branch banking reports. Using AML&F as a case illustration for pastoral companies, the policies detailed in the surviving minute books of the London-based Board of Directors were broad in nature and did not address the type of accounting information sought, if any, to assess applications for loans.[18] (For illustrative purposes, Appendix F records extracts of minutes of matters of lending policy found in the Minute Books of the AML&F Board during 1867-1879). More specific client information was found in reports submitted annually by the Company's General Manager in Australia to the Board of Directors in London.[19] These reports featured the General Manager's "remarks" on examination of loan accounts at the various Australian offices of the Company as at the end of each calendar year. These remarks focused on the security, if any, involved with advances to pastoralists and generally addressed the safety of the advance (featuring views from time to time on station affairs and the general prospects of the station).[20] There was reference in these reports to station profitability in a few instances. The following statements were written on occasions "the operations on this a/c for year show a loss" or "the operations on this a/c do not show any profit for the year". Such statements evidently related to the excess of disbursements over receipts (typically including wool proceeds) as shown in their clients' current accounts (162/35). Other than station managers employed by AML&F to run company controlled stations, there was no evidence found of pastoralists being required to submit periodic or ad hoc accounting information to AML&F. However, the management of the Company appears to have been content to examine, among other things, the movements in current account balances on a periodic basis for the purpose of assessing a pastoralist's capacity to meet loan obligations.

In the case of banks, a specific illustration involving the Cumming family in dealings with the Bank of Australasia provides an indication of the bank's lending arrangements in the 1860s.[21] The following extracts of comments included in surviving business records of the bank (Australia & New Zealand Banking Group Ltd Group Archive, Melbourne) elucidate a prime concern for considerations of wealth and reputation:

> The Messrs Cumming are wealthy settlers, and undoubted for these advances on the whole £29,893 - which does not exceed the value of one year's produce from their respective stations (Advances at Branches Exceeding £10,000, 15 October 1866, Statements, Superintendent's Department, A/148/1).

> The three Messrs Cumming guarantee each other's liabilities which amount on the whole to £24,186. Their joint clip of wool last year realised about £35,000, being well known here and in London as of first quality. Their sheep are to a great extent kept on their own freehold land, and the accounts are safe and valuable (Advances at Branches Exceeding £10,000, 14 October 1867, Statements, Superintendent's Department, A/148/1).

> The Cummings are quite undoubted for the advances made to them and to require security therefore would result in the loss of this really valuable connection (Advances at Branches Exceeding £10,000, 12 October 1868, Statements, Superintendent's Department, A/148/1).

It can be assumed without recklessness that the bank did not request or obtain periodic financial statements from the Cumming family if it was regarded as an insult to require security from them in this colonial era. However, the sales value of the annual wool clip appears to have been important input in assessments of the ability of pastoralists to service loan obligations.

In summary, the economic factors identified appear to have affected pre-Federation pastoral accounting in the Western District. Bookkeeping barter was a product of barter transactions on account of currency problems and station remoteness from banks. Taxation arrangements became more complex as the economy grew and the size and funding requirements of the public sector expanded. The advent of income tax was linked to the early 1890s economic depression which appears to have been a catalyst for the development of the organized accounting profession in Victoria. Pastoral financiers, at least to the late 1870s, did not appear to focus on an examination of periodic statements of financial performance and financial position for their view of a pastoralist's capacity to pay. Instead, the evidence suggests the lending decisions of financiers were based on judgements of the wealth and reputation of individual pastoralists and on monitoring movements in clients' current accounts wherein wool proceeds for the annual clip were commonly deposited.

Other Factors

Three other environmental factors related to operating conditions in the Western District appear to have impacted upon the structure and usage of pre-Federation pastoral accounting information. These are the mode of pastoral operation, climate and the early employment practices adopted in connection with shearers.

Unlike nineteenth century pastoralists in the British Isles, pioneering Western District pastoralists were able to achieve cost advantages by running large flocks of sheep on vast expanses of land and subsequently on land bound by copious stretches of fencing (Gibson, 1991, pp.104-105). In this context, the Western District pastoralist adopted close supervisory arrangements for livestock by means of the engagement of station hands such as shepherds and boundary riders. This reliance on direct supervision of resources and personal ledger accounts that reflected the specific costs of individual station workers meant that the pastoralist had little need to implement detailed cost control systems. Hence, the cost advantages available due to the mode of pastoral operation adopted by pioneering pastoralists is a probable determinant of the lack of focus on the maintenance of detailed cost records evident in this study.

Climate appears to have had an influence on pastoral accounting practices in pre-Federation Victoria. As pointed out in Chapter 7, there was evidence of the practice of budgeting found for only one of the 23 entities in the research sample. Perhaps written budgets were viewed as inappropriate due to the seasonal nature of the pastoral industry. Support for this view came from the descendants of two Western District pastoral pioneers. In an oral history interview held on 24 July 1990, Robert Jamieson III (who became the station manager at the family's Bolac Plains station in 1923) stated "when I was manager I never budgeted. Well I did budget but I didn't put it down [in writing] because I didn't know what the season was going to be" (Carnegie, 1990-91). Similarly, in an oral history interview held on 3 December 1990, Norman Dennis remarked "the question of budget [preparation] would have meant crystal ball gazing, it wouldn't have been worth the time of compiling if they even had such things in those [colonial] days" (Carnegie, 1990). As pointed out earlier in this chapter, climate might have also contributed to the apparent unwillingness of professional accountants in many cases to regularly restate valuations of certain pastoral assets but particularly land. Perhaps climate generally created conditions of uncertainty under which both pastoralists and professional accountants were, on occasions, unwilling to reflect in accounting records.

As discussed in Chapter 7, stock and stores records were found to have been generally prepared in advance of shearing tally records. An explanation for this finding relates to the early employment practices involving those who undertook shearing work. Kiddle (1961, p.67) explained that a pastoralist "tried to depend on his own men and a few extra hands at shearing, but as his flocks increased this soon became impracticable". This purported dependence on station hands for shearing would have meant this task was recognized as forming part of their regular work requirements and would have been compensated on the basis of agreed pay rates for designated terms of employment. In such cases, piece-work rates would not have been applicable. The propensity for recording accurate details of individual shearing performance would have increased in line with the need to make greater use of itinerant shearers.

This discussion indicates that certain operating conditions appear to have affected pre-Federation pastoral accounting in the Western District. Although pastoralists in the British Isles were also affected by climate, they could not physically mount operations of the scale implemented in the Western District.

Conclusion

This chapter has endeavoured to present explanations for the accounting practices observed in pre-Federation pastoral industry engagement in the Western District. Generalized conclusions have been drawn about the probable impact of cultural, legal and political, professional, educational, economic and certain other factors. No attempt has been made to rank any of the key environmental factors identified in any order of importance.

Culture appears to have impacted upon the structure and usage of the surviving pre-Federation pastoral accounting information examined. Under the cultural perspective adopted in this study, culture provides the context within which local accounting practices can be explained. This chapter has discussed the apparent impact of an organisational culture of interpersonal communal exchanges and the pastoralist's paternalistic control of his isolated station community to explain the personification of financial recording systems in the absence of accountability relationships. It has also addressed the apparent impact of national culture both in terms of the development in Victoria of colonial liberalism and the existence or advent of accountability relationships. This study has also shown that pre-Federation pastoral accounting practice became increasingly influenced by a professional culture as circumstances arose which necessitated the use of professional accounting services. Legal factors also played a role in shaping pre-Federation pastoral accounting practices as it is evident that legislation was necessary to compel the payment by pastoralists of the relevant levies assessed upon them. Political factors, although shown to be important, often masquerade for prevailing world views or national culture.

Professional accountants were involved in pastoral accounting in the Western District in the period before the incorporation of the IIAV in 1887. Hence, the availability of professional accounting skills from at least the early 1870s was a determinant of accounting change. Although not clearly evident in this study, the advent and growth of an organized accounting profession may have assisted members of accounting bodies in developing their pastoral client-base. The strong emphasis of professional accountants on the preparation of financial information for nineteenth century pastoral operations is consistent with the thrust of the IIAV Examining Committee in preparing "Book-keeping" examination papers during 1891-99 and also the focus of Vigars in his book on pastoral accounting first published in 1900.

Educational factors also appear to have influenced pre-Federation pastoral accounting practice. The Scottish majority of pastoral pioneers in the Western District were raised during the era of the "Scottish Enlightenment". Such exposure to "practical applicability" would assist to explain their propensity to establish both financial and volume recording systems at the time of, or shortly after, their settlement in the district. Studies by the sons of pastoral pioneers at private boarding schools in subjects such as arithmetic and bookkeeping or similar presented opportunities for the constructive transfer of knowledge acquired in the classroom to the pastoral industry. However, it is difficult in many cases to assess the direct impact of a private school education on pastoral accounting. It is likely the influence of local formal education was more often experienced, albeit indirectly, on the establishment of accountability relationships such as on the advent of deceased estates.

Economic factors consisting of currency problems, heightened economic complexity and the early 1890s economic depression appear to have impacted upon pre-Federation pastoral accounting. At a microeconomic level, the lending policies and practices of pastoral financiers including their requirements, if any, for examining accounting information also had implications for accounting practice. Other major environmental factors identified were the mode of pastoral operation adopted, climate and the early employment practices adopted for shearing. These other probable determinants of accounting practice related to operating conditions in the Western District and presented certain opportunities and challenges that were typically outside the experiences of pastoralists in the British Isles at the time.

Overall, there appears to have been a broad range of environmental factors which impacted upon the structure and usage of surviving pre-Federation pastoral accounting information. In the complete absence of an examination of the impact of local, time-specific cultural factors, less comprehensive explanations would have been presented of the accounting practices found to be adopted in the Western District. Hence, for interpretive history, it is apt for culture to be incorporated as a key contextual factor in order to assist in affording historical evidence the vitality it once possessed.

NOTES

1. One of the earliest documented calls, if not the earliest, for the establishment of an organized accounting profession was made by Edward Wild of Melbourne in 1874 (Carnegie & Varker, 1995).
2. A thoughtful discussion on "education and indoctrination" in the context of accounting is provided by Chambers (1994). According to Chambers (1994, p.79) "all education and technical instruction are indoctrination". In criticising traditional methods of teaching accounting, Chambers (1994, p.79) argued that early (and even "modern") textbooks generally did not "demonstrate in what way the products of following the rules [enunciated] were serviceable in managing the financial affairs of merchants".
3. The provisions of the Memorandum of Association of the IIAV remained unchanged during the passing of the years (Macdonald, 1936, pp.11-12).
4. Thomas Brentnall played a leading role in the development of an organized accounting profession in Australia and became the first President of The Institute of Chartered Accountants in Australia which was established in 1928. It was the first accounting body outside Britain to hold a Royal Charter (Brentnall, 1938, pp.70-72; Graham, 1978, pp.vii, 3 & 10-11).
5. In the nineteenth century, it was common for a professional accounting body to admit foundation members based on admissions of relevant experience and without examination, while persons admitted subsequently were required to pass formal examinations administered by the body in order to demonstrate minimum levels of competence. Brentnall (1898, p.329), for example, provides an illustration of this dichotomy in the case of a proposal to obtain legal recognition for members of the organized accounting profession in Victoria.
6. William Henry Tuckett commenced practice in Melbourne as a public accountant, estate agent, trade assignee among other things in 1868 (Sutherland Smith, 1992, p.57). According to *The Official Post Office Directory of Victoria 1875*, James Knight Bickerton was already practising as an accountant in Melbourne in 1875. Peter Wares Tait publicized in the *Camperdown Chronicle* of 17 December 1875 that he had commenced practice as an accountant in Camperdown and stated his willingness "to take charge of station books, &c.". Frederick Courthorpe Downes had a large practice in Ballarat (*Ballarat Courier*, 6 September 1902) but no evidence was found to indicate when he commenced practice. Surviving business records of the AIIA indicate that Frederick Courthorpe Downes was the President of that body in 1897 and 1898.

7. As a member of the IIAV, Oehr (1899, pp.298-299) claimed that professional accountants should possess the skills to open and keep proper executorship accounts and that executors who found figures to be "unintelligible" should use the services of a professional accountant.

8. The first examinations of the IIAV were held in January 1889. The subjects examined were Bookkeeping; Auditing; Adjustment of Partnership and Executorship Accountants; The Rights and Duties of Liquidators, Trustees and Receivers; Principles of the Law of Insolvency and of Joint Stock Companies, and Mercantile Law and the Law of Arbitration and Awards (IIAV, 1907, p.26). The earliest "Bookkeeping" examination paper of all those surviving is dated June 1891 (Australian Society of Certified Practising Accountants Archives, Melbourne). A new scheme of examinations was introduced in 1899 when "Intercolonial" examinations were held jointly with the Institute of Accountants in South Australia and the Sydney Institute of Public Accountants (Macdonald, 1936, p.26; Graham, 1978, p.4).

9. The Victorian Treasurer proposed an income tax in the Budget Statement submitted to Parliament during November 1894 (Mills, 1925, p.89). Hence, in setting the July 1894 examination papers, the IIAV Examining Committee appears to have anticipated later developments in colonial revenue raising.

10. The CAA was incorporated in New South Wales on 17 August 1899 under the *Companies Act* 1874 (Walton, 1970b, p.41). Vigars first appeared in the *Sands Sydney Suburban and Country Commercial Directory, 1902* in both the "Accountants" listing and in a list of the members of the CAA. No earlier listing of CAA members was published in this directory. Walton (1970b, p.42) pointed out that F.E. Vigars was among the names "which appear in its [CAA's] early records". It is probable that Vigars was a member of the CAA by the end of December 1901.

11. *Practical Bookkeeping* (first published in Australia in 1880) by John Scouller, while focusing on double entry bookkeeping, contained an appendix to the second edition (believed to be published in 1882) and also subsequent editions which featured a revenue account for a colliery showing expenses per ton of output (Goldberg, 1977, pp.227 & 234). The discussion of this account confirmed Scouller's recognition of the difference between fixed and variable costs (1882, p.83).

12. For instance, Daniel Hechstetter, the German manager of an English copper works during 1597-1633, was almost undoubtedly influenced by his father and also his brother at Keswick where cost accounting techniques were ascertained to be in use by c.1600 (Edwards, Hammersley & Newell, 1990, pp.61 & 63-66). William Jenkins gained valuable experience as a clerk for many years under accountant James Walkinshaw at Dowlais Iron Company (Boyns & Edwards, 1997, p.31). Archille Dufaud, a director of Société Fourchambault (SF), attended Cyfarthfa in Wales in 1823 and subsequently recommended the adoption of costing and other practices observed there at the SF foundry at Fourchambault, France (Thuillier, 1959, p.42).

13. Like Thomas Brentnall and Rudolph John Oehr, West Outtrim Strangewood was a member of the IIAV.

14. In particular, Mepham (1988a) wrote about Alexander Malcolm, John Mair, William Gordon and Robert Hamilton which he described as the four most important Scottish accounting authors during this period of ascendancy (p.153). The first Scottish book on accounting was Robert Colinson's *Idea Rationaria* which was published in 1683 (Parker, 1974). A more detailed account of accounting in Scotland in the eighteenth century is found in Mepham (1988b).

15. It seems that George Russell was privately tutored by Wallace for he also attended private lectures on chemistry presented by a Mr. D.B. Reid who was assistant to Dr. Hope, at that time Professor of Chemistry at the University of Edinburgh (Brown, 1935, pp.38-39). Professor Wallace was made an honorary Doctor of Laws in recognition of his contribution to learning and to the University (University of Edinburgh, 1957, p.218).

16. In 1843, Charles Myles Officer was placed sixteenth in a class of 108 students and won a prize for scholarship (The Edinburgh Academy, 1843, p.40).

17. The "Plan of Education" in the handwriting of the School's first headmaster, Dr. J.E. Bromby, indicated the planned availability of bookkeeping studies. The Plan of Education reads as if written before the opening of the School in April 1858 (Melbourne Church of England Grammar School Archives).

18. The AML&F was selected as the pastoral company case illustration because of the availability of records of lending policies and practices from relatively early times in the Colony in comparison with other pre-Federation pastoral companies whose records have survived. AML&F was also found to have made advances to Robert Jamieson pioneer in the 1880s.

19. These reports are contained in the "General Purpose Committee Minute Book" (1866-1893) and "Committee Reports on Accounts" (1894-1948) held at The Noel Butlin Archives Centre, Australian National University, Canberra (162/35 and 162/36 respectively).

20. For Robert Jamieson, the General Manager's remarks for the year ended 31 December 1885 were merely as follows "an undoubted advance, which I presume is temporary. We hold titles to Stony Point lands 5,799 a[cres] worth 25,000 pounds and his Bolac Plains estate is free" (Box 162/35).

21. The Cumming family case involving the Bank of Australasia was selected because it represented the earliest instance of surviving banking records from all enquiries made to banks whose archives hold pre-Federation records pertaining to pastoral entities in the research sample. During this period, the Bank of Australasia was dealing with brothers John Cumming the younger, and also George and William Cumming.

CHAPTER 9

CONCLUSION

This study has been concerned with the nature of accounting information prepared by non-corporate entities for pre-Federation pastoral industry engagement in the Western District of Victoria during the period 1836 to 1900. Based on examinations of surviving business records, it has presented evidence of the structure and usage of pastoral accounting information prepared in an unregulated financial reporting environment. Probable explanations for the pre-Federation pastoral accounting practices observed have been rendered. The study has endeavoured to augment our understanding of accounting's past. It also provides insights into accounting's present and might enable a broadening of our perspectives of accounting's future.

This final chapter presents an overview of the major findings of this study and discusses a case for lost relevance of accounting information prepared for Western District pastoralists in the closing decades of the nineteenth century. The chapter also addresses the contemporary relevance of the study and outlines opportunities for future research.

Summary of Major Findings

This study has shown that there was a broad range of financial and volume records prepared for pre-Federation pastoral industry engagement in the Western District by the 23 entities which comprised the research sample. In the absence of accountability relationships, the accounting records commonly prepared were personalized ledgers combined with various records of non-financial operating statistics. In such cases, there was found to be a general focus on the use of these statistics to measure production performance, particularly lambing and wool production. For wool production, the focus on input/output relationships was in both physical and financial terms. The evidence of the periodic determination of lambing and various wool performance measures would have enabled a longitudinal comparison of station operating performance and, in the case of wool production only, station financial return.

The personalized ledgers examined were not structured to permit the determination of periodic financial performance and financial position. They were thus not used to measure underlying attributes of economic activity and, in effect, were ends in themselves. However, they contained information relating to the status of financial dealings with individual parties. They represented a combined debtors' and creditors' record and contained key personnel information. In addition, they effectively presented vignettes of station life. The personalized ledgers illustrated a commitment to the maintenance of records which accurately reflected the financial dealings with station personnel and other parties involved with the station community. As such, they communicated to those who read them the essential features of economic reality from an individualized perspective.

Personalized station ledgers appeared to be symbolic of the station culture which shaped the world views of the pastoralist. These ledgers appeared to be dominated by world views that reflected a culture of interpersonal communal exchanges in isolated interdependent station communities and the pastoralist's paternalistic control of his community. It follows that personalized ledgers came to define and were defined by an organisational culture as the context within which prevailing world views were determined. Although personalized ledgers provided evidence of bookkeeping barter, it is apparent that barter in itself was only one aspect of the organisational culture in isolated station communities and that the ledger records were not merely maintained to make barter easier.

In cases where accountability relationships did not exist, it is evident that the pastoral accounting information prepared was used essentially for internal purposes. Particularly as this study found evidence of only one instance of budgeting, it would appear that the accounting systems were primarily maintained for control rather than planning purposes. Personalized ledgers provided evidence to enable the pastoralist or station manager to monitor strictly the status of financial positions of dealings with a range of parties and to provide documentation, where necessary, to settle disputes or satisfy queries. Documentary evidence is not only important as a reference for what has happened, it is also relevant in assessments about what may happen in the future. Personalized ledgers contained certain personnel and performance particulars including wage rates (periodic or piece rate) and particulars of contractor performance on a unit basis. Such information was likely to have been relevant in setting future wage rates and in deciding whether to re-appoint certain contractors respectively.

Stock and stores records were found to have generally been relied upon in advance of other types of volume records. These records enabled a pastoralist or station manager to reflect and exercise control over station livestock and stores and allowed assessments to be made of the accountability of those who were held responsible for the supervision of those resources. The recording of non-financial production statistics including shearing tallies and bale particulars allowed the pastoralist or station manager to monitor production performance and to assess the impact of changes in production methods, climate and, in the case of wool production, changes in shearing personnel. Such operating systems provided a means to measure and improve productivity. Systems which went beyond recording input/output relationships in physical unit terms incorporated the externality of selling (market) prices, a factor which was not within the control of any one pastoralist. However, this interest in financial return based on inputs (sheep shorn) and/or outputs (per pound) shows a concern for depicting performance based on wool production from varying perspectives.

Ram fleece weights and bale records focused on particular facets of the quality of production. There were only two cases found of the determination of individual ram fleece weights, a practice which aided in the selection of rams of superior productivity for stud purposes. These records provided a means to enhance future wool productivity. Bale records included details of bale wool type for each bale in the annual clip. In only one case (Millear, Maidment and Austin/Millear) was there any further analysis of bale wool types. These records showed for each wool type the total number of bales and the total weights of the bales involved. As it was common practice for stud performance to be assessed externally by means of a pastoralist's performance at popular sheep and wool shows held throughout the Western District and in Melbourne, assessments of quality were often represented by the number and grade of sashes displayed in the station homestead and publicity in newspapers and other outlets.

This study found little evidence of a concern for expenditure control in the absence of accountability relationships. Instead, there appeared to be a stronger focus on the maintenance of records which depicted cash position. As usual in commercial arrangements, information about one's cash position would have been important to nineteenth century pastoralists. The currency of their bank account balances would have been apparent, if not from their own records, then certainly from those kept by banks. Ledger records representing debtor and creditor relationships appeared to complement depictions of a pastoralist's cash position in providing detailed evidence of future expected outgoings and incomings on an individualized basis.

The impact of externalities was central to the development of accounting. The nature of information required for accountability purposes and by the government had a stronger financial focus with a much greater emphasis on the preparation of periodic financial statements. In cases involving accountability relationships, the act of preparing financial statements for pastoral operations seemed to be symbolic of the national culture which shaped the world views of those involved as accountors. The notion of rendering account in accountability relationships is a long-standing tenet of English society and was formulated at law under the Australian legal system which was based on the English legal system. As stewards of others' resources, Western District accountors evidently met their obligation to periodically report to accountees on their activities and on the financial performance and position of the entities under their control. The Victorian government was interested in the financial affairs of pastoralists by means of, among other things, the imposition of death duties (1870) and income tax (1895). The advent of deceased estates on the death of pastoral pioneers brought an obligation for executors to account on a periodic basis for the resources under their effective control. The introduction of death duties in 1870 and the requirement to submit a statement of assets and liabilities of the deceased to the Master-in-Equity were stimuli on many occasions for the appointment of professional accountants. The later requirement to present financial information to government for income tax purposes further strengthened the focus on the measurement of financial outputs. Where accountability relationships had not existed previously, the impact of this sharpened focus on financial outputs was generally staggered until 1895, as the advent of accounting change was often linked to the mortality of the pastoral pioneers involved.

Although legislation was necessary to apply financial burdens upon pastoralists in the form of the stock assessment, death duties, land tax and income tax, it is evident that the prevailing world views implicit in colonial liberalism impacted upon pastoral accounting and contributed to the sharpened focus on the measurement of financial outputs. As a culture, colonial liberalism developed from around the mid 1850s and embodied the rejection of world views implicit in settler capitalism. Within urban communities, the prevailing world views which emerged represented a national culture which eventually affected accounting practice as the colonial liberalists gained political influence and as legislation was passed from 1870 to impose financial burdens on pastoralists in bids to repress their wealth and influence. Clearly, legal factors played a role in the implementation of government levy collection arrangements in pre-Federation Victoria. Political factors, although important, often masquerade for prevailing world views or national culture which was found to be an underlying influence on pastoral accounting in this study.

From the early 1870s, the availability of professional accounting skills had an impact on pastoral accounting in the Western District. The world views of professional accountants were shaped by their educational and commercial background in accounting. These world views of the preferred structure and usage of accounting information represented a professional culture. Understandably, professional accountants were keen to inculcate practices they had come to learn and understand even if some or most of them had never used the outputs of recording systems implemented by themselves for pastoral or other industry engagement. Their specialized skills, particularly their command of double entry accounting, set them apart from those who were proficient in other professions, crafts or occupations. In the closing decades of the nineteenth century, pastoral accounting became increasingly influenced by a professional culture as circumstances emerged which necessitated the use of the services of professional accountants. From 1887 on the incorporation of the IIAV, professional culture was intended to be captured and monopolized by those who became members of professional bodies in an organized accounting profession. As evident in the surviving examination papers of the IIAV on "Bookkeeping", an ability to measure financial outputs was the hallmark of a "qualified" professional accountant while Vigars (1901, p.4) was infact concerned with the widespread adoption of "a complete system of [double entry] Book-keeping" by pastoralists.

The advent of double entry accounting and periodic financial reporting was not necessarily seen to be a superior means of handling Western District station operations. Prior to the appointment of professional accountants in cases where accountability relationships had not previously existed, personalized ledgers were evidently an integral part of a workable system within the station community for running pastoral affairs on a day to day basis. In some cases, the financial reporting systems introduced by professional accountants were added as an overlay. The continued use of personalized ledger systems in such circumstances sharpens the case for station organizational culture to be depicted as an important environmental factor. The evidence in balance sheets prepared by professional accountants of valuations which either remained constant or were subject to infrequent change also casts doubts on their usefulness for pre-Federation pastoral engagement.

With the possible exception of one case (Armytage), the influence of professional accountants on the structure and usage of pre-Federation accounting information of a non-financial operating nature is problematic. On the appointment of professional accountants, the pre-existing operating systems were retained for day to day station operations. Whatever impact, if any, professional accountants had on the structure and usage of non-financial operating information, it did not result in the paradigm shift as observed in cases following their involvement with financial recording systems. Professional accountants also appear to have overlooked any scope that existed to become involved in financial and production budgeting. Despite the sharpened emphasis on the preparation of periodic financial statements, periodic profit results did not commonly feature in surviving inter-station comparative reports. Instead, there was a strong emphasis on the analysis of inter-station performance measures for wool production. Such measures were possibly regarded as more cogent indicators of station productivity and financial return than any based on the capital/income dichotomy (and particularly those which involved the use of asset valuations which lacked contemporaneity). There were also only two cases found of the use of accounts prepared by professional accountants to ascertain return on investment (assets).

A range of educational, economic and other factors appear to have influenced pre-Federation pastoral accounting practice. Probable educational factors included the achievements of the "Scottish Enlightenment" and the private school education commonly provided to sons of pastoral pioneers. The enlightenment exposed Scottish pastoral pioneers to the notion of "practical applicability" which appears to explain, at least partly, the common early emphasis on both financial and volume record systems. A private school education permitted the constructive transfer of knowledge acquired at school to pastoral industry engagement and probably conditioned the locally educated progeny to accept the involvement of professional accountants on the later advent of accountability relationships. Probable economic factors included currency problems, economic growth and the 1890s economic depression which affected the timing of the introduction of income tax. Currency problems and station remoteness from banks contributed to the adoption of barter and the practice of bookkeeping barter in personal ledger records. Economic growth contributed to the increased complexity of commerce as the public sector expanded and taxation arrangements became more involved in line with this growth. At a microeconomic level, the policies and practices of pastoral lenders seem to have impacted on accounting practice. Other probable environmental factors included the mode of pastoral operation and the vagaries of the seasons. The reliance by pioneering Western District pastoralists on direct supervision of livestock rather than detailed cost control systems appears to explain, at least in part, the absence of detailed cost record systems for lambing and wool production. The variable impact of climate and its direct impact on production performance may have contributed to both the apparent unwillingness to prepare budgets and the propensity for professional accountants to be generally hesitant in stating assets such as land and livestock at their current valuations as at each balance date.

From 1893, accounting authors and others in Australia stressed the importance for pastoralists to maintain a "proper" set of books. These authors emphasized the periodic measurement of financial outputs and commonly advocated the adoption of double entry accounting systems by pastoralists. This study of surviving pre-Federation accounting records of 23 Western District pastoral entities has provided evidence that effective pastoral accounting for day to day station operations did not equate with "proper" professional accounting as advocated by Musson (1893), Buckley (1897), Hombsch (1897), Goldsbrough Mort & Co. Ltd (1897), Anon (1899) and Vigars (1900). It also provides evidence that accounting in early pre-Federation station communities embraced both financial and volume record systems and was not merely concerned with the lubrication of barter.

A Case of Relevance Lost?

The phrase "Lost Relevance" was used by Johnson and Kaplan (1987, p.12) in their provocative and widely-cited work titled *Relevance Lost: The Rise and Fall of Management Accounting*. In the context of corporations in the USA, Johnson and Kaplan referred to the stagnation in the innovation of management accounting practices from around 1925. They attributed this stagnation to the "dominance of the external financial accounting statements during the twentieth century" (1987, p.13). The authors argued that prior to the mid 1920s, management accounting practices developed and flourished in an environment where corporations were not burdened by any demands for external financial reporting (1987, p.xii). In support of this argument, Fleischman and Parker (1991), in their study of 25 sets of surviving records of British industrial firms from 1760 to 1850, found substantial evidence of mature cost management in four major areas of activity (cost control techniques, accounting for overhead, costing for routine and special decision making, and standard costing). Similarly, in a study of surviving records of numerous Welsh companies engaged principally in metal manufacture from 1700 to 1830, Jones (1985) provided insights into the use made of accounting information for planning, decision making and control purposes (Edwards, 1989b). Reporting on the accounting practices of two charcoal iron making firms in the Sheffield region, England, Edwards and Boyns (1992) identified the integration of cost and financial records from 1690 as their most remarkable observation. Johnson and Kaplan (1987, p.13) attributed the shift in focus from the 1920s to the preparation of cost-based income statements and balance sheets to management yielding "the design of their cost management systems to financial accountants and auditors".

This study has provided some evidence with respect to pastoral performance measurement of a shift in focus to a strong emphasis on the measurement of financial outputs. It has demonstrated that financial recording systems were commonly captured by professional accountants in the closing decades of the colonial era. Professional accountants evidently perceived pastoralists' financial recording systems to be inadequate and appear to have devoted most, if not all, of their energies to the implementation of double entry accounting systems and the preparation of periodic financial statements. While they did not dismantle pre-existing station operating systems which provided information to evaluate the efficiency of internal processes, professional accountants appear to have had little, if any, impact on the structure and usage of pre-Federation accounting information of a non-financial operating nature. The study points to the failure of professional accountants to goad pastoral clients into managerial accounting innovations as they did in financial accounting directions. Thus, the expansion and enhancement of the domain of double entry accounting appears to have been central to the success of the accounting professionalization project in the colonial era.

The evidence suggests that the Western District pastoralists involved may not have found periodic financial statements to be effective for day to day station operations, even though they may have been comforted by advice received from accountants that they had implemented "proper" professional accounting systems. Evidence of the adoption of dual accounting systems indicates the pastoralists or station managers in at least these cases continued to use pre-existing financial and volume recording systems for day to day station operations after the engagement of professional accountants. Similarly, the concentration on non-profit performance measures in surviving inter-station comparative reports shows that dependable and informative performance measures for wool production did not rely upon the preparation of periodic financial statements. The general absence of contemporaneity evident in asset valuations stated in pre-Federation balance sheets prepared by professional accountants would have at least cast doubt on their suitability for financial decision making. It seems that the professional accountants involved had a strong preference for presenting financial reports based on objective, verifiable and realized financial transactions. As Dodd (1994, p.113) explained in the context of monetary exchange, "to transmit and receive information . . . is not simply to project an independent body of facts through space and time, but to bring those facts into being as facts" (also see Power, 1996, p.21). This study elucidates an accepted notion of objectivity which enabled professional accountants to represent certain dated (financial) facts as facts through time.

In accounting for pastoral operations in an unregulated financial reporting environment, professional accountants evidently relied on periodic financial statements for their view of Western District pastoral entities. This emphasis seems to have isolated them from the real value-creating processes in pastoralism. They appeared to largely neglect a potential involvement in pastoral production processes as they did not, for example, focus on the measurement and improvement of productivity nor concern themselves with attaching costs to a range of activities in production processes. Professional accountants undoubtedly considered they had much to offer pastoralists in the establishment and maintenance of double entry accounting systems. However, it seems that their tunnelled vision was of the ilk which Johnson and Kaplan (1987, p.12) detected in concluding the pace of innovation in management accounting seemed to stop in the USA by around the mid 1920s.

Implications of the Study

There are five major implications of this study. Firstly, the study illustrates the importance of field-based case study research in augmenting our understanding of accounting's past. Secondly, it shows how culture, as a key contextual variable, can assist in explaining historical accounting practices in a local, time-specific context. Thirdly, it provides some evidence which suggests that a key determinant of the professionalization of accounting in the colonial era was the expansion and enhancement of the domain of double entry accounting. It also provides some insights into the origins of the present concentration on financial accounting systems and financial reporting issues in Australia. Finally, the evidence of a regard for the efficiency of production by pre-Federation Western District pastoralists themselves in some respects predates similar concerns with efficiency exhibited by contemporary manufacturing and public sector management. These implications are now discussed in turn.

Importance of Field-Based Case Study Research

This study shows the importance of field-based case study research to examine accounting systems in their organisational and social context. There are serious limitations inherent in confining research to publications written by accountants themselves. As this study of 23 sets of surviving business records found, accounting records were not only maintained at stations but the pastoralists involved generally focused on the integrated use of financial and non-financial operating information for pre-Federation pastoral industry engagement. Bridges's (1975) study of the history of Australian farm recording from 1788 to 1972 was based on publications written primarily by accountants and portrays a perspective on the development of pastoral accounting through reliance on the opinions and prescriptions expressed in these writings. His view is at variance with the findings of this study which indicate that effective pastoral accounting for day to day station operations did not equate with "proper" professional accounting practice. According to Johnson and Kaplan (1987, p.138), Littleton's widely-cited work titled *Accounting Evolution to 1900* was similarly constricted as the author did not examine surviving company business records in writing about the history of cost accounting.[1] Instead, Littleton (1933) relied upon publications written by accountants themselves. This study provides evidence that field-based case study research permits more specific conclusions to be drawn about accounting development including the explanation of paradigm shifts in accounting's past.

Culture as a Theoretical Perspective

There is a growing literature on the impact of culture in shaping the accounting environment of a country. This study presents a logical development of this literature in using culture as a theoretical perspective to assist in explaining historical accounting practices in a local, time-specific context. In the complete absence of an examination of local, time-specific cultural factors, less comprehensive explanations are likely to be drawn about accounting practices of bygone eras. Hence, for interpretive history, the use of culture as an explanatory variable assists in affording historical evidence the life it once possessed.

Professionalization of Accounting

The study provides some evidence which suggests that the expansion and enhancement of the domain of double entry accounting was a key determinant of the professionalization of accounting in Australia, particularly in the period following the early 1890s economic depression in Eastern Australia. While double entry accounting was portrayed as "proper" professional accounting, its widened adoption seems to have enabled the organized accounting profession to expand its services in overcoming what Davison (1978, p.112) described as "a popular fear of bad bookkeeping "stemming from the economic crises.

Double entry accounting, as a mystery to the laity, also served to mark off the accounting profession from other professional groups.

The organized accounting profession today continues to promote rationales which assist to expand and enhance the domain of accrual accounting in regulated financial reporting environments. The justification that full accrual accounting or "commercial accounting" provides information useful for making and evaluating decisions about the allocation of scarce resources and satisfies accountability considerations is now confidently articulated for mandated financial reporting practices, irrespective of the organisational and social context.[2] Whenever accounting is "normalized" through the adoption of its traditional product or when the traditional product is extended to embrace new forms of quantification, the impacts typically include an improvement in the demand for professional accounting services.

Origins of Current Financial Reporting Emphasis

This study also provides some insights into the origins of the present dominance of the financial accounting function and the emphasis on financial reporting by the organized Australian accounting profession (Weekes, 1986; Ireland, 1990; Parker, 1990, 1995, 1996; Avigdor, 1993; Lowry, 1993; Carnegie & Wolnizer, 1995, 1996). The Australian Society of Certified Practising Accountants (ASCPA) and The Institute of Chartered Accountants in Australia (ICAA), as the two major Australian professional accounting bodies, emphasize financial reporting by means of pronouncements prepared and issued on their behalf by the Australian Accounting Research Foundation (AARF). The AARF is the jointly sponsored research arm of the ASCPA and ICAA (AARF, 1992).[3] The major professional pronouncements comprise accounting and auditing standards, accounting concept statements, auditing practice statements, and accounting and auditing guidance releases.

Present reforms of the Australian public sector involve the adoption of full accrual accounting for financial reporting purposes by reporting entities in the sector. Such accounting reforms have also been imposed upon public not-for-profit organizations such as repositories of cultural, heritage and scientific collections (hereafter "collections") (Boreham, 1994b; Clark, 1994; Carnegie & Wolnizer, 1995, 1996; Griffin, 1995; Parker, 1995; Walker, 1995a, b). Commenting on proposals to place values on publicly-owned collections for financial reporting purposes, Parker (1995, p.81) stated "let us hope that the accounting profession's enthusiasm for its traditional product does not drag public sector and not-for-profit organisations into the abyss". Further addressing this issue, Carnegie and Wolnizer (1996) proposed "a

244   *Pastoral Accounting in Colonial Australia*

means of averting a spurious and stultifying notion of accountability envisaged by those who advocate the valuation of collections for financial reporting purposes" (p.94) in outlining a "broader and more functional notion of accountability" described as "enabling accountability in museums" (EAM) (p.84). Parker (1996) advocated "broad scope accountability", a concept aimed at serving a broad community-based constituency. Broad scope accountability would be discharged through reporting a combination of financial and non-financial quantitative information supported by a wide range of qualitative data (Parker, 1996, p.9).

The recent establishment in Australia of an Urgent Issues Group (UIG) provides a further illustration of organized accounting profession's emphasis on financial reporting. The UIG's role "is to provide timely guidance on urgent financial reporting issues" (AARF, 1994, p.D2). Similarly, following the corporate failures of the 1980s in Australia, the ASCPA and ICAA commissioned a major study on ways to bridge the so-called "expectation gap" (ASCPA & ICAA, 1994; Boreham, 1994a, p.64).[4] The reforms proposed in that study all related to financial reporting and auditing and provide further evidence of the emphasis on financial reporting issues by the organized Australian accounting profession. This emphasis on financial reporting issues does not assist in addressing the problems highlighted by Johnson and Kaplan (1987, p.1) who stated:

> Today's management accounting information, driven by the procedures and cycle of the organization's financial reporting system, is too late, too aggregated, and too distorted to be relevant for managers' planning and control decisions.

Kaplan and Norton (1996, p.7) expressed similar concerns about the current concentration on financial outputs derived under the "historical-cost financial accounting model" in stating:

> . . . financial measures tell the story of past events, an adequate story for industrial age companies for which investments in long-term capabilities and customer relationships were not critical for success. These financial measures are inadequate, however, for guiding and evaluating the journey that information age companies must make to create future value through investment in customers, suppliers, employees, processes, technology and innovation.

Regard for Efficiency in the Colonial Era

Despite the orientation of the organized accounting profession in Australia, there have been certain recent developments in management accounting practices and management techniques which focus on efficiency, effectiveness and quality concepts. The concept of efficiency is concerned with the relationship between input and output in both physical and financial terms (L.D. Parker, 1986, p.13). This study has provided evidence that pre-Federation Western District pastoralists were concerned with the efficiency of production processes although the introduction by accountants of "proper" financial recording systems concentrated attention on financial outputs. As the evidence showed, the pre-Federation pastoralists themselves were generally concerned with measuring and evaluating performance in financial and non-financial operating terms and commonly focused directly on the real value-generating processes of their operations. This appears to be a focus now being rediscovered by contemporary manufacturing and public sector management. Practices and techniques such as activity-based costing (Cooper, 1988), performance and value-for-money auditing (L.D. Parker, 1986; Guthrie, 1990) and total quality management (Cooper & Kaplan, 1991, pp.200-205) are broadly concerned with either the efficiency and effectiveness of operations or the quality of outputs as to keys to long-term profitability. These developments have influenced the management control process (Anthony, Dearden & Govindarajan, 1992, pp.497-521). In the manufacturing sector, these developments are regarded as integral to the "new" manufacturing environment (Hilton, 1991, pp.163-219). In the Australian public sector, similar developments are occurring in combination with the widespread adoption of accrual-based financial reporting systems (Guthrie & Parker, 1990; Roberts, 1993, p.86). It remains to be seen whether there will be a focus in the Australian public sector on measuring and evaluating performance in accordance with the specific organisational objectives of public sector entities.

Opportunities for Further Research

Examination of accounting development in surviving business records of Australian firms is still in its infancy. However, the study of the intricacies of double entry accounting records for its own sake does not offer insights into the structure and usage of accounting information prepared generally for industry engagement. As stated by Edwards (1989b, p.316):

> There has been a tendency for writers to concentrate on the quality
> of double entry bookkeeping procedures and to cast doubt on the

usefulness of surviving accounting statements and, from this, a
lack of interest in such documentation has been inferred.

There is considerable scope in Australia and elsewhere to undertake
interpretive history studies of surviving business records of all types in
order to augment our understanding of accounting's past and to provide
insights into accounting's present and future.[5] As evident from this
study, the examination of leather-bound ledgers alone delimits the
opportunities for recognising whatever diversity existed in accounting
systems of earlier times. Similarly, historical studies of accounting
development based on articles and books on accounting techniques can
result in simplistic descriptions of actual accounting practice during the
period examined.

In terms of specific research studies, there is scope to extend this
study by examining the surviving post-Federation Western District
business records of non-corporate pastoral entities. An extension of this
study would permit further specific conclusions to be drawn about the
structure and usage of accounting information for Western District
pastoral industry engagement. However, it may only be possible to
extend the study to around 1950 as surviving business records after that
time may not be available for privacy reasons.

Examinations of surviving pre-Federation pastoral business records
prepared elsewhere in Victoria or in other Australian colonies would
permit more generalized conclusions to be drawn about the structure and
usage of pre-Federation pastoral accounting information. Similarly, a
study of this nature could be undertaken in other countries subject to the
availability of a sample of surviving pastoral business records. Any
studies of pastoral business records undertaken overseas would permit
the findings to be compared with those of this study and enable
explanations of any variations in practice to be rendered.

A study of this nature could also be undertaken in other Australian
industries to augment the literature on accounting development. A
broader view of accounting development in any country is possible
when research findings based on surviving business records are available
for a range of industries rather than for a particular industry in a certain
region of a country.

Whatever future research this study may motivate, it is important
to recognize that the study of accounting's past offers the potential for
accountants to enhance their own self-understandings as members of a
professional elite. It also offers the scope to broaden perspectives of
accounting's future. Whatever the future holds for accounting, it is
important for accountants, accounting standard-setters, and regulators
among others to reflect upon Porter's statement:

There is strength in numbers, and anyone who proposes to wield them more effectively must ask not only about their validity but also about how the world might be changed by adopting new forms of quantification (1996, p.53).

An understanding of accounting's past is the key to understanding accounting as it enters the third millenium. As accounting becomes increasingly implicated in the lives of all, may accounting history inform and enhance discussion about accounting and its future development.

NOTES

1. The material on cost accounting history is contained in Littleton (1933) Chapters 20-22.
2. Under the conceptual framework for regulated financial reporting being developed by the organized Australian accounting profession, reports prepared using full accrual accounting are known as "general purpose financial reports". A "general purpose financial report" is defined as a "financial report intended to meet the information needs common to users who are unable to command the preparation of reports tailored so as to satisfy, specifically, all of their information needs" (AARF, 1990, para.5).
3. The principal objectives of the AARF are to "improve the quality of financial reporting and auditing in Australia; contribute to the international development of financial reporting and auditing; and contribute to the development of commercial law and practice in Australia" (AARF, 1992).
4. The "expectation gap" was defined in the study as "the difference between the expectations of users of financial reports and the perceived quality of financial reporting and auditing services delivered by the Accounting Profession (the Profession)" (ASCPA & ICAA, 1994, p.3).
5. Boyns (1993, p.327) indicated that the examination of costing records of British firms is also in its infancy.

APPENDICES

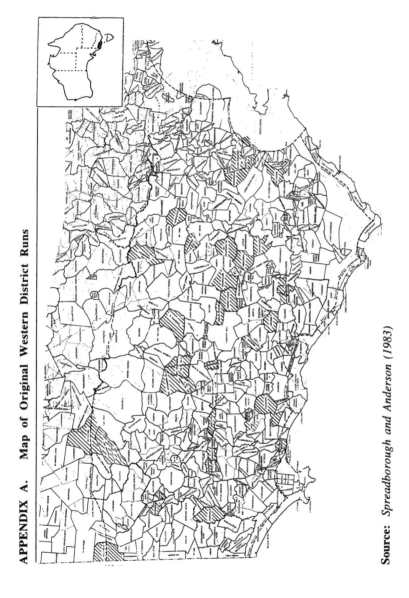

APPENDIX A.   Map of Original Western District Runs

Source: *Spreadborough and Anderson (1983)*

249

APPENDIX B: Official Form to be Completed Under Act 2 *Victoria,* No.27

THE CLYDE COMPANY *and 2* VICTORIA NO. 27

(Copy, on the official form, of returns made to the Commissioner of Crown Lands for the six months ending 31 Dec. 39, plus a note of returns made as at 30 June 40.)
SCHEDULES REFERRED TO
SCHEDULE A

First day of *January* 1840

HALF YEARLY RETURN of the number of PERSONS employed, or residing at, and of the number and description of the Live Stock on, the Licensed Station of *The Clyde Company* called *The run of the Clyde Comp*ˢ situated in the District of *Geelong,* adjacent to the County of *Grant,* of which District *Foster Fyans* [E]squire is the Commissioner; rendered in conformity with the Provisions of the Act of the Governor and Council, 2 Victoria, No.27

1.	STATION	
2.	Names of Proprietors of Stock herein returned	*Theodore Walrond, Frederick Adamson, John S. Wood, William Wood, Patrick Wood, Philip Russell, William Cross*
3.	Person Superintending	*George Russell*
4.	Estimated Extent of Run	*Twenty Thousand Acres*
5.	Number of Acres in Cultivation	*None*
6.	How Watered	*By the rivers Leigh & Murrabull*

7. Persons at Stations

Free	Male	*26 (Twenty Six)*
	Female	*2 (Two)*
Bond	Male	*None*
	Female	*None*
	Total	*28 (Twenty Eight)*

8. Stock on Station

Horses	*15 (Fifteen)*
Cattle including Calves above six months old	*212 (Two Hundred & Twelve)*
Sheep including weaned Lambs	*6,974 (Six Thousand nine Hundred and Seventy four)*

9.	Number of Licenses	*1 (One)*
10.	Brand	*C C*

APPENDIX B (cont'd)

[On the back of the sheet is the following. The heading and first name are in Captain Fyans's writing, the other names in George Russell's.]

Nominal List of Persons on the Establishment

Mr George Russell
Robert Muirhead
William Thomson
Joseph Simmons
Richard Jhonson
David Oswald
George Tugnelt
John Russell
Henry Younger
James Thomson

Andrew Baxter
Frederick Smith
Charles Brichby
Thomas Barnes
John Moffatt
James Clancey
Patrick Raynolds
and Wife
Charles Younger
Thomas Marlow

Thomas Tilson
John Kimbers and
Wife
Malcolm Bowie
David Sharp
Andrew Scott
Roderick Gollan
George Rhodes
William Nicholas

[At the foot of the sheet is a note by George Russell showing the sum due in assessment, and bound up with it is a smaller paper carrying a similar calculation. These are reproduced below.]

Cattle	£	1	.	6	.	6
Sheep		14	.	10	.	7
Horses				3	.	9
	£	16	.	-	.	10

Source: *Reproduced from Brown (1952, pp.350-351).*

APPENDIX C: Inventory of Primary Records of the
Australian Institute of Incorporated
Accountants Sighted at the Public Records
Office, Victoria, Laverton

- Memorandum and Articles of Association
- Notice of change of Registered Office, dated 1 March 1893
- Notice of change of Registered Office, dated 28 June 1893
- Notice of change of Secretary, dated 28 June 1893
- Statement for the year ended 31 December 1897
- Notice of meeting / Report of the Council / Statement for the year ended 31 December 1898
- Notice of meeting / Report of the Council / Statement for the year ended 31 December 1899
- Notice of change of Secretary, dated 12 December 1906
- Notice of passage of Resolution, relating to changes to Articles of Association, dated 9 February 1909.

Source: *Government of Victoria - Public Records Office of Victoria, Laverton VPRS 933 Australian Institute of Incorporated Accountants, Unit No. 2810*

APPENDIX D. Summary of the Content of Examinations on "Book-keeping"(a) held by The Incorporated Institute of Accountants, Victoria during 1891-99

Date of Examination	Details	Q1.	Q2.	Q3.	Q4.	Q5.	Q6.	Q7.	Q8.
		Type of Question/Nature of Entity/Requirements(b)							
June 1891	Subject I.	D							
March 1892	Subject I.	P/F/SI	P/P/A	P/ST/A	P/ST/J	P/P/A	P/C/A		
August 1893	Subject I.	P/P/A	P/ST/SA	P/F/ET	D	P/F/J	P/F/J		
February 1894(c)	Students'	D	D	D	P/PC/J	P/M/J	P/C/J		
July 1894	Students'	D	D	P/NS/SI	P/ST/A				
February 1895	Students'	D	P/ST/A	P/C/J	P/ST/A(d)	P/C/A(d)			
	Associates'	D	P/ST/A	P/NS/SI	P/NS/SI	P/NS/SI	P/E/A		
August 1895	Students'	P/NS/SI	P/C/A	P/NS/SI	P/C/A	P/E/A			
	Associates'	P/C/A	P/P/A	D	P/P/A	P/E/SI	P/NS/AD	P/P/A	P/E/A
March 1896	Students'	D	P/E/A	D	D	P/C/A			
	Associates'	P/ST/A	D	D	D	D	P/NS/A		
October 1896	Associates'(e)	D	P/P/A	P/ST/A	P/P/A	P/P/A	P/F/SA		
	Students'	D	P/C/A	D	P/E/A	P/E/A	P/P/A		
March 1897	Intermediate(f)	P/P/A	D	P/NS/SI	D	D			
	Associates'(g)		P/NS/SI		D			P/NS/SI	
September 1897(g)	Students'	D	D	D	P/C/A	P/ST/SA			
	Intermediate	D	D	P/NS/SI	P/ST/A	P/P/A			
June 1898	Students'			P/P/A	D				
	Intermediate			P/SO/A	P/NS/SI				
	Associates'		D	P/E/A	D				
November 1898	Students'	P/NS/AD	P/F/SA	P/C/A	D	P/C/A	P/NS/SI		
	Intermediate	P/F/A	P/NS/AD	P/F/SA	P/E/A	P/C/A			
	Associates'	P/E/A	D	P/P/A	P/P/A	P/E/A			
April 1899	Students'	D	D	P/C/A	P/NS/SI	D			
	Intermediate	D	D	P/C/A	D	P/C/A			
	Associates'	D		P/C/A	P/C/A		P/E/A		

APPENDIX D. (cont'd)

Notes:

(a) From August 1895, the "Book-keeping" examinations were retitled and became known as "Book-keeping and Accounts; incl. Partnership and Executorship Accounts". (For simplicity, the title "Book-keeping" is used to describe this series of examinations in this study).

(b) The key to the codes (Type of Question/Nature of Entity/Requirements) shown in this appendix is detailed hereunder:

Type of Question	Nature of Entity		Requirements	
D = Descriptive	C	= Company	A	= Accounts
P = Practical	E	= Executorship	AD	= Average Date (to find)
	F	= Firm	ET	= Equated Time of Debt (to determine)
	M	= Merchant	J	= Journal Entries
	NS	= Not Specified	SA	= Statement of Affairs (for creditors)
	P	= Partnership	SI	= Specimen Rulings of Books and Illustrative Entries
	PC	= Partnership to Company		
	SO	= Station Owner		
	ST	= Sole Trader		

(c) From 1894, the IIAV conducted separate examinations in "Book-keeping" for students and associates (that is, candidates for associateship) (IIAV, 1895).

(d) The first questions in the surviving examination papers which included the item depreciation appeared in these examination papers.

(e) The October 1896 Associates' Examination was the first examination to be held over two nights (questions 1-4 were to be attempted on the first night while questions 5-7 were to be attempted on the second night).

(f) From July 1896, students' examinations were either "Preliminary" or "Intermediate". Preliminary examinations embraced "Composition, Dictation, Grammar, Arithmetic, and Algebra to Single Equations" (IIAV, 1896, p.12).

(g) From March 1897, the Associates' Examination questions were numbered consecutively from number one for both sittings.

APPENDIX E: Reproduction of the First Question Set on Station Accounting in Surviving "Bookkeeping" Examination Papers of The Incorporated Institute of Accountants, Victoria

3.-A., B., and C. are equal partners in a Station, the value of which at 30th June, 1896, stood as follows: 100,000 Sheep at 5/-, 3,500 Cattle at 30/-, and 125 Horses at £3 per head. Improvements had cost £5,500, Freehold Land 25,000 acres worth £2 10/- per acre, 10,000 acres conditional purchased land paid up to 9/- per acre, on which there remained a liability of 11/- per acre to make freehold.

The liabilities were on a Mortgage of £20,000, due to Bankers £6,300, Sundry Creditors £1,250, and balance owing to station hands £675. Stock bills were current (payable) for £1,500.

The partners' over-drawings up to the 30th June, 1896, had been-A., £1,500; B., £1,200; and C., £1,000; on which it was provided that interest at the rate of 5% per annum should be charged.

At the 31st December, 1896, it was decided that A. and B. should buy out their partner, C.

When the stock were mustered prior to the purchase of C.'s share, it was found that there had been a loss of 20,000 Sheep, an increase of 300 Cattle, and 25 Horses, to be dealt with on the basis of the above valuations.

The books then showed the following expenditure for the six months: Wages, £1,275; Shearing Expenses, £2,300; Goods and Stores, £520; Station Expenses, £155; Land Tax, £350; Rates, £196; and Vermin Destruction, £330.

The Wool Clip of 1,500 bales had fetched a nett average of £11 10/- per bale. Stock Sales had amounted to £1,360, and Skins and Hides £25.

Depreciation at the rate of 10% per annum had to be written off the improvements, and the balance required to pay up the C.P.'s provided for.

The partners had drawn a sum of £1,500 in anticipation of their respective shares of profits in the following proportions, viz.: A., £600; B., £400; and C., £500; but on this no interest had to be paid.

Prepare a Profit and Loss Account and Balance-Sheet, and also a Statement showing the amount which A. and B. had to provide to buy out C.

Source: *Reproduced from IIAV, Associates' "Bookkeeping" Examination, June 1898 (Australian Society of Certified Practising Accountants Archives, Melbourne).*

APPENDIX F: Australian Mortgage (Mercantile) Land and Finance Company Ltd Extracts of Minutes of the London-based Board of Directors on Matters of Lending Policy (1867-79)

---

22 July 1867   **Advances in Australia**
                        Referring to proposed loan by the Manager in Melbourne to Mr Henry Ricketson; the Secretary was instructed to reply the Board is of the opinion, that it is not desirable to advance (unless in exceptional cases) a larger sum than £20,000 to any one man, unless the security includes freehold land.

12 January 1870   **Reduction of Colonial Accounts**
                        That in the opinion of the Directors the time has arrived when it is advisable that a reduction in the amount advanced on mortgages should be made and instructions sent to the Managers in the Colony that a reduction in the amount on all accounts above £10,000 be made annually of at least 10% for the next three years, and intimation of such instructions be given to the Mortgagors and that on properties taken over by the Company on the amount of their advance unless a profit of at least 6 per cent per annum can be shown, the necessary steps be taken to dispose of such properties.

28 September 1870   **Settlers Advances to be Reduced**
                        On the suggestion of Mr McLachlan it was considered desirable that the Manager in Melbourne should be written to by this mail to again call his attention to the increasing amount of the advances to the Settlers and large overdrafts at the Bank contrary to the wishes of the Board, as already expressed in former communications under dates 9 October 1868, 18 June 1869 and 28 January 1870.

5 June 1872   **Advances on Deposit of Deeds**
                        It was resolved that the Manager in Victoria should in future be authorised to make temporary advances not exceeding £10,000 to any single borrower on the security only of a simple deposit of Deeds.

29 June 1875   **Advances to Colonial Directors**
                        Adverting to the clause in the Letter of Instructions to the Colonial Manager dated 24 December 1874 relative to Advances to Directors - It was now agreed upon that an advance might be made at any time to a Director provided the amount did not exceed the value of his ensuing clip of wool.

30 September 1879   **Tel. re Finance & Wool Advances**
                        After some remarks from the Chairman (Mr. Gibbs) on the subject of Finance, the Board being unanimous in the desire that a more restrictive policy should be pursued in Melbourne, it was decided that the following telegram be sent to the Melbourne Manager "Jewess (we cannot see hope of improvement) endeavour to keep wool advances with margin on present values".

APPENDIX F (cont'd)

---

14 October 1879   **Special Finance**
Melbourne Special letter no.106 was read, also a paragraph in Special no.73 to Melbourne on the subject of borrowing on freehold land. The whole policy of the Company was then discussed, and although no definite conclusion was arrived at, the Board were unanimous in wishing that the business of the Company in Australia should be kept within safer limits, and that the Melbourne Manager should clearly understand that the limit of capital assigned to him by the London Board should never be exceeded.

Source: *AML&F, Minute Books held at The Noel Butlin Archives Centre, Australian National University, Canberra (162/2; 162/3; 162/4).*

BIBLIOGRAPHY

Anderson, H., (1969), *The Flowers of the Field: A History of Ripon Shire*, Melbourne: Content Publishing Co.

Anon., (1893), "The Status of Accountants", *The Australasian Insurance and Banking Record*, Vol.17, No.10, 20 November, p.1014.

Anon., (1899), "Farm Bookkeeping", *Queensland Agricultural Journal*, Vol.4, No.3, March, pp.175-179.

Anon., (1965), "George Armytage was Born in Derbyshire: Early Youth in Brussels", *Colac Herald*, 6 August, p.9.

Ansari, S.L. and Bell, J., (1991), "Symbolism, Collectivism and Rationality in Organisational Control", *Accounting, Auditing & Accountability Journal*, Vol.4, No.2, pp.4-27.

Anthony, R.N., Dearden, J. and Govindarajan, V., (1992), *Management Control Systems*, seventh edition, Homewood: Irwin.

Arpan, J.S. and AlHashim, D.D., (1984), *International Dimensions of Accounting*, Boston: Kent Publishing Co.

Arpan, J.S. and Radebaugh, L.H., (1985), *International Accounting and Multinational Enterprises*, second edition, New York: John Wiley & Sons.

Australasian, (1873), 10 May; (1898), 19 March.

Australian Accounting Research Foundation, (1990), *Statement of Accounting Concepts SAC2 "Objective of General Purpose Financial Reporting"*, August, Melbourne: AARF.

Australian Accounting Research Foundation, (1992), *Facts About the Australian Accounting Research Foundation*, Melbourne: AARF.

Australian Accounting Research Foundation, (1994), *Urgent Issues Group Charter*, October, Melbourne: AARF.

(The) Australian Encyclopaedia, (1963), Vol.2, Sydney: The Grolier Society of Australia.

(The) Australian Encyclopaedia, (1963), Vol.6, Sydney: The Grolier Society of Australia.

(The) Australian Encyclopaedia, (1963), Vol.7, Sydney: The Grolier Society of Australia.

(The) Australian Institute of Incorporated Accountants, (1892), *Memorandum and Articles of Association*, Melbourne: AIIA.

Australian Society of Accountants, (1963), *History of the Australian Society of Accountants and its Antecedent Bodies*, Melbourne: Australian Society of Accountants.

Australian Society of Certified Practising Accountants and The Institute of Chartered Accountants in Australia, (1994), *A Research Study on*

Financial Reporting and Auditing - Bridging the Expectation Gap, ASCPA and ICAA.

Avigdor, J., (1993), "Defining a Role that Survives Restructuring", *New Accountant*, 18 March, p.22.

Bailey, J.D., (1966), *A Hundred Years of Pastoral Banking: A History of the Australian Mercantile Land & Finance Company 1863-1963*, London: Oxford University Press.

Ballarat Courier, (1902), 6 September.

Ballarat Star, (1892), 15 July.

Barnard, A., (1957), "The Significance of Wool in the Australian Economy, 1850-1950", paper read to the Wool Seminar, Australian National University, as dated 14 June.

Bassett, M., (1954), *The Hentys: An Australian Colonial Tapestry*, London: Oxford University Press.

Bate, W., (1990), *Light Blue Down Under: The History of Geelong Grammar School*, Melbourne: Oxford University Press.

Baxter, W.T., (1946), "Credit, Bills and Bookkeeping in a Simple Economy", *The Accounting Review*, Vol.21, No.2, April, pp.154-166.

Baxter, W.T. (ed.), (1950), *Studies in Accounting Theory*, London: Sweet & Maxwell.

Baxter, W.T., (1956), "Accounting in Colonial Accounting" in Littleton, A.C. and Yamey, B.S. (eds.), *Studies in the History of Accounting*, London: Sweet & Maxwell, pp.272-288.

Baxter, W.T., (1983), "Accounting Roots and their Lingering Influence" in Gaertner, J.F. (ed.), *Selected Papers From The Charles Waldo Haskins Accounting History Seminars*, Monograph No.4, The Academy of Accounting Historians, pp.135-151.

Bean, C.E.W., (1950), *Here, My Son*, Sydney: Angus & Robertson.

Belkaoui, A., (1985a), *Accounting Theory*, second edition, Orlando: Harcourt Brace Jovanovich.

Belkaoui, A., (1985b), *International Accounting: Issues and Solutions*, Westport: Greenwood Press.

Belkaoui, A., (1989), "Cultural Determinism and Professional Self-Regulation in Accounting", *Research in Accounting Regulation*, Vol.3, pp.93-101.

Billis, R.V. and Kenyon, A.S., (1930), *Pastures New*, Melbourne: McCarron, Bird & Co.

Billis, R.V. and Kenyon, A.S., (1974), *Pastoral Pioneers of Port Phillip*, second edition, Melbourne: Stockland Press (first published in 1932 by Macmillan & Company, Melbourne).

Birnberg, J.G., (1980), "The Role of Accounting in Financial Disclosure", *Accounting, Organizations and Society*, Vol.5, No.1, June, pp.71-80.

Blainey, G., (1958), *Gold and Paper: A History of The National Bank of Australasia Limited*, Melbourne: Georgian House.

Bloom, R. and Naciri, M.A., (1989), "Accounting Standard Setting and Culture: A Comparative Analysis of the United States, Canada, England, West Germany, Australia, New Zealand, Sweden, Japan and

Switzerland", *The International Journal of Accounting Education and Research*, Vol.24, No.1, pp.70-97.

Boehm, E.A., (1971), *Prosperity and Depression in Australia 1887-1897*, London: Oxford University Press.

Boreham, T., (1994a), "How to Get Auditors to Live up to Expectations", *Business Review Weekly*, 31 January, pp.64-65.

Boreham, T., (1994b), "Valuing Heritage Assets: Is it Worth the Cost and Trouble?", *Business Review Weekly*, 14 November, pp.116-118.

Boyns, T., (1993), "Cost Accounting in the South Wales Coal Industry, c. 1870-1914", *Accounting, Business & Financial History*, Vol.3, No.3, December, pp.327-352.

Boyns, T. and Edwards, J.R., (1996), "Change Agents and the Dissemination of Accounting Technology: Wales' Basic Industries", *Accounting History*, NS Vol.1, No.1, May, pp.9-34.

Boyns, T. and Edwards, J.R., (1997), "Cost and Management Accounting in Early Victorian Britain: A Chandleresque Analysis", *Management Accounting Research*, Vol.8, pp.19-46.

Brentnall, T., (1898), "Interesting Address to Young Accountants", *Bankers' Magazine of Australasia*, Vol.12, No.4, 15 November, pp.242-247 and Vol.12, No.5, 15 December, pp.328-331.

Brentnall, T., (1938), *My Memories*, Melbourne: Robertson & Mullins.

Bride, T.F. (ed.), (1969), *Letters from Victorian Pioneers*, Melbourne: William Heinemann (first published in 1898 for the Trustees of the Public Library, Museums by Robt. S. Brain, Government Printer, Melbourne).

Bridges, A., (1975), "History of Australian Farm Recording 1788-1972", unpublished MEc. dissertation, University of New England.

Brown, P.L. (ed.), (1935), *The Narrative of George Russell of Golf Hill*, London: Oxford University Press.

Brown, P.L. (ed.), (1941), *Clyde Company Papers*, Vol.1 1821-35, London: Oxford University Press.

Brown, P.L. (ed.), (1952), *Clyde Company Papers*, Vol.2 1836-40, London: Oxford University Press.

Brown, P.L. (ed.), (1958), *Clyde Company Papers*, Vol.3 1841-45, London: Oxford University Press.

Brown, P.L. (ed.), (1959), *Clyde Company Papers*, Vol.4 1846-50, London: Oxford University Press.

Brown, P.L. (ed.), (1963), *Clyde Company Papers*, Vol.5 1851-53, London: Oxford University Press.

Brown, P.L., (1966), "Armytage, George (1795-1862)", *Australian Dictionary of Biography*, Vol.1, Melbourne: Melbourne University Press, p.27.

Brown, P.L., (1967), "Russell, Philip (1796?-1844) and George (1812-1888)", *Australian Dictionary of Biography*, Vol.2, Melbourne: Melbourne University Press, pp.408-409.

Brown, P.L. (ed.), (1968), *Clyde Company Papers*, Vol.6 1854-58, London: Oxford University Press.

Brown, P.L. (ed.), (1971), *Clyde Company Papers*, Vol.7 1859-73, London: Oxford University Press.

Brown, P.L., (1974), "Russell, Philip (1822?-1892) and Thomas (1828-1920)", *Australian Dictionary of Biography*, Vol.6, Melbourne: Melbourne University Press, p.77.

Brownhill, W.R., (1990), *The History of Geelong and Corio Bay*, Geelong: Geelong Advertiser (first published in 1955 by Wilke & Co., Melbourne).

Buckley, J., (1897), "Bookkeeping for Farmers" in Part II of Lindley-Cowen, L. (ed.), *The West Australian Settler's Guide and Farmer's Handbook*, Perth: Bureau of Agriculture, pp.342-360.

Buckley, J.W., Buckley, M.H. and Chiang, H.F., (1976), *Research Methodology and Business Decisions*, National Association of Accountants and the Society of Industrial Accountants of Canada.

Burke, B., (1958), *Burke's Genealogical & Heraldic History of the Landed Gentry of Ireland*, Pine L.G. and Scot, F.S.A. (eds.), fourth edition, London: Burke's Peerage.

Burtchaell, G.D. and Sadleir, T.U., (eds.), (1935), *Alumni Dublinenses: A Register of the Students, Graduates, Professors and Provosts of Trinity College in the University of Dublin (1593-1860)*, Dublin: Alex. Thom & Co.

Butlin, N.G., (1957), "Australian Pastoral Development, 1860-1900", paper read to the Wool Seminar, Australian National University, 3 July.

Butlin, N.G., (1958), "The Distribution of Sheep Population Preliminary Statistical Picture, 1860-1956", paper read to the Wool Seminar, Australian National University, as dated 7 October.

Butlin, N.G., (1964), *Investment in Australian Economic Development 1861-1900*, Cambridge: Cambridge University Press.

Butlin, S.J., (1953), *Foundations of the Australian Monetary System 1788-1851*, Melbourne: Melbourne University Press.

Butlin, S.J., (1961), *Australia and New Zealand Bank*, London: Longmans.

Camperdown Chronicle, (1875), 17 December; (1894), 10 November.

Cannon, M., (1967), *The Land Boomers*, Melbourne: Melbourne University Press.

Cannon, M., (1973), *Life in the Country. Australia in the Victorian Age: 2*, West Melbourne: Thomas Nelson.

Carnegie, G.D., (1990), "Oral History Interview with Norman Dennis and Sheila Dennis", unpublished manuscript.

Carnegie, G.D., (1990-91), "Oral History Interviews with Robert Jamieson No.III", unpublished manuscript.

Carnegie, G.D., (1991a), "Oral History Interview with Dame Ella and Helen Macknight,", unpublished manuscript.

Carnegie, G.D., (1991b), "Oral History Interview with Eoin C. Smith,", unpublished manuscript.

Carnegie, G.D., (1993a), "Pastoral Accounting in Pre-Federation Victoria: A Case Study on the Jamieson Family", *Accounting and Business Research*, Vol.23, No.91, pp.204-218.

Carnegie, G.D., (1993b), "The Australian Institute of Incorporated Accountants (1892-1938)", *Accounting, Business & Financial History*, Vol.3, No.1, March, pp.61-80.

Carnegie, G.D., (1994), "The Structure and Usage of Accounting Information in Pre-Federation Pastoral Industry Management in the Western District of Victoria (1836-1900)", unpublished Ph.D dissertation, The Flinders University of South Australia.

Carnegie, G.D., (1995), "Pastoral Accounting in Pre-Federation Victoria: A Contextual Analysis of Surviving Business Records", *Accounting, Auditing & Accountability Journal*, Vol.8, No.5, pp.3-33.

Carnegie, G.D. and Parker, R.H., (1994), "The First Australian Book on Accounting: James Dimelow's 'Practical Bookkeeping Made Easy'", *Abacus*, Vol.30, No.1, March, pp.78-97.

Carnegie, G.D. and Varker, S.A., (1995), "Edward Wild: Advocate of Simplification and an Organised Profession in Colonial Australia", *The Accounting Historians Journal*, Vol.22, No.2, December, pp.131-149.

Carnegie, G.D. and Wolnizer, P.W., (1995), "The Financial Value of Cultural, Heritage and Scientific Collections: An Accounting Fiction", *Australian Accounting Review*, Vol.5, No.1, pp.31-47 (reprinted with permission in Nudds, J.R. and Pettitt, C.W. (eds.), *The Value and Valuation of Natural Science Collections*, London: The Geological Society, 1997).

Carnegie, G.D. and Wolnizer, P.W., (1996), "Enabling Accountability in Museums", *Accounting, Auditing & Accountability Journal*, Vol.9, No.5, pp.84-99.

Chambers, R.J., (1994), "Historical Cost - Tale of a False Creed", *Accounting Horizons*, Vol.8, No.1, March, pp.76-89.

Chambers, R.J. and Wolnizer, P.W., (1991), "A True and Fair View of Position and Results: The Historical Background", *Accounting, Business & Financial History*, Vol.1, No.2, March, pp.197-213.

Chatfield, M., (1977), *A History of Accounting Thought*, revised edition, New York: Robert E. Krieger Publishing Co.

Chua, W.F. and Poullaos, C., (1993), "Rethinking the Profession-State Dynamic: The Case of the Victorian Charter Attempt, 1885-1906", *Accounting, Organizations and Society*, Vol.18, Nos.7, 8, pp.691-728.

Civelli, D., (1991), "In Tune with the Past", *Geelong Advertiser*, Weekend Magazine, 16 February, pp.1-2.

Clark, C., (1994), "Valuing Heritage Assets", (Postscript), *Business Review Weekly*, 12 December, p.105.

Colac Herald, (1888), "The History of Colac and District" (published as a series); (1892), 15 April; (1965), 6 August.

Collier, J., (1911), *The Pastoral Age in Australasia*, London: Whitcombe & Tombs.

Colligan, M., (1990), *Boomtime: Australia 1871-1890*, The Colonial Collection, Australia Post.

Collins, M. and Bloom, R., (1991), "The Role of Oral History in Accounting", *Accounting, Auditing & Accountability Journal*, Vol.4, No.4, pp.23-31.

Commonwealth of Australia, (1921), *Historical Records of Australia*, Series 3, Vol.3, Sydney (William Applegate Gullick, Government Printers): The Library Committee of the Commonwealth Parliament.

Connell, R.W. and Irving, T.H., (1992), *Class Structure in Australian History*, second edition, Melbourne: Longman Cheshire.

Cooper, R., (1988), "The Rise of Activity-Based Costing - Part One: What is an Activity-Based Cost System?", *Journal of Cost Management*, Vol.2, No.2, Summer, pp.45-54.

Cooper, R. and Kaplan, R.S., (1991), *The Design of Cost Management Systems*, New Jersey: Prentice-Hall.

Critchett, J.F., (1990), *A Distant Field of Murder*, Melbourne: Melbourne University Press.

Cumming, W.H., (1992), "A Short History of the William Cumming Family of Mt. Fyans, Stonehenge, Myrngrong, Wooroglin and including Strathallyn and Barnie Bolac, Woorigoleen and Fyans Lodge", unpublished manuscript.

Curr, E.M., (1968), *Recollections of Squatting in Victoria*, Adelaide: Libraries Board of South Australia (first published in 1889 by George Robertson, Melbourne).

Davison, G., (1978), *The Rise and Fall of Marvellous Melbourne*, Melbourne: Melbourne University Press.

Denholm, D., (1967), "Tregurtha, Edward Primrose (1803-1880)", *Australian Dictionary of Biography*, Vol.2, Melbourne: Melbourne University Press, pp.538-539.

Dennis, A.W., (1963), "Six Generations: A History of the Dennis Family", Tarndwarncoort, Warncoort, unpublished manuscript.

Denoon, D., (1983), *Settler Capitalism: The Dynamics of Dependent Development in the Southern Hemisphere*, New York: Oxford University Press.

de Serville, P.H., (1983), "Hood, Robert (1821-1891) and Robert Alexander David (1863-1934)", *Australian Dictionary of Biography*, Vol.9, Melbourne: Melbourne University Press, pp.359-360.

de Serville, P.H., (1991), *Pounds and Pedigrees*, Melbourne: Oxford University Press.

de Ste. Croix, G.E.M., (1956), "Greek and Roman Accounting" in Littleton, A.C. and Yamey, B.S. (eds.), *Studies in the History of Accounting*, London: Sweet & Maxwell, pp.14-74.

Dimelow, J., (1871-73), *Practical Book-keeping Made Easy*, Ballarat: Pinkerton's Steam Print. (This book comprises three sets which were published between 1871 and 1873.)

Dingle, T., (1985), "Pastoralists, Farmers and the Changing Landscape of the Western District" in Sherwood, J., Critchett, J. and O'Toole, K. (eds.), *Settlement of the Western District from Pre-Historic Times to the Present*, Warrnambool: Warrnambool Institute Press, pp.99-114.

Dodd, N., (1994), *The Sociology of Money: Economics, Reason and Contemporary Society*, Cambridge: Polity Press.

Dunstan, D., (1984), *Governing the Metropolis - Politics, Technology and Social Change in a Victorian City: Melbourne 1850-1891*, Melbourne: Melbourne University Press.

Dunstan, K., (1991), "Life with Melbourne's Ruling Class", *The Sunday Age*, Agenda, 31 March, pp.1-2.

(The) Edinburgh Academy, (1843), *Prize List, Public Exhibition Day of The Edinburgh Academy, Friday, 28th July 1843*, Edinburgh.

Edwards, J.R., (1989a), *A History of Financial Accounting*, London: Routledge.

Edwards, J.R., (1989b), "Industrial Cost Accounting Developments in Britain to 1830: A Review Article", *Accounting and Business Research*, Vol.19, No.76, pp.305-317.

Edwards, J.R. and Boyns, T., (1992), "Industrial Organisation and Accounting Innovation: Charcoal Ironmaking in England 1690-1783", *Management Accounting Research*, Vol.3, pp.151-169.

Edwards, J.R., Hammersley, G. and Newell, E., (1990), "Cost Accounting at Keswick, England, c.1598-1615: The German Connection", *The Accounting Historians Journal*, Vol.17, No.1, June, pp.61-80.

Edwards, P.D. and Joyce, R.B., (eds.), (1967), *Australia/Anthony Trollope*, St. Lucia: University of Queensland Press, (Anthony Trollope's *Australia and New Zealand* was published in 1873 by Chapman and Hall, London).

Elton, G.R., (1969), *The Practice of History*, London: Fontana.

Farmer, R. and Richman, B., (1966), *International Business: An Operational Theory*, Homewood: Irwin.

Fayle, R.D., (1984), "An Historical Review of the Development of Income Tax in Australia", *Taxation in Australia*, Vol.18, February, pp.666-676.

Fifoot, C.H.S., (1970), *History and Sources of the Common Law: Tort and Contract*, New York: Greenwood Press.

Fitzpatrick, B., (1941), *The British Empire in Australia: An Economic History; 1834-1939*, Melbourne: Melbourne University Press.

Fleischman, R.K. and Parker, L.D., (1990), "Managerial Accounting Early in the British Industrial Revolution: The Carron Company, a Case Study", *Accounting and Business Research*, Vol.20, No.79, Summer, pp.211-221.

Fleischman, R.K. and Parker, L.D., (1991), "British Entrepreneurs and Pre-Industrial Revolution Evidence of Cost Management", *The Accounting Review*, Vol.66, No.2, April, pp.361-375.

Fleischman, R.K., Kalbers, L.P. and Parker, L.D., (1996), "Expanding the Dialogue: Industrial Revolution Costing Historiography", *Critical Perspectives on Accounting*, Vol.7, No.3, June, pp.315-337.

Fleischman, R.K. and Tyson, T.N., (1993), "Cost Accounting During the Industrial Revolution: The Present State of Historical Knowledge", *Economic History Review*, Vol.46, No.3, August, pp.503-517.

Fleischman, R.K. and Tyson, T.N., (1997), "Archival Researchers: An Endangered Species?", unpublished working paper, March.

Fletcher, B., (1976), *Colonial Australia Before 1850*, Melbourne: Thomas Nelson.

Forth, G., (1979), "The Winter Cooke Papers: A Valuable Record of the Pastoral Age in Western Victoria", *Western Victoria Journal of Social Issues*, No.3, September, pp.28-37.

Forth, G., (1982), "The Squatters' Golden Age in the Western District of Victoria", *Regional Journal of Social Issues*, No.10, May, pp.34-39.

Forth, G., (1984), "An Anglo Irish Family in Australia Felix", unpublished Ph.D thesis, Monash University.

Frank, W.G., (1979), "An Empirical Analysis of International Accounting", *Journal of Accounting Research*, Vol.17, No.2, Autumn, pp.593-605.

Garden, D., (1984), *Hamilton: A Western District History*, North Melbourne: Hargreen Publishing Co.

Gavens, J., (1990), "An Historical Perspective of Integration of the Australian Accounting Profession" in Parker, R.H. (ed.), *Accounting in Australia: Historical Essays*, New York: Garland Publishing, pp.381-407.

Geelong Advertiser, (1850), 20 November; (1851), 7 July.

Geelong Church of England Grammar School, (1907), *History and Register*, Geelong: GCEGS.

(The) Geelong College, (1863), *Annual Report, Prize List, and Prospectus of The Geelong College*, Session 1863, Geelong.

(The) Geelong College, (1875), *Annual Report, Prize List, and Prospectus of The Geelong College*, Session 1875, Geelong (this item is partially numbered).

Geertz, C., (1973), *The Interpretation of Cultures*, New York: Basic Books.

Geertz, C., (1983), *Local Knowledge*, New York: Basic Books.

Geertz, C., (1988), *Works and Lives*, Stanford: Stanford University Press.

Gibbney, H.J. and Smith, A.G. (eds.), (1987), *A Biographical Register 1788-1939: Notes from the Name Index of the Australian Dictionary of Biography*, Vol.2, Canberra: Australian Dictionary of Biography.

Gibson, C.J., (1974), "Station Bookkeeping and City Accountants", *The Chartered Accountant in Australia*, Vol.44, No.11, June, pp.19-23.

Gibson, R.W., (1971), *Disclosure by Australian Companies*, Melbourne: Melbourne University Press.

Gibson, R.W., (1979a), "Accounting Records and Social History: Early Times at Ensay Station", *Western Victoria Journal of Social Issues*, No.2, May, pp.3-21.

Gibson, R.W., (1979b), "Development of Corporate Accounting in Australia", *The Accounting Historians Journal*, Vol.6, No.2, Fall, pp.23-38.

Gibson, R.W., (1991), "Cost and Management Accounting in Australia", *Accounting History*, Vol.3, No.2, pp.104-110.

Gillison, J., (1958), *Wool and Ships: The Story of John Sanderson and Co.*, Melbourne: John Sanderson & Co.

Goldberg, L., (1965), *An Inquiry into the Nature of Accounting*, Sarasota: American Accounting Association.

Goldberg, L., (1977), "The Search for Scouller: An Interim Report", *Accounting and Business Research*, Vol.7, No.3, Summer, pp.221-235.

Goldsbrough, Mort & Co. Ltd, (1897), *A Practical Treatise on Wool and Sheep Breeding, Edible Scrubs, the Economical Use of Tank Water, Station Book-keeping, etc.*, Sydney: John Andrew & Co.

Graham, A.W., (1978), *Without Fear or Favour: A History of The Institute of Chartered Accountants in Australia 1928-1978*, Sydney: Butterworths.

Gray, C.M., (1932), *Western Victoria in the Forties: Reminiscences of a Pioneer*, reprinted from Hamilton "Spectator" by Hamilton "Spectator", Hamilton.

Gray, S.J., (1980), "The Impact of International Accounting Differences from a Security Analysis Perspective: Some European Evidence", *Journal of Accounting Research*, Vol.18, No.1, Spring, pp.64-76.

Gray, S.J., (1988), "Towards a Theory of Cultural Influence on the Development of Accounting Systems Internationally", *Abacus*, Vol.24, No.1, March, pp.1-15.

Green, M., (1968), *Paninga (Some Time Age): The History of Woorndoo and District*, Mortlake: Mortlake Publishing Company (this item does not contain page numbers).

Greenwood, G., (1955), "National Development and Social Experimentation, 1901-14" in Greenwood, G. (ed.), *Australia: A Social and Political History*, Sydney: Angus & Robertson, pp.196-257.

Gregory, E.B., Gregory, M.L. and Koenig, W.L., (1985), *Coast to Country: Winchelsea, A History of the Shire*, North Melbourne: Hargreen Publishing Co.

Griffin, D., (1995), "Valuing Heritage Assets is Costly and Irrelevant", (Letters), *New Accountant*, 31 August, p.12.

Griffith, R.G. De B., (1965), *Probate Law and Practice in Victoria*, Sydney: The Law Book Co.

Griffiths, N., (1982), "The Days of the Society's Beginnings", *The Australian Accountant*, Vol.52, No.1, January/February, pp.42-43.

Guide to Collections of Manuscripts Relating to Australia, Canberra: National Library of Australia.

Guthrie, J., (1990), "Performance Audit - International Developments" in Guthrie, J., Parker, L. and Shand, D. (eds.), *The Public Sector: Contemporary Readings in Accounting and Auditing*, Sydney: Harcourt Brace Jovanovich, pp.285-291.

Guthrie, J. and Parker, L., (1990), "Public Sector Accounting and the Challenge of Managerialism" in Guthrie, J., Parker, L. and Shand, D. (eds.), *The Public Sector: Contemporary Readings in Accounting and Auditing*, Sydney: Harcourt Brace Jovanovich, pp.454-469.

Halevy, E., (1949), *England in 1815*, London: Ernest Benn.

Hamilton, J.C., (1981), *Pioneering Days in Western Victoria*, Warrnambool: Warrnambool Institute Press (first published in 1914 by Exchange Press, Melbourne).

Hamilton Spectator, (1863), 17 July; (1870), 2 February; (1893), 20 July.

Hamilton, T., (1991), *A Squatting Saga*, Sorrento: Arden Press.

Hebb, I., (1970), *The History of Colac and District*, Melbourne: Hawthorn Press (first published in series in *Colac Herald*, 1888).

Henderson, A. (ed.), (1936), *Early Pioneer Families of Victoria and Riverina*, Melbourne: McCarron, Bird & Co.

Henderson, A. (ed.), (1941), *Henderson's Australian Families: A Genealogical and Biographical Record*, Melbourne: author.

Henning, G.R., (1980), "Historically Speaking: Some Nineteenth Century Origins of Australian Accounting Bodies", *Management Forum*, Vol.6, No.3, September, pp.206-213.

Hetherington, J., (1964), *Witness to Things Past*, Melbourne: F.W. Cheshire.

Hilton, R., (1991), *Managerial Accounting*, New York: McGraw-Hill.

Hofstede, G., (1980), *Culture's Consequences: International Differences in Work-Related Values*, Beverly Hills CA: Sage Publications.

Hofstede, G., (1987), "The Cultural Context of Accounting" in Cushing, B.E. (ed.), *Accounting and Culture*, Sarasota: American Accounting Association, pp.1-11.

Hombsch, F.W., (1897), "Farm Bookkeeping" (Address), *Journal of Agricultural and Industry* (South Australia), Vol.1, No.5, December, p.453.

Hone, J.A., (1969a), "Armytage, Charles Henry (1824-1876) and Frederick William (1838-1912)", *Australian Dictionary of Biography*, Vol.3, Melbourne: Melbourne University Press, pp.51-52.

Hone, J.A., (1969b), "Currie, John Lang (1818-1898)", *Australian Dictionary of Biography*, Vol.3, Melbourne: Melbourne University Press, pp.510-511.

Hone, J.A., (1972), "Dennis, Alexander (1811-1892)", *Australian Dictionary of Biography*, Vol.4, Melbourne: Melbourne University Press, pp.53-54.

Hone, J.A., (1974a), "Macknight, Charles Hamilton (1819-1873)", *Australian Dictionary of Biography*, Vol.5, Melbourne: Melbourne University Press, pp.178-179.

Hone, J.A., (1974b), "Officer, Charles Myles (1827-1904) and Suetonius Henry (1830-1883)", *Australian Dictionary of Biography*, Vol.5, Melbourne: Melbourne University Press, pp.357-358.

Hood, R., (1991), *Merrang and the Hood Family*, Warrnambool: Deakin University Press.

Hopwood, A.G., (1983), "On Trying to Study Accounting in the Contexts in which it Operates", *Accounting, Organizations and Society*, Vol.8, No.2/3, pp.287-305.

Hopwood, A.G., (1985), "The Tale of a Committee that Never Reported: Disagreements on Intertwining Accounting with the Social", *Accounting, Organizations and Society*, Vol.10, No.3, pp.361-377.

Hopwood, A.G. and Johnson, H.T., (1986), "Accounting History's Claim to Legitimacy", *The International Journal of Accounting Education and Research*, Vol.21, No.2, Spring, pp.37-46.

Howden, J. McA., (1900), "The Legalising of the Profession of Accountants", *Bankers' Magazine of Australasia*, Vol.14, No.1, 29 August, p.14.

(The) Incorporated Institute of Accountants, Victoria, (1887), *List of Members, Memorandum and Articles of Association*, Melbourne: IIAV.

(The) Incorporated Institute of Accountants, Victoria, (1895), *Ninth Annual Report*, 10 June, Melbourne: IIAV.

(The) Incorporated Institute of Accountants, Victoria, (1896), *Report and Balance Sheet for 1896 with List of Members*, Melbourne: IIAV.

(The) Incorporated Institute of Accountants, Victoria (1907), *History, Report of Council for year 1906-1907*, Melbourne: IIAV.

Ijiri, Y., (1975), *Theory of Accounting Measurement*, Studies in Accounting Research No.10, Sarasota: American Accounting Association.

Ireland, A., (1990), "Management Accounting R.I.P.?", *Charter*, Vol.61, No.5, June, pp.42-45.

Jackson, J.G.C. (1956), "The History of Methods of Exposition of Double-entry Book-keeping in England" in Littleton, A.C. and Yamey, B.S. (eds.), *Studies in the History of Accounting*, London: Sweet and Maxwell, pp.288-312.

Jacobs, C.P., (1969), *Proceedings in the Master's Office (with Precedents)*, Melbourne: The Law Book Co.

Johnson, H.T., (1972), "Early Cost Accounting for Internal Management Control: Lyman Mills in the 1850's", *Business History Review*, Vol.46, No.4, Winter, pp.466-474.

Johnson, H.T., (1978), "Management Accounting in an Early Multidivisional Organization: General Motors in the 1920's", *Business History Review*, Vol.52, No.4, Winter, pp.490-517.

Johnson, H.T. and Kaplan, R.S., (1987), *Relevance Lost: The Rise and Fall of Management Accounting*, Boston: Harvard Business School Press.

Jones, H., (1985), *Accounting, Costing and Cost Estimation, Welsh Industry: 1700-1830*, Cardiff: University of Wales Press.

Juchau, R., (1993), "Truth in Accounting - Charles Musson, An Early Australian Advocate?", *Accounting History*, Vol.5, No.1, pp.59-62.

Kaplan, R.S., (1986), "The Role of Empirical Research in Management Accounting", *Accounting, Organizations and Society*, Vol.11, No.4/5, pp.429-452.

Kaplan, R.S. and Norton, D.P., (1996), *The Balanced Scorecard: Translating Strategy into Action*, Boston: Harvard Business School Press.

Keith, B.R. (ed.), (1961), *The Geelong College 1861-1961*, Geelong: Geelong College Council and the Old Collegians' Association.

Kiddle, J.B. (ed.), (1937), *Liber Melburniensis 1848-1936*, Melbourne: Robertson & Mullens.

Kiddle, M.L., (1961), *Men of Yesterday: A Social History of the Western District of Victoria, 1834-1890*, Melbourne: Melbourne University Press.

Kininmonth, P. and Kininmonth, P., (1987), *Mount Hesse: History, Humour and Hazards on a Sheep Station 1837-1985*, Malvern: Robert Anderson & Associates.

Kitson Clark, G., (1967), *The Critical Historian*, London: Heinemann.

Lang, J., Unpublished manuscript of accounts of various incidents with respect to Larra station in the Western District (situated near Derrinallum) supplied by J.L. Currie, E. Currie, A. Currie, P.H. Lang, W.T. Manifold and others, undated (original held at Titanga, Lismore by Chris Lang).

Larson, M.S., (1977), *The Rise of Professionalism: A Sociological Analysis*, Berkeley: University of California Press.

Littleton, A.C., (1933), *Accounting Evolution to 1900*, New York: American Institute Publishing Co.

Littleton, A.C. and Yamey, B.S. (eds.), (1956), *Studies in the History of Accounting*, London: Sweet & Maxwell.

Loft, A., (1986), "Towards a Critical Understanding of Accounting: The Case of Cost Accounting in the U.K., 1914-1925", *Accounting, Organizations and Society*, Vol.11, No.2, pp.137-169.

Lovell, C.R., (1962), *English Constitutional and Legal History*, New York: Oxford University Press.

Lowry, J., (1993), "Management Accounting's Diminishing Post-Industrial Relevance: Johnson and Kaplan Revisited", *Accounting and Business Research*, Vol.23, No.90, Spring, pp.169-180.

Macdonald, K.M., (1985), "Social Closure and Occupational Registration", *Sociology*, Vol.19, No.4, November, pp.541-556.

Macdonald, O.R., (1936), "Historical Survey 1887-1936" in *The Commonwealth Accountants' Year Book 1936*, Melbourne: Commonwealth Institute of Accountants.

Macintyre, S., (1991), *A Colonial Liberalism: The Lost World of Three Victorian Visionaries*, Melbourne: Oxford University Press.

Martindale, H.G., "The Jamieson Papers", unpublished manuscript, undated (original held at Stony Point, Darlington by Robert Jamieson III MBE).

Maskell, R.E., (1944), "Fifty Years of Progress: The History of the Federal Institute of Accountants 1894-1944", *The Federal Accountant*, Vol.26, 25 July, pp.201-251.

McAlpine, R.A., (1982), *The Shire of Hampden 1863-1963*, fifth impression, Morphet Press Print (first published in 1963 by Terang Express).

McGregor, P. and Oaten, L., (1985), *Mount Elephant: A History of the Derrinallum and Darlington District*, Warrnambool: authors.

McLean, T., (1995), "Contract Accounting and Costing in the Sutherland Ship Building Industry, 1818-1917", *Accounting, Business & Financial History*, Vo.5, No.1, pp.109-146.

McNaughtan, I.D., (1955), "Colonial Liberalism, 1851-92", in Greenwood, G. (ed.), *Australia: A Social and Political History*, Sydney: Angus & Robertson.

Mellor, S.G., (1974), "Miller, Henry (1809-1888)", *Australian Dictionary of Biography*, Vol.5, Melbourne: Melbourne University Press, pp.252-253.

Mennell, P., (1892), *The Dictionary of Australasian Biography*, London: Hutchinson & Co.

Mepham, M.J., (1988a), "The Scottish Enlightenment and the Development of Accounting", *The Accounting Historians Journal*, Vol.15, No.2, Fall, pp.151-176.

Mepham, M.J., (1988b), *Accounting in Eighteenth Century Scotland*, New York: Garland Publishing.

Mills, P.A., (1988), *The Legal Literature of Accounting: On Accounts by Diego del Castillo*, New York: Garland Publishing.

Mills, P.A., (1990), "Agency, Auditing and the Unregulated Environment: Some Further Historical Evidence", *Accounting, Auditing & Accountability Journal*, Vol.3, No.1, pp.54-66.

Mills, S., (1925), *Taxation in Australia*, London: Macmillan & Co.

Milsom, S.F.C., (1969), *Historical Foundations of the Common Law*, London: Butterworths.

Mitchell, T., (1839), "Three Expeditions into the Interior of Australia", 2 vols., original manuscript held at Mitchell Library, Sydney.

Mowle, P.C., (1948), *A Genealogical History of Pioneer Families in Australia*, Sydney: John Sands.

Musson, C.T., (1893), "Book-keeping for Farmers and Orchardists", *Agricultural Gazette of New South Wales*, Vol.4, pp.162-186.

Nair, R.D. and Frank, W.G., (1980), "The Impact of Disclosure and Measurement Practices on International Accounting Classifications", *The Accounting Review*, Vol.55, No.3, July, pp.426-450.

Napier, C.J., (1989), "Research Directions in Accounting History", *British Accounting Review*, Vol.21, No.3, September, pp.237-254.

New South Wales, Statutes. *An Act further to restrain the unauthorised occupation of Crown Lands and to provide the means of defraying the expense of a Border Police*, 2 Victoria, No.27, 22 March 1839.

New South Wales, Statutes. *Companies Act 1874*, Act No.19, 1874.

Nobes, C.W. and Parker, R.H. (eds.), (1995), *Comparative International Accounting*, fourth edition, Hemel Hempstead, Hertfordshire: Prentice Hall International.

Notman, G.C., (1989), *But a Heartbeat in Time: Tales of Town and Stations at Skipton, Australia 1839-1989*, Skipton: author.

Nunan, J., (1971), *Squatters & Soldiers: Trawalla 1839-1971*, The Back-to-Trawalla Committee for Trawalla School Centenary Celebrations 1971, Trawalla.

Oehr, R.T., (1899), "How to Become a Skilled Accountant", *Banker's Magazine of Australasia*, Vol.13, No.5, 29 December, pp.291-300.

Oman, J.R. and Lang, P.S., (1980), *Brown's Water Holes: History of Lismore 1840-1960*, Geelong: authors.

Palmer, J.A. (ed.), (1973), *William Moodie - A Pioneer of Western Victoria*, Mortlake: author.

Palmer, J.A., (1980), *The Great Days of Wool: 1820-1900*, Adelaide: Rigby Publishers.

Parker, L.D., (1986), *Value-For-Money Auditing: Conceptual, Development and Operational Issues*, Auditing Discussion Paper No.1, Melbourne: AARF.

Parker, L.D., (1990), "Management Accounting: Ripe Not R.I.P.", *Charter*, Vol.61, No.8, pp.46-49.

Parker, L.D., (1995), "Price Tags not Needed on Every Heritage Item", (Postscript), *Business Review Weekly*, 30 January, p.81.

Parker, L.D., (1996), "Broad Scope Accountability: The Reporting Priority", *Australian Accounting Review*, Vol.6, No.1, March, pp.3-15.

Parker, R.H., (1961), "Australia's First Accountancy Body - The Adelaide Society of Accountants", *The Chartered Accountant in Australia*, Vol.32, No.6, December, pp.337-340.

Parker, R.H., (1969), *Management Accounting: A Historical Perspective*, New York: Augustus, M. Kelley.

Parker, R.H., (1974), "The First Scottish Book on Accounting: Robert Colinson's *Idea Rationaria* (1683)", *The Accountant's Magazine*, Vol.78, No.819, September, pp.358-361.

Parker, R.H., (1978), "British Men of Account", *Abacus*, Vol.14, No.1, June, pp.53-65.

Parker, R.H., (1982), "Bookkeeping Barter and Current Cash Equivalents in Early New South Wales", *Abacus*, Vol.18, No.2, September, pp.139-151.

Parker, R.H., (1986), "Accounting in Australia", *Australian Accountant*, Vol.57, No.10, November, pp.85-86.

Parker, R.H., (1989), "Importing and Exporting Accounting: The British Experience" in Hopwood, A.G. (ed.), *International Pressures for Accounting Change*, Hemel Hempstead, Hertfordshire: Prentice-Hall International, pp.7-29.

Parker, R.H. and Carnegie, G.D., (1997), "Accountants and Empire: The Case of Co-Membership of Australian and UK Accountancy Bodies to 1914", paper presented at the British Accounting Association conference, Birmingham.

Parnaby, J.E., (1951), "The Economic and Political Development of Victoria, 1877-1881", unpublished Ph.D thesis, University of Melbourne.

Parsons, T., (1973), "Culture and the Social System Revisited" in Schneider, L. and Bonjean, C. (eds.), *The Idea of Culture in the Social Science*, London: Cambridge University Press, pp.33-46.

(The) Pastoral and Agricultural Society of Deniliquin, (1979), *A Trial of Years: 100 Shows, and the Deniliquin District*, Deniliquin.

Pastoral Review Pty Ltd, (1910), *The Pastoral Homes of Australia*, Vol.1, Melbourne.

Pastoralists' Review, (1909), May.

Pattillo, J.W., (1965), *The Foundation of Financial Accounting*, Baton Rouge: Louisiana State University.

Pine, L.G. (ed.), (1958), *Burke's Genealogical & Heraldic History of the Landed Gentry of Ireland* by B. Burke, fourth edition, London: Burke's Peerage.

Pollard, S., (1965), *The Genesis of Modern Management: A Study of the Industrial Revolution in Great Britain*, Cambridge, Massachusetts: Harvard University Press.

Pollock, F. and Maitland, F.W., (1968), *The History of English Law*, Vol.1, London: Cambridge University Press (first published in 1898).

Port Phillip Gazette, (1843), 16 September.

Porter, T.M., (1996), "Making Things Quantitative" in Power, M. (ed.), *Accounting and Science: Natural Inquiry and Commercial Reason*, Cambridge: Cambridge University Press, pp.36-56 (first published in 1994 in *Science in Context*, Vol.7, No.3, Autumn, pp.389-408).

Port Fairy Gazette, (1903), 6 November.

Portland Guardian & Normanby General Advertiser, (1854), 23 February.

Poullaos, C., (1993), "Making Profession and State, 1907-1914: The ASCPA's First Charter Attempt", *Abacus*, Vol.29, No.2, pp.196-229.

Poullaos, C., (1994), *Making the Australian Chartered Accountant*, New York: Garland Publishing.

Powell, J.M., (1970), *The Public Lands of Australia Felix*, London: Oxford University Press.

Power, M. (1996), "Introduction: From the Science of Accounts to the Financial Accountability of Science" in Power, M. (ed.), *Accounting and Science: Natural Inquiry and Commercial Reason*, Cambridge: Cambridge University Press, pp.1-35 (first published in 1994 in *Science in Context*, Vol.7, No.3, Autumn, pp.355-388).

Power, P.M., (1977), *From These Descended*, Kilmore: Homestead Books.

Powling, J.W., (1980), *Port Fairy: The First Fifty Years 1837-1887, A Social History*, Melbourne: William Heinemann.

Previts, G.J. and Merino, B.D., (1979), *A History of Accounting in America*, New York: John Wiley & Sons.

Previts, G.J., Parker, L.D. and Coffman, E.N., (1990a), "Accounting History: Definition and Relevance", *Abacus*, Vol.26, No.1, March, pp.1-16.

Previts, G.J., Parker, L.D. and Coffman, E.N., (1990b), "An Accounting Historiography: Subject Matter and Methodology", *Abacus*, Vol.26, No.2, September, pp.136-158.

Radebaugh, L.H. and Gray, S.J., (1993), *International Accounting and Multinational Enterprises*, third edition, New York: John Wiley & Sons.

Report from the Select Committee of the House of Commons on Petitions relating to the Corn Laws of this Kingdom: Together with the Minutes of Evidence and an Appendix of Accounts, (1814), London: James Ridgway.

Riahi-Belkaoui, A. and Picur, R.D., (1991), "Cultural Determinism and the Perception of Accounting Concepts", *The International Journal of Accounting Education and Research*, Vol.26, No.2, pp.118-130.

Riponshire Advocate, (1879), 25 January; (1880), 31 December.

Roberts, B., (1993), "Towards a More Commercial Focus" in *Readings in Accounting Developments in the Public Sector 1992-93*, Melbourne: ASCPA.

Roberts, S.H., (1935), *The Squatting Age in Australia*, Melbourne: Melbourne University Press.

Rohner, R.P., (1984), "Toward a Conception of Culture for Cross-Cultural Psychology", *Journal of Cross-Cultural Psychology*, Vol.15, No.2, June, pp.111-138.

Ronald, H.B., (1978), *Wool Past the Winning Post: A History of the Chirnside Family*, South Yarra: Landvale Enterprises.

Ross, C.S., (1901), *The Scottish Church in Victoria, 1851-1901*, Melbourne: M.L. Hutchinson.

Russell, G.K., (1991), "Some Records are Intact", *Geelong Advertiser*, Letter to the Editor, 2 March, p.6.

Sabel, C.F., (1982), *Work and Politics: The Division of Labor in Industry*, New York: Cambridge University Press.

Schoenfeld, H.M., (1983), "Major Influences which Shape Accounting Systems: An Attempt of an Interpretational - Historical Analysis" in Gaertner, J.F. (ed.), *Selected Papers From The Charles Waldo Haskins Accounting History Seminars*, Monograph No. 4, The Academy of Accounting Historians, pp.153-172.

Schreuder, H., (1987), "Accounting Research, Practice, and Culture: A European Perspective" in Cushing, B.E. (ed.), *Accounting and Culture*, Sarasota: American Accounting Association, pp.12-22.

Scotch College, (1870), *Annual Report, Honor List, & Prospectus*, Melbourne: Scotch College.

Scouller, J., (1882), *Practical Bookkeeping*, second edition, Melbourne: George Robertson & Co.

Seidler, L.J., (1983), "An Overview of External Forces Affecting The Evolution of Accounting Theory" in Gaertner, J.F. (ed.), *Selected Papers From The Charles Waldo Haskins Accounting History Seminars*, Monograph No.4, The Academy of Accounting Historians, pp.57-62.

Serle, G., (1971), *The Rush to be Rich: A History of the Colony of Victoria, 1883-1889*, Melbourne: Melbourne University Press.

Serle, G., (1986), "Mackinnon, Donald (1859-1932)", *Australian Dictionary of Biography*, Vol.10, Melbourne: Melbourne University Press, pp.312-315.

Shann, E., (1930), *An Economic History of Australia*, London: Cambridge University Press.

Shaw, M.T., (1981), "Jonathan Shaw 1826-1905: A Forgotten Pastoralist", *Victorian Historical Journal*, Vol.52, No.1, February, pp.57-62.

Sherington, G., (1990), *Australia's Immigrants 1788-1988*, second edition, Sydney: Allen & Unwin.

Shire of Glenelg, (1963), *Shire of Glenelg Centenary, 1863-1963*, Casterton.

Smith, A., (1987), *Como*, Melbourne: The National Trust (Victoria).

Southall, I., (1950), *The Weaver from Meltham*, Melbourne: Whitcombe & Tombs.

South Australia, Statutes. *Associations Incorporation Act* 1858, Act No.21.

Spreadborough, R. and Anderson, H., (1983), *Victorian Squatters*, Melbourne: Red Rooster Press (the pages featuring maps were not numbered).

Stewart, D., (1854), "Dissertation: Exhibiting the Progress of Metaphysical, Ethical, and Political Philosophy, Since the Revival of Letters in Europe", in Hamilton, W. (ed.), *The Collected Works of Dugald Stewart*, Vol.1, Edinburgh: Thomas Constable & Co.

Strachan, H.M., (1927), *Some Notes and Recollections*, Melbourne: author.

Strangward, W.O., (1899), "Accountants and Auditors", *Bankers' Magazine of Australasia*, Vol.13, No.4, 30 November, pp.218-226.

Sutherland, A., (1977a), *Victoria and its Metropolis, Past and Present*, Vol.1, Melbourne: Today's Heritage (first published in 1888 by McCarron, Bird & Co., Melbourne).

Sutherland, A., (1977b), *Victoria and its Metropolis, Past and Present*, Vol.2A, with contributed papers by Ellery, R.L.J. *et al.*, Melbourne: Today's Heritage (first published in 1888 by McCarron, Bird & Co., Melbourne).

Sutherland Smith, G., (1992), "The Firm of W.H. Tuckett and Sons", *Accounting History*, Vol.4, No.2, pp.57-58.

Sydney Gazette, and New South Wales Advertiser, (1821), 30 June.

ten Have, O., (1976), *The History of Accounting* (translated by van Seventer, A.), second edition, Palo Alto: Bay Books.

Terang Express, (1922), 27 November; (1927), 22 November.

Thuillier, G., (1959), *Georges Dufaud et les Débuts du Grand Capitalisme dans la Métallurgie, en Nivernais, au XIXe Siècle*, Paris: SEVPEN.

Tosh, J., (1991), *The Pursuit of History: Aims, Methods and New Directions in the Study of Modern History*, second edition, New York: Longman.

Turner, H.G., (1973), *A History of the Colony of Victoria from its Discovery to its Absorption into the Commonwealth of Australia*, Vol.2 A.D. 1854-1900, Melbourne: Heritage Publications (first published in 1904 by Longmans, Green & Co., London).

University of Dublin, (1993), *University of Dublin Calendar*, Part 1, 1993-94, Dublin: University of Dublin.

University of Edinburgh, (1833), *The Edinburgh University Almanack*, Edinburgh: Maclachlan & Stewart; London: Baldwin & Craddock.

University of Edinburgh, (1957), *The University Portraits*, compiled by Rice, D.T./biographies by McIntyre, P., Edinburgh: Edinburgh University Press.

vanden Driesen, I.H. and Fayle, R.D., (1987), "History of Income Tax in Australia" in Krever, R.E. (ed.), *Australian Taxation: Principles and Practice*, Melbourne: Longman Cheshire, pp.27-36.

Victoria, *Parliamentary Debates, Session 1894-5*, Legislative Council and Legislative Assembly, Vol.76, 1895.

Victoria, Statutes. *Companies Statute* 1864, Act No.190.

Victoria, Statutes. *Duties on the Estates of Deceased Persons Statute* 1870, Act No.388.

Victoria, Statutes. *The Land Tax Act* 1877, Act No.190.

Victoria, Statutes. *Companies Act* 1890, Act No. 1074.
Victoria, Statutes. *Income Tax Act* 1895, Act No.1374.
Victoria, Statutes. *Companies Act* 1896, Act No.1482.
Vigars, F.E., (1900), *Station Book-keeping. A Treatise on Double Entry Book-keeping for Pastoralists and Farmers*, Sydney: William Brooks & Co.
Vigars, F.E., (1901), *Station Book-keeping. A Treatise on Double Entry Book-keeping for Pastoralists and Farmers*, Sydney: William Brooks & Co.
Wadham, S., Wilson, R.K. and Wood, J., (1964), *Wadham and Wood. Land Utilization in Australia*, fourth edition, Melbourne: Melbourne University Press.
Walker, B., (1995a), "Why Valuing Heritage Assets is Archaic", *New Accountant*, 11 May, pp.11 and 13.
Walker, B., (1995b), "Pine in the Sky: Heritage Asset Values", *New Accountant*, 22 June, pp.11-12.
Wallace, W.A., (1985), "The Economic Role of the Audit in Free and Regulated Markets" in *Auditing Monographs*, New York: Macmillan Publishing Co., pp.9-56.
Walsh, R.J. and Stewart, R.E., "Agency Theory and Management Accounting: A Case Study of an International Company", unpublished paper, University of Glasgow, 1986.
Walton, S.J.T., (1970a), *History of The Institute of Chartered Accountants in Australia and Its Antecedent Bodies with References to Personalities Concerned*, Part 1, Sydney: Institute of Chartered Accountants in Australia.
Walton, S.J.T., (1970b), *History of The Institute of Chartered Accountants in Australia and its Antecedent Bodies with References to Personalities Concerned*, Part II, Sydney: Institute of Chartered Accountants in Australia.
Ward, R., (1969), "Black, Niel (1804-1880)", *Australian Dictionary of Biography*, Vol.3, Melbourne: Melbourne University Press, pp.171-172.
Warrnambool Standard, (1880), 18 May; (1991), 23 February.
Weekes, W.H., (1986), "Whatever Happened to Management Accounting?", *The Chartered Accountant in Australia*, Vol.57, No.1, July, pp.44-46 and 70.
Were, J.B. & Son., "Were's Statistical Service: Strachan & Co. Limited", Melbourne, 17 August, 1934.
West, B.P., (1996), "The Professionalisation of Accounting: A Review of Recent Historical Research and its Implications", *Accounting History*, NS Vol.1, No.1, May, pp.77-102.
West Bourke & South Grant Guardian, (1869), 11 September.
Wild, E., (1874), *Bookkeeping by Double Entry Made Easy*, Melbourne: Sands and McDougall.
Wolnizer, P.W., (1987), *Auditing as Independent Authentication*, Sydney: Sydney University Press.

Wood, B.C., (1991), *"Woodlands" From Black Swamp to Balmoral*, Hamilton: author.

Woods, C., (1972), "Johnston, James Stewart (1811-1896)", *Australian Dictionary of Biography*, Vol.4, Melbourne: Melbourne University Press, pp.485-486.

Yamey, B.S., (1962), "Some Topics in the History of Financial Accounting in England, 1500-1900", in Baxter, W.T. and Davidson, S. (eds.), *Studies in Accounting Theory*, London: Sweet & Maxwell, pp.14-43.

Young, D., (1967), *Edinburgh in the Age of Reason*, Edinburgh: The University Press.

INDEX

Pastoral Accounting in Colonial Australia

For Product Safety Concerns and Information please contact our EU
representative GPSR@taylorandfrancis.com
Taylor & Francis Verlag GmbH, Kaufingerstraße 24, 80331 München, Germany

www.ingramcontent.com/pod-product-compliance
Ingram Content Group UK Ltd.
Pitfield, Milton Keynes, MK11 3LW, UK
UKHW021606240425
457818UK00018B/413

* 9 7 8 1 1 3 8 9 9 4 7 8 2 *